THE NEW NATURALIST

A SURVEY OF BRITISH NATURAL HISTORY

WADERS

The aim of this series is to interest the general reader in the wild life
of Britain by recapturing the inquiring spirit of the old naturalists.
The Editors believe that the natural pride of the British public in the
native fauna and flora, to which must be added concern for their
conservation, is best fostered by maintaining a high standard of
accuracy combined with clarity of exposition in presenting the
results of modern scientific research.

THE NEW NATURALIST

WADERS

W. G. HALE

COLLINS
ST JAMES'S PLACE, LONDON

William Collins Sons & Co Ltd
London · Glasgow · Sydney · Auckland
Toronto · Johannesburg

TO

MARIE

First published 1980
© W. G. Hale 1980

ISBN 0 00 219727 8

Filmset by Jolly & Barber Ltd, Rugby

Made and Printed in Great Britain by
William Collins Sons & Co Ltd, Glasgow

CONTENTS

PLATES

7

EDITORS' PREFACE

A recent development in the New Naturalists series has been the publication of several successful books dealing with groups of birds, instead of monographs on single species such as the Fulmar, the Yellow Wagtail, the Greenshank, the Redstart, the House Sparrow and the Wren. These monographs were welcomed by the specialist reader, but rising costs have compelled us to discontinue their production. It is clear that many naturalists, including those who are not primarily ornithologists, are interested in authoritative accounts describing the various species of birds in greater detail than is possible in the many excellent volumes concerned with the whole British avifauna. We believe that by producing these books dealing with groups of birds we are able to make this sort of information available to the general reader for whom the New Naturalist series is written.

We have been fortunate in finding in Professor W. G. Hale an author who, we believe, has dealt with his subject as successfully as did those who wrote the previous books on Finches, Birds of Prey, Tits and Thrushes, which have already appeared in this series. Like the other authors, Professor Hale is clearly an enthusiast, who has devoted his life to the study of this and allied subjects. He is well known for his detailed investigations of the Redshank, one of the waders described in this book. But he is certainly not a 'one bird man', for he has always meticulously observed all forms of wildlife with which he has come in contact. He has the advantage of having made detailed studies of the soil fauna, so he is in the unusual position of having worked on both invertebrates and vertebrates. This has given him an unusual appreciation of the problems of the whole ecosystem. In this book he demonstrates this understanding in his account of the bio-energetics of the birds, which makes a useful contribution to the understanding of the part they play in the web of life of the areas they inhabit.

Wetlands, the areas where waders are generally observed, are probably our most endangered habitat. In all parts of the world, but particularly in Britain, marshes and bogs are being drained and used for agriculture, with the total loss of their conservation importance. Professor Hale has not only studied the life of wetlands, he has played an important part in the struggle to preserve the wetlands themselves. His work and his enthusiasm played an important part in the successful battle to preserve the Ribble estuary, which is among the most important international sites for waders. It is Professor Hale's combination of meticulous observation, scientific study and emotional involvement which makes this book one which will not only give its readers instruction and enjoyment, but will enable them also to play an informed part

9

in the further struggle to preserve our disappearing wetlands so as to ensure that waders and other species continue to flourish in and around the British Isles.

AUTHOR'S PREFACE

THIS book is a general and personal view of wading birds, a group which has fascinated me for as long as I can remember. The Redshank was my favourite bird before I knew what it was and I identified it on my seventh birthday from the figure of its egg in Seebohm's 'Coloured Figures of the Eggs of British Birds' which my father gave to me as a present. Before this I had spent many hours watching Lapwings, Curlews and Snipes in the foothills of the Pennines in East Lancashire, and whilst I was prepared to watch any birds, these always had a special interest for me. I discovered the estuarine waders one sunny August day with K. G. Spencer, when the tide 'banked' and waders by the thousand settled on islets on the salt marsh near Crossens, on the Ribble. On many occasions I tried in vain to persuade those doyens of Lancastrian ornithology, Clifford Oakes and Edmund Battersby, to come with me in search of waders on the marshes. They taught me that there were enough problems to satisfy anyone in one's own back yard, but ironically it was the latter who persuaded me to look at birds other than in Lancashire, and to recognise the fact that there are animals other than birds – a nearly impossible act of faith for many bird watchers.

There are many who enter professional biology through an initial interest in birds and often this interest wanes in favour of some other group of organisms. For me, this did not happen but other groups of animals attained the level of fascination of the birds, as I experienced what must surely rank as one of the best undergraduate invertebrate courses ever given. Waders still ranked highly and I remember vividly that my supervision, as a research student working on Collembola (Springtails), consisted largly of beer, ornithology, cricket and ideas. The airing of ideas and problems can be as important as their solution, and were I to retrace the steps of my career I would again follow the route littered with the ideas of Professor J. B. Cragg and the arguments with John Coulson which began at an EGI Conference longer ago than I care to remember and are still continuing. I like to think that I introduced some ornithological ideas to my own Ph.D. students working in the field of soil zoology. In regular sojourns to the Liverpool Museum (alas, no longer possible) during this soil zoology period, I spent many hours with Reg Wagstaffe (at temperatures in the high 90s!) talking about waders. It was probably this that turned my head and the wheel full circle. I realised that life was too short not to spend it looking at Redshanks, and where better than the Ribble to do so. I have spent many hours flying over the Ribble through the kindness of Wing Commander Roland Beamont (much to the envy of my ornithological research students) looking at waders from the air, and many hundreds of hours on the mud flats and salt marsh, often accompanied by my friend (and former research student) Malcolm Greenhalgh and my ever reliable assistant Martin Greenwood. On more occasions than I would wish I have actually been in the Ribble, much to the amusement of my research students. From all of them I have learned something and I hope that they have learned something from being with me. They have all, in some way or other, contributed to this book, but I would hasten to add that they would not necessarily contribute to all of my opinions. At some stage or other they have all disagreed with me, which in my estimation makes them all good students. Drs M. E. Greenhalgh and R. C. Taylor were in many ways the pioneers of my feeding ecology and geographical variation groups to be followed by Dr Bob Ashcroft, Dr Julian Greenwood, Peter Rose, Sheila Rynn, Ian Bainbridge, Bill Sutherland, John Swift, Kevin Briggs, Martin Kendrick, Barry Yates and Martin Jamieson and in rather different fields of ornithology John Foster and Michael Thompson. Members of the Liverpool Ornithologists' Club, the Merseyside Ringing Group and the South West Lancashire Ringing Group have helped me in many ways and had free access to the Department. I would like to acknowledge the help and contributions made to the work of my research group by my colleague Dr Philip Smith and by Dr Philip Burton, Dr John Goss-Custard, Dr Janet Kear, Professor G. V. T. Matthews and the late Dr J. G. Harrison. Dr John Goss-Custard has kindly commented on parts of the manuscript and the rest has been subjected to the ministrations of my present research students. I am grateful to all of them for their help and constructive criticisms; the faults that remain are mine alone.

For the photographs to illustrate the book I went in the main to two internationally known bird photographers, Dr David Cooke and Dr Pamela Harrison; their work speaks for itself and I am grateful to them for allowing me to use these photographs and to all the other photographers whose pictures are listed on pages 7 and 8. The sketches are by Diane Breeze and the manuscript was typed by Mrs Helen Orme, my secretary, who also dealt with the many administrative problems with her unwaning efficiency.

W. G. HALE
Department of Biology
Liverpool Polytechnic
July, 1978

INTRODUCTION

PLOVERS, Sandpipers and their close relatives, collectively termed Waders, are together placed in the Sub-order Charadrii, in the Order Charadriiformes, which also includes the gulls, terns and auks. Significant monographs have appeared over the years on several individual species, for example the Lapwing (42, 229), the Greenshank (163), the American Woodcock (219), the Dotterel (164) and the Snipe (243) but no comprehensive account of the waders as a whole has been published in Europe since Seebohm's 'Geographical distribution of the Family Charadriidae' in 1887. A detailed literature of the group up to 1924 was compiled by Low (139), with a second edition (139a) up to 1928, and very general accounts have been given of British waders by Arnold (3), Vesey-Fitzgerald (248) and Bayliss Smith (223). The 'Shorebirds of North America' (233) provides a more up to date account of the group, but significant additions to our knowledge of these birds have been provided more recently by the establishment of the Wader Study Group, which publishes a regular Bulletin, the initiation of the 'Birds of Estuaries Enquiry' by the British Trust for Ornithology and an increasing interest in feeding ecology of waders originally centred on the effect of Oystercatchers on cockle fisheries. A great deal of information has also been obtained through ringing and it is the aim of this book to bring together some of this new material which has extended our understanding of the biology of wading birds.

The Waders of Europe, the Shorebirds of North America, the Sub-order Charadrii of the systematist are neither wholly waders nor wholly shorebirds. In the breeding season they are birds of open spaces – the northern tundras, grasslands and arid regions further south. But in the non-breeding season they are mainly to be found on the coast where many species form conspicuous flocks and the collective name for this group of birds is derived from their habits during this season. In Europe the term 'waders' was coined because most species tend to be associated with wetland areas and water when feeding; the Trans-atlantic term 'shorebird' is equally applicable since most species spend much of the time outside the breeding season on the shore where they obtain their food between the tides. Even the scientific name, Charadrii, is derived from the Greek 'Charadra' – a gully – a habitat normally occupied outside the breeding season. It is no accident that the names for these birds originate from the non-breeding seasons. Most species are known to observers only at those times, as many return to the high arctic to breed; therefore their habits on the breeding ground are familiar to few ornithologists. Because of

13

this the behavioural and morphological adaptations and their feeding and breeding biology are interpreted and explained on the basis of observations of only a few species throughout their lives, or on more species during only part of their life cycle. In this book I have attempted to review the biology of waders with equal emphasis on the breeding and non-breeding seasons.

In a work of this type it is not possible to cover fully the biology of the smaller groups of the sub-order. I have therefore concentrated mainly on the larger groups – the sandpipers and plovers. The biology of individual species is covered adequately elsewhere (253, 8, 55). However, I have considered the success of the group as a whole, and examined those aspects of the biology which have led to this success and evolutionary trends within the group. The main emphasis is on those birds which occur regularly in western Europe but some aspects of wader biology have been worked on only in North America and I have had to draw on the results of this work to provide a fuller picture of the annual cycle. This is, then, not just another book on British waders but an attempt to examine the biology of Holarctic waders in general throughout the year with particular reference to those species occurring in Britain and western Europe.

CHAPTER I

THE WADERS

THE SPECIES SPECTRUM

THERE can be little doubt that, during the course of their evolutionary history, many species of waders have died out and that other species are still evolving now. There are 202 species of waders in existence today (Appendix 1) and by far the majority of these are placed in two families, the Sandpipers (*Scolopacidae*) and the Plovers (*Charadriidae*); it is mainly with these two groups that this book is concerned. Together with the Oystercatchers (*Haematopodidae*) they form the waders or shorebirds as they are generally recognised. The other nine families contain only 49 species between them and these have become adapted to rather different environments than those occupied by the Plovers and Sandpipers.

There are twelve families recognised in the Sub-order Charadrii, as follows:

Family Jacanidae	Lilly Trotters	7 species
Family Rostratulidae	Painted Snipe	2 species
Family Haematopodidae	Oystercatchers	6 species
Family Recurvirostridae	Avocets and Stilts	6 species
Family Burhinidae	Stone Curlews	9 species
Family Charadriidae	Plovers	62 species
Family Glareolidae	Coursers and Pratincoles	17 species
Family Scolopacidae	Sandpipers and Snipe	85 species
Family Dromadidae	Crab Plover	1 species
Family Ibidorhynchidae	Ibis-bill	1 species
Family Thinocoridae	Seed Snipes	4 species
Family Chionididae	Sheath-bills	2 species

Only six of these families have Holarctic representatives – Haematopodidae, Recurvirostridae, Burhinidae, Charadriidae, Glareolidae and Scolopacidae, and it would be appropriate to consider briefly the general biology of each of these, and the relationships between them, before considering the habits and characteristics of the group as a whole.

Oystercatchers: Family Haematopodidae

Typically the Oystercatchers are black and white birds with a characteristic, long, chisel-like, red bill and red legs. Some of them are completely black. All of them are noisy birds. Only one of the six species of Oystercatcher occurs in the British Isles and western Europe, *Haematopus ostralegus*, a cosmopolitan species occurring in Europe, Asia, Australia, North America and South America. In the old literature it was referred to, perhaps more correctly, as a 'Sea-pie' and the name 'Oystercatcher' appears to date from 1731 when Catesby, in his 'Natural History of Carolina' used it in relation to birds feeding on an oyster bed exposed by the tide at low water. However, as Latham (131) points out in his 'General Synopsis of Birds', Oystercatchers are capable of opening oysters and probably fed on them when they occurred more abundantly round the European coast.

Oystercatchers are amongst the few waders to find food for their young (Pratincoles, Stone Curlew and Snipe being others) and offer it to them, and it takes over a year for a young Oystercatcher to become as effective a feeder as adult birds. They normally breed for the first time at three years of age and lay a clutch of three or four eggs which are ovoid in shape and not so pointed as those of Plovers and Sandpipers. They are particularly well camouflaged on pebbly beaches. The male makes a number of scrapes, and the female selects the one in which to lay. Incubation begins with the last egg and the scrape is deepened and increasingly decorated with pebbles and vegetation as incubation progresses. The incubation period is between 24 and 27 days and the young leave the nest within a few hours of hatching. The fledging period of young is about 32 days, but the young may remain with their parents after fledging if only molluscs are available as food, when they are fed by the parents. Chicks normally crouch if threatened by a potential predator but are capable of swimming and diving soon after hatching.

Two clutches may be laid in the same breeding season and lost clutches may be replaced.

At the end of the breeding season most British Oystercatchers move south but few leave the British Isles. The wintering population is supplemented by birds from Iceland and the Faeroes which winter mainly in the west, and by some Scandinavian birds which occur mainly in the south.

Avocets and Stilts: Family Recurvirostridae

Avocets and Stilts are black and white birds with long legs and bills. Two species of this family occur in western Europe, and the British Isles, the Avocet (*Recurvirostra avosetta*) and the Black-winged Stilt (*Himantopus himantopus*). Whilst the former has a very characteristic, up-curved bill, the latter has a long straight bill. Both are wetland birds and feed in shallow water, the Avocet using a side to side sweeping motion of its slightly-open bill which filters out small invertebrates from the water. Avocets take very little vegetable matter, and the diet consists mainly of crustaceans, molluscs, annelids, insects and their larvae, and sometimes small fish and young amphibians. They feed mainly in water a few centimetres deep, but it is not unusual to see them feeding on mud recently uncovered by the receding tide. Occasionally Avocets will wade up to the belly in water and will swim and 'upend'. On dry land they sometimes pick up insects in the bill tip, and chicks, which have a very short bill on hatching, will pick at any potential food. Stilts, on the other hand, probe deeply into mud but chiefly pick their food from the surface or from floating vegetation, taking a variety of aquatic insects and their larvae; like Avocets, they will take annelids, molluscs and even young amphibia and small fish.

The Avocet's range extends as far east as northern China and south to the Mediterranean and Iraq. The British Isles are at the north-western limit. The Black-winged Stilt normally breeds no further north than the west coast of France, but spreads east to China, into South Africa, Australia and South and North America. It has bred once in Britain in 1945 when three pairs laid eggs in the Trent valley and three young fledged. The Avocet bred regularly in south-eastern England in the 18th century but was extinct by the middle of the 19th century. It was again established as a breeding bird in Suffolk in 1947 where it has since increased under the protection of the Royal Society for the Protection of Birds and there is now a regular wintering flock of some 60 birds in Devon and Cornwall.

The Black-winged Stilt is a rare visitor to the British Isles and its occurrence is sporadic.

Avocets breed colonially in saline lagoons and salt marshes where the nests are often subject to flooding. The three to five eggs are laid in a scrape in the ground which is often built up with vegetation if flooding is threatened. The incubation period is from 22–24 days and the fledging period about 40 days.

Black-winged Stilts nest in small colonies of up to ten pairs, on small islands, floating vegetation or sun-baked mud. The incubation period is about 25 days and the fledging period about 30 days.

Both Avocets and Stilts are single-brooded but will lay repeat clutches if the first is lost. In both cases both parents incubate and tend the young, which are good swimmers and capable of diving. Family parties tend to stay together after hatching.

Stone Curlews: Family Burhinidae

Stone Curlews are relatively large birds which, superficially, are rather Plover-like in build, and have short, thick bills. They are uniformly coloured sandy-brown and resemble Bustards, to which they were once placed close in the systematic list. They are now known to be more closely related to Plovers. Only one species *Burhinus oedicnemus* occurs in the British Isles as a summer visitor. Their large eyes are related to their nocturnal habits, and they usually feed at dusk and in the hours of darkness. They take mainly grasshoppers and beetles, but also crustaceans, molluscs, annelids, seeds and even small amphibians, reptiles and rodents. They are birds of chalk downs, open heaths

and dry sandy soils and nowadays are limited as British breeding birds to the south-east of England. In the last century the species bred as far north as the North Riding of Yorkshire but its distribution has been adversely affected by the cultivation of much of the marginal land which it once occupied, and by scrub covering what was once downland – an effect of the reduction in rabbit populations due to myxomatosis.

Stone Curlews often hunt their prey in a manner very similar to that of the Grey Heron, with long motionless periods following a slow, deliberate walk. Prey is caught by a quick dart of the bill when hunting in this way, but often the birds will feed by picking seeds and insects from the ground in the manner of Plovers.

In Britain, Stone Curlews are at the north-western part of their breeding range which extends southward into North Africa and eastwards to central Russia and Burma.

The British breeding population returns from wintering in Iberia and southern France early in March but eggs are normally not laid until the beginning of May. Usually there is no nest and the two eggs are deposited in a scrape on open ground, often amongst surface stones and pebbles, the smaller of which may be moved to the edge of the scrape to form a ring round it. Both parent birds incubate and hatching occurs after 25–27 days. The young leave the scrape within a day and are able to fly some six weeks later. Both parent birds bring food to the young chicks and usually drop it on the ground in front of them for the young to pick up. The family parties stay close together, even after the young have fledged, but the young become increasingly independent during the fledging period. Late in the breeding season, family parties group together to form flocks, usually of some 20–100 birds, and the size of these flocks suggests that the recent estimate of 200–400 breeding pairs in Britain may be too small, and probably the number exceeds 500 pairs. This figure compares with a possible 2000 pairs in the late 1930s.

Occasionally Stone Curlews are double-brooded and, as in most waders, replacement clutches are laid if the first is lost. They are retiring birds during the day, and both adults and young will crouch when danger threatens.

Plovers: Family Charadriidae

The Plovers are a large and distinct family of birds with short bills and legs of a medium length. They are not so much associated with the shore as sandpipers but like them, they flock outside the breeding season. As a group the Plovers are not well represented in the British avifauna. Of the 62 species only four breed commonly in the British Isles, the Lapwing *Vanellus vanellus*, Golden Plover *Pluvialis apricarius*, Ringed Plover *Charadrius hiaticula* and Little Ringed Plover *C. dubius*. The Dotterel *Eudromias morinellus* is a rare breeder and the Kentish Plover *Charadrius alexandrinus* last bred in 1956. Even if wintering or migrating birds are taken into account, the only other common species is the Grey Plover *Squatarola squatarola*.

The shape of the bill is remarkably similar in all Plovers, being shorter than the head, but having a bulbous tip with sensory nerve endings. For the most part Plovers find their food by sight, but touch may well play a part in night feeding, which is common in Plovers. One of the most interesting aspects of the feeding of Plovers is the 'pattering' which often occurs when a bird stops running and then rapidly vibrates one foot against the ground. It then pauses, head on one side looking at the ground and frequently, after a few seconds, takes an earthworm or a cranefly larva. 'Pattering' clearly brings food items to the surface of the ground; it does not simply dislodge them. It is possible that 'pattering' has the same effect as rain in attracting earthworms to the surface, and it could well be this habit that has given rise to the name Plover (Pluvius (Lat.) =rain) or Rain-bird, as it is recorded frequently in the old literature, though surprisingly not in the Handbook. (Spencer (229) cites 11 references in British literature before 1900).

Because of their short bills Plovers are unable to take food items which are not at or near the surface of the soil. Often, they will penetrate the soil to the full depth of the bill but the end result is usually a broken earthworm. Insects are the most important food of Plovers, particularly during the breeding season. During the early breeding season Plovers will move quite long distances from their breeding areas to feed, and both Lapwings (229) and Asiatic Golden Plovers *Pluvialus dominica* (215) use central areas for feeding. A similar situation occurs in Golden Plovers and it has been suggested (215) that this complex system has evolved to prevent food shortage within the breeding areas. In the northern species it may well be that the birds simply cannot get food on the breeding areas when they first return in spring, but again this clearly prevents the reduction of future food supplies in the nesting area. Plovers will also take seeds, leaves of some plants and occasionally algae. Usually quantities of stones and shell fragments are found in the stomach and these are almost certainly eaten deliberately to help grind down the harder insect parts.

In Britain in winter the inland nesting Plovers tend to move to lower coastal feeding areas which are less likely to freeze over, but for the most part they still feed inland, where earthworms may play a more important role in the diet. The shore Plovers move south but in the case of Ringed Plovers British birds are replaced by more northerly nesting birds.

All Plovers tend to lay four eggs which depend for their survival on the effectiveness of their camouflage. Ringed Plovers, often nesting on sand, lay pale finely spotted eggs whilst Lapwings lay darker more boldly marked eggs on agricultural land or marginal grassland.

The nest is little more than a scrape in the ground, to which are added fragments of vegetation or pebbles and shells, as the eggs are laid and sometimes throughout incubation. Both sexes generally share the incubation, except in the Dotterel where most of the incubation is carried out by the male. In the smaller species incubation takes some 20 days and in the larger species 30 days. As in most waders the young leave the nest within a few hours of hatching and are cared for by both parents, but again the Dotterel is an exception in that the male usually tends the chicks alone, the female often leaving the nesting area, or mating with another male. It is interesting that in the southern hemisphere, the Mountain Plover *Eupoda montana*, probably the Dotterel's nearest relative, behaves in the same way – the males remain with the chicks until after fledging, the females leaving during the fledging period; in the Sociable Plover *Chettusia gregaria*, however, the reverse is the case and the males flock during the fledging period. In the smaller Plovers the fledging period is of the order of three weeks but it may be as long as six weeks in some of the larger species.

Territoriality appears to be important in Plovers. The territory is established in early spring and held against other birds of the same species. This can result in a very even distribution of pairs over the available habitat, for example among Golden Plover, Dotterel and Lapwing. However, once the territory is established and maintained for a short time during incubation, its importance seems to wane, certainly in Lapwing and Golden Plover. In both these species the territory is not used to any extent for feeding until after the hatch of the eggs, by which time there is little, if any, territory defence. Clearly territoriality initially causes a dispersion of the nesting pairs but in some Plovers it seems to play little part in forming an exclusive area in which to rear the brood.

Some Plovers are quite remarkable migrants and Lesser Golden Plovers cover very large distances during migration. Of equal interest is the dispersal of the Lapwing which, as a breeding species, is found right across central Eurasia, from the east coast of Russia to Iberia. Ringing recoveries have shown that nestlings ringed in western Europe might be found half way across Eurasia as far east as Longitude 90°E. This degree of dispersal is remarkable and probably accounts for the lack of geographical variation in the Lapwing in that it illustrates at least a potential for an extensive gene flow, which would militate against geographical variation.

Coursers and Pratincoles: Family Glareolidae

The majority of species in this family occur in Africa and southern Asia, but they are also found in Australia and the more temperate parts of Europe and Asia. Outside the breeding season they are notorious wanderers, usually in groups, and this has resulted in three species finding their way to the British Isles. The Black-winged Pratincole *Glareola nordmanni* is the rarest vagrant of the three species, the Cream-coloured Courser *Cursorius cursor* next and the Collared Pratincole *Glareola pratincola* least rare in Britain. The family does not occur in America.

The Coursers are Plover-like birds with long legs and short wings and are specially adapted to dry, desert conditions. They feed largely on insects and everywhere tend to be sparsely distributed. They are, like most waders, cryptically coloured and are fast runners. It seems likely that variations in food supply may cause fluctuations in the time of breeding which varies greatly in different parts of the range. They lay two or three eggs of a characteristic shape and coloration, though in the Cream-coloured Courser the eggs are streaked and spotted, unlike those of other waders in that the markings are fine and the ground coloration paler. Other Coursers' eggs are more Plover-like.

Most Coursers incubate their eggs, although in some cases they merely shield them from the sun by standing over them, and the Egyptian Plover *Pluvianus aegyptius*, partially buries its eggs in sand where the heat of the sun plays an important part in incubation, although at night an adult (probably the female) will incubate. In this species the young are also partially covered in sand by the adult when danger threatens.

Their migrations are puzzling. Many wander south after the end of the breeding season but others move north and west and have been recorded as far north as Finland and Sweden.

A good deal more is known of the Pratincoles, which are also known as Swallow-Plovers because of their long wings and forked tails. No nest is made and the two or three eggs are deposited in a scrape in the sand or mud. They are typical wader eggs, though more ovate than in most species, and those of the Collared Pratincole resemble eggs of the Little Tern *Sterna albifrons*. Pratincoles tend to nest colonially, the size of the colony ranging from tens to hundreds of pairs and the incubation period is about 18 days. The young are usually tended by both parents and are unusual in waders in that, in the early stages of the the fledging period, they are fed on food regurgitated by the adults and placed on the ground in front of the chick. The chicks begin to feed themselves at the age of nearly two weeks and are capable of flight some four weeks after hatching. When nesting colonially the young congregate once they are capable of feeding themselves. Unlike other waders the young crouch with their heads raised.

Sandpipers, Snipes and Phalaropes: Family Scolopacidae

Whilst the Plovers tend to be colourful birds, which are cryptic because of the disruptive nature of their plumage, the Sandpipers and Snipes are generally dull coloured birds, with little contrast in their plumage, but similarly cryptic. There is a much greater size range within the group than in the Plovers, and a great diversity of bill forms is associated with a much greater adaptive radiation (see Chapter 2).

The Curlews are amongst the most distinctive members of this family, being large birds with down-curved bills and a characteristic song. Two species are found in the British Isles, the European Curlew *Numenius arquata*, which is extremely common, and the Whimbrel *N. phaeopus*, which is limited as a breeding bird to northern Scotland but familiar as a migrant elsewhere. The Hudsonian Whimbrel, which is the same species as the European Whimbrel, is recognisable in the field, and this has now been recorded on three occasions in the British Isles. The Slender-billed Curlew *N. tenuirostris*

has been recorded only once, though several other records exist which for one reason or another are said to be unacceptable.

Incubation in Curlews is normally carried out by both sexes and lasts 26–30 days in the European Curlew and 24–28 days in the Whimbrel. In the former there is a tendency for the female to leave after tending the young for 2–3 weeks but the male remains for the period of fledging which is between 5 and 6 weeks. A similar fledging period is found in the Whimbrel. In this species both birds normally tend the young which, as in all Curlews, leave the nest when dry and feed themselves.

The Tringine Sandpipers, or Tattlers, are noisy birds varying in size between the Common Sandpiper *Tringa hypoleucos* and the Greenshank *T. nebularia*, both of which breed in the British Isles. The Redshank *T. totanus* is probably the commonest British breeder in this group but the Wood Sandpiper *T. glareola* has now nested in Scotland since 1959. The Green Sandpiper *T. ochrophus* has bred twice (1919 and 1959) and the Spotted Sandpiper *T. macularia* once (1975). The Spotted Redshank *T. erythropus*, Green and Wood Sandpipers occur as regular passage migrants in the British Isles, and the Lesser Yellowlegs *T. flavipes*, Greater Yellowlegs *T. melanoleuca*, Solitary Sandpiper *T. solitaria*, Terek Sandpiper *T. cinereus* and Spotted Sandpiper *T. macularia* occur as vagrants.

One interesting feature of all the species which have been studied to any great extent so far is that they have an elaborate display flight and ground display prior to copulation (though the former may be absent in the Spotted Redshank). All the species of this group normally lay a clutch of four eggs. Most nest on the ground but two of them, the Solitary and Green Sandpipers, and occasionally the Wood Sandpiper, lay in abandoned nests of tree-nesting birds, normally passerines. In the smaller species the incubation period is about 20 days, in the larger, for example Greenshank, about 24 days. In the Redshank it is 23 days. The incubation is normally carried out by both birds of a pair although in the Spotted Redshank the male is mainly concerned and in the Greenshank the female. In most species both parents tend the young, but during the latter part of the fledging period only one parent may be present, usually the male. The young fly at about three weeks in the smaller species (e.g. Common Sandpiper) and between 28 and 33 days in the larger species (e.g. Redshank and Greenshank).

In Phalaropes the roles of the sexes are largely reversed; the female is the more brightly coloured, is the more demonstrative and performs a display flight. The male incubates the eggs (18–20 days) and tends the young, though the female may be present during the fledging period which lasts about 20 days.

Phalaropes are birds of the water and the Grey Phalarope *Phalaropus fulicarius*, a passage migrant and occasional winter visitor to the British Isles, spends most of its life associated with the sea, though some nest near fresh water pools. The Red-necked Phalarope *P. lobatus*, nests in the northern and western islands of Scotland, and in one locality in Ireland. In the British Isles it is on the edge of its range which is circumpolar. Wilson's Phalarope *P. tricolor* is a Nearctic species which is apparently increasing as a vagrant in the British Isles. It is not a bird of the sub-arctic tundras, as are the other two species, but nests further south in North America and winters in South America. It is more a wading bird than the other two species but will 'spin' as they do in feeding, stirring up the water and pecking food from the surface with its fine bill.

There are 23 species of Woodcock and Snipe only two of which, the European Woodcock *Scolopax rusticola* and the Common Snipe *Capella gallinago*, breed in the British Isles. The Great Snipe *C. media* and the Jack Snipe *Lymnocryptes minima* are both winter visitors and passage migrants but the former has a very small wintering population and has been recorded in the British Isles only some 200 times.

All these species are shot as game birds and because of this there is more information available about the biology of Common Snipe and Woodcock than there is for most waders. A Woodcock caught in February 1798 at Cleuston Wood, Dorset was amongst the earliest birds ever to be ringed and released. Both species are well known for their spring displays, the Woodcock for its roding in woodland clearings and the Snipe for its 'drumming' over open bogs.

Courtship display is poorly developed in this group of species and in the Woodcock particularly little is known. Probably the roding male is called down by the female and there is apparently little in the way of preliminaries to copulation. The Common Snipe has a ground display and the Great Snipe has a communal gathering of both males and females at a 'lek' usually at dusk and continuing into the night. In both Woodcock and Snipe normally only the female incubates but in the latter the male is present during the fledging period. The incubation period in Common Snipe is 18–20 days and from 20–23 days in the Woodcock, whereas the fledging period of both species is about 20 days. Young Snipe take food from the parents during the first week out of the nest but from then on, like Woodcock, feed themselves.

It is probable that all species of the group are double brooded, but it does not follow that all pairs are always double brooded; they are not. Records of Woodcocks carrying young between the legs in flight have regularly been doubted, though several of the reports seem perfectly good. I have never personally witnessed this in Woodcock and Snipe but I have seen it on two separate occasions, involving six chicks, in Redshank, when the adult bird carried them in exactly this manner over a dry wall, so that I would judge the Woodcock records to be true.

There are some 23 species of Sandpipers which can be described as 'Calidritine' Sandpipers but only one of these, the Dunlin *Calidris alpina*, is a relatively common breeder in the British Isles; two others, the Temminck's Stint *C. temminckii* and the Ruff *Philomachus pugnax* are rare breeders, though the latter was at one time common in parts of England. The Knot *Calidris canutus*, Sanderling *C. alba* and Purple Sandpiper *C. maritima* are passage migrants and winter visitors, and the Curlew Sandpiper *C. testacea* and Little Stint *C. minuta* are passage migrants. Of the remaining fifteen species only four have not been recorded in the British Isles and eleven can be regarded as rare vagrants. In order of increasing rarity these are Pectoral Sandpiper *C. melanotus*, Buff-breasted Sandpiper *Tryngites subruficollis*, White-rumped (Bonaparte's) Sandpiper *Calidris fuscicollis*, Baird's Sandpiper *C. bairdii*, Broad-billed Sandpiper *Limicola falcinellus*, Least Sandpiper *Calidris minutilla*, Semi-palmated Sandpiper *C. pusillus*, Sharp-tailed Sandpiper *C. acuminata*, Stilt Sandpiper *Micropalama himantopus*, Western Sandpiper *Calidris mauri* and Red-necked Stint *C. ruficollis*.

There is a well developed nuptial display in most species of this group, involving a display flight and a ground display; this will be considered in Chapter 4.

All species normally lay 4 eggs and all are ground nesting. The Dunlin is typical of this group in having an incubation period of 21–22 days, during which both sexes share egg covering, and a fledging period of about 25 days. It is atypical in that the female gradually takes over during fledging and is usually left with the chicks at the end of the period, whereas in most species of waders it is the male which is left with the chicks. This applies to Temminck's Stint where the fledging period is a little shorter – 18 days. The Ruff, of course, is unique, the female doing all the incubating (21 days) and tending young, the fledging period of which is not known accurately but is about 24 days. Most of the other Calidritine Sandpipers share incubation, with the exception of the White-rumped, Pectoral and probably the Buff-breasted Sandpipers where the female alone incubates and rears the young. All species are normally single brooded though Temminck's Stint has been recorded as double-brooded and in parts of its range the Sanderling is double-brooded, each bird of a pair incubating one clutch simultaneously. The various breeding strategies are considered further in Chapter 4.

The Bar-tailed Godwit *Limosa lapponica* is a common passage migrant and winter visitor but there are no records of the two American Godwits in the British Isles. In Godwits both parents incubate, and the female appears to take the larger share. The Black-tailed Godwit incubates for 23–24 days and the Bar-tailed Godwit 21–22 days and the young, which fly in about four weeks, are tended by both parents.

In courtship display there is both a display flight and ground display.

Most authorities now treat the American Dowitchers as two species, the Long-billed Dowitcher *Limnodromas scolopaceus* and the Short-billed Dowitcher *L. griseus*. Both occur as vagrants in the British Isles, and there are well over 100 accepted records.

The Turnstone *Arenaria interpres*, is a common shore bird in the British Isles, both as a passage migrant and as a winter visitor. Like other waders, the Turnstone flocks in winter but these flocks seldom exceed 100 birds. They are to be found mainly on rocky shores where they search beneath stones and in

weed for their food. They often associate with Purple Sandpipers. At the beginning of the breeding season Turnstones are very vocal, both males and females having a form of song. However, there appears to be no well developed display flight or courtship display. Incubation is carried out by both sexes, but predominantly the female and lasts 22–23 days. The young are tended by both adults and fly at about three weeks old.

RELATIONSHIPS

Birds were first recognised in the fossil record in the Jurassic, some 140 million years ago, but half this period was to pass before the first recognisable waders or shorebirds occurred in the rock strata. Two groups of fossils from the late Cretaceous are of interest in searching for the origins of waders: firstly, several specimens which have been referred to the genus *Palaeotringa*, a small sandpiper-like bird found in the Cretaceous rocks of New Jersey; and, secondly, specimens referable to two genera, *Cimolopteryx* and *Ceramornis* (both Family Cimolopterigidae) from the Cretaceous of Wyoming. The latter seems, on the basis of the four specimens which have been found, to be the ancestor of the Avocets and Stilts (Family Recurvirostridae), or closely related to them. *Palaeotringa* appears to be something of a 'catch-all' genus, into which all early wader-like birds have been placed. However, it is probable that by the late Cretaceous two major groups of waders had evolved. By the early Eocene, Gulls and Auks occurred on both sides of what is now the Atlantic Ocean, so that the divergence of these groups from the basic Charadriiform stock occurred at least 50 million years ago. It is likely though that waders as we know them have been evolving for at least 70 million years, and during this period many forms must have died out, so that now we are left with a group of birds in which some twelve present-day families are recognised, containing 202 extant species (see Appendix 1).

At the end of the Cretaceous the climate was milder than at present. There is good evidence to suggest that, for most geological time, ice-caps were absent from the earth's surface, and even though fossils might well be found south of the normal breeding range of the species concerned, it seems likely that the first waders were birds of a warm temperate climate. Seebohm (217) suggested that since many waders are largely arctic species these birds had their origins in the arctic basin. There can be little doubt that he was right in implying that the Pleistocene ice ages played an important part in the evolutionary history of the group but the probability is that some forms proved to be adaptable to the changing colder climate and it is from these that the arctic waders have evolved.

The fossil record of wading birds is poor and provides little information on the possible relationships of the different families. The classification of the group has been largely based on the structure of the skeleton and external morphology but two recent pieces of work have contributed considerably to our knowledge of possible phylogeny. Jehl (109) examined the relationship using the colour pattern of downy young, and Sibley (220) used the electrophoretic patterns of egg white proteins in a study of the relationships of birds in general.

From these studies several points of importance arise which are illustrated in Fig. 1.

1. It appears that the Jacanas and Painted Snipes, *Jacanidae* and *Rostratulidae*, are related more closely to each other than to other families.
2. The Stone Curlews, Oystercatchers, Avocets and Stilts, *Burhinidae*, *Haematopodidae* and *Recurvirostridae*, form a closely related group.

The chicks of the three families all have a similar dorsal pattern and Jehl (109) and Fjeldså (49) suggest that this indicates a phylogenetic relationship. Since the chicks occupy such different habitats it seems unlikely that the patterning is a result of convergence and both protein and osteological studies indicate a relationship between Oystercatchers, Avocets and Stone Curlews. There are also behavioural similarities between the groups, but the similarities of protein patterns between these three families and the Plovers provide what is probably the strongest evidence for their relationship.

The Ibis-bills *Ibidorhynchidae* do not appear to be closely related, though in some classifications such a relationship has been indicated.

3. The Coursers *Glareolidae* are most closely related to Plovers which in turn are related to the Stilts, Avocets and Oystercatchers.
4. The true Sandpipers *Scolopacidae* do not appear to be closely related to the Plovers but the Phalaropes *Phalaropodinae* are related to the Sandpipers.
5. Turnstones *Arenaria* are more closely related to Sandpipers *Scolopacidae* than to Plovers *Charadriidae*.
6. *Arenaria* seems to be a Tringine offshoot, whereas the Surf Bird *Aphriza* is of Calidritine origins.
7. Dowitchers appear to be more closely related to Snipes than to Godwits.
8. The Seed Snipes *Thinocoridae* are probably more closely related to the Sheathbills *Chionididae* than to other groups.
9. The affinities of the Crab Plover *Dromodidae* are uncertain.
10. It may well be that the Charadriidae are no more closely related to the Scolopacidae than they are to the gulls, so that the waders may not be the collection of closely related forms that the systematic approach has suggested, but a polyphyletic group – one in which the constituent subgroups have disparate origins.

On the basis of his study of downy chick patterns, Jehl has suggested a tentative phylogeny for the waders. Fig. 1 is based largely on Jehl's work but includes some modification made in the light of more recent findings. What is clear from this is the antiquity of many of our familiar waders, which is

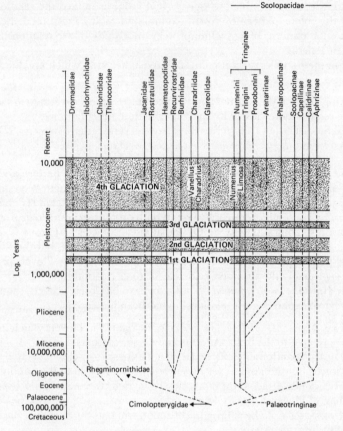

FIG. 1. Probable evolutionary relationships of wading birds. Solid lines indicate known fossil record.

particularly emphasised where fossils are known to occur (solid line). Where there is such a long evolutionary history it is often difficult to pinpoint phylogenetic relationships and convergences may cloud the issue. The waders may well be a polyphyletic group but to those who watch them and work with them they have the singular fascination of a group of birds which has survived several ice ages and tens of millions of years of evolution because of the adaptations they possess. In many ways these adaptations obscure relationships and it is quite possible that we may never know the true origins of these birds.

RARITIES

The British Isles are on the extreme western edge of the range of most European wading birds and because of this any contraction of the range results in the species in question becoming rarer as a British breeding bird. This is probably what has happened in the past to such species as the Avocet, Black-tailed Godwit and Ruff whose return as breeding birds to Britain has probably resulted from a range extension. This too is probably the case in Temminck's Stint and Wood Sandpiper, and it may well be that other waders which have bred in the past, such as Kentish Plover, will again breed following a future range extension.

1971 was the first year in which Temminck's Stint was known to rear young successfully in Scotland, this being the fifth breeding record. Since then a few pairs have bred each year. In the case of the Ruff, after it became extinct in Norfolk in 1871 only sporadic breeding records occurred until 1963 when the species bred successfully on the Ouse washes, and now over twenty Reeves nest each year. Sites in Lancashire have also provided suitable breeding areas for Ruff, and three out of four nests hatched chicks in 1976.

Godwits similarly are making a come-back in Britain. The Black-tailed Godwit *Limosa limosa* became extinct in the British Isles before the middle of the 19th century but since 1952 has bred regularly and in increasing numbers on the Ouse washes and in several other areas in England and Scotland.

There are other species which have bred very occasionally, such as Black-winged Stilt, Turnstone and Spotted Sandpiper, but these were isolated instances of birds well outside their normal breeding ranges, and not a serious attempt to establish a breeding population. In the case of the Spotted Sandpiper, this was the first recorded instance (1975) of a Nearctic species breeding in the British Isles, and was of particular interest in view of the apparent increase in the numbers of American waders reaching Europe in recent years.

The Turnstone has been suspected to breed on several occasions, but proof has been lacking until recently. During the examination of an egg collection made by Mr A. Yates of Morecambe, I came across a clutch of four Turnstone's eggs taken on the Outer Hebrides on 30 April, 1938. Mr Yates has confirmed this record both verbally and by correspondence.

The occurrence of isolated instances of breeding and the arrival of rare vagrants are of little or no biological significance (Appendix 2, Table 1). However, they could be of significance if they eventually gave rise to regular patterns of migration which might be important in subsequent climatic changes or where behaviour patterns are modified which might lead to changes in habitat selection (see Chapter 2). In these circumstances they could have significance and clearly have had in the past when range extensions have occurred following climatic changes, for example in the late Pleistocene (see Chapter 3).

Particularly in the case of the American waders (Appendix 2, Table 2), there is some debate as to whether or not the increases in records of the nineteen recorded species in the British Isles, constitute a real increase in numbers. Prior to 1958 there were some 350 records of these species in the British Isles, but since then 1301. There has been a very large increase in the number of competent recorders since 1958. As a result attention has been drawn to the previously almost unwatched localities in which rarities are likely to occur, so that often there are more bird watchers than birds in these areas. However, there has not been a similar increase in the records of rarities originating from the European continent (Appendix 2, Table 3). In fact of the 14 rare species with a total of 601 records, only one third of these (206) have been recorded since 1958. The likelihood is that there is a real increase in the vagrancy of North American birds which has been attributed to changes in weather patterns due to the southerly shift of the Icelandic low pressure area (252).

Most of the records of American waders (75%) occur in autumn, the majority on the west coast of the British Isles. The early autumn records (July and early August) occur mainly on the east coast which suggests that these are of birds which have summered in northern Europe, having crossed the Atlantic in the previous autumn. If this is the case they must have over-wintered on the eastern side of the Atlantic, and may well have attempted to breed in northern Europe. Since the species in question, or their near relatives, have existed for many thousands of years, it is unlikely that this is the first occasion on which such trans-Atlantic journeys have occurred. It is also unlikely that these species will form viable breeding populations in Europe. Their occurrence is interesting but biologically insignificant until such time as one of these species is capable of taking advantage of a niche which is not already occupied by a European breeding species.

Amongst the records of rare waders which have been claimed for the British Isles are those to be found in the list of the so-called 'Hastings Rarities' recorded in that area between 1892 and 1930 (171, 80). All these were removed from the British List in 1962, but rare visitors which have occurred since have provided grounds for questioning this action. There can now be little doubt that at least some of the Hastings Rarities were perfectly admissible records. All the Hastings waders are shown in Appendix 2, Table 1, where a comparison is made between monthly records of each species for the periods 1958 and before, 1958–72, and 1972–76. In several cases, e.g. Black-winged Stilt, Lesser Golden Plover, the Hastings records occurred in months in which the majority of recent observations has been made, so suggesting that the Hastings records may well have been perfectly good ones. This is of relatively little biological importance other than to indicate that some of the Hastings birds are probably more common visitors than has previously been supposed, and that many waders are capable of making long and arduous flights involving extensive overseas crossings more frequently than the records indicate.

All these rarities, with the exception of those establishing small breeding populations, are, by definition, outside their normal geographical range which is determined by the adaptations which each species possesses to fit it for the habitat in which it lives. Each species occupies its own niche in a particular habitat, within a limited breeding range. Suitable habitat and geographical barriers normally limit the ranges of different species, but these limitations vary with time, and occasionally other factors allow the colonisation of different habitats, and range extension. In general the geographical distribution of species is determined by the distribution of suitable habitat, and therefore habitat will be considered next before an account of geographical distribution and variation.

CHAPTER 2

HABITATS AND ADAPTATION

HABITAT SELECTION

PERHAPS the most obvious characteristic of any bird species is that it tends to be found in the same general sort of habitat no matter where in its range it is encountered. In itself this is not surprising and may be entirely a function of the fact that the particular species in question is unable to live elsewhere and not due to the active selection of a given part of the environment by the individuals concerned. If the former is the case then a change in habitat preference would require a genetical change in a species; if the latter is true then a change in behaviour would suffice to enable a species to colonise a new habitat. Whilst habitat preferences can clearly be seen to exist, it is no simple matter to single out those features of the environment which result in a species being successful or are indicators of a suitable environment.

It is now generally thought that there are two elements to habitat selection; firstly, an innate response and secondly, a response resulting from experience where the usual behaviour might be modified. Hand-reared Oystercatchers and Lapwings, which have had no contact with adult birds and therefore cannot have an element of post-natal learning (from parent birds) in their behaviour, produce nesting scrapes on bare ground; similarly raised Redshanks select tufts of vegetation in which to produce a scrape. Thus, the

34

selection of the immediate habitat of the nest appears to be genetically determined and not learned. In marked contrast to this the roosting behaviour of a semi-urban population of Redshank in Kendal, Cumbria, is of interest. Here, the birds have adopted a roof-top day-time roost, presumably as a result of disturbance, resorting to roosting on flooded fields or islands in the river at night. Over 50 birds are regularly involved in the behaviour which has clearly resulted from a modification of the normal behaviour in the light of experience.

Most waders select different types of habitat during the breeding and non-breeding seasons. Generally speaking the breeding habitat is much more species specific whilst the wintering habitat is for the most part the same for many species of wading birds.

Considering first the breeding habitat, the Lapwing is probably the species to which most attention has been given. There have been two B.T.O. Lapwing Habitat Enquiries (170, 137), an extensive study of habitat selection by Klomp (117) and two monographs on the species have considered the habitat in greater (229) or lesser detail (42). Lapwings are birds of farm-land now; they prefer open spaces away from buildings and avoid trees and woodland areas. Klomp (117) suggested that this might be associated with the ability to drive away crows in an open situation. The same author found that Lapwings prefer grey-brown meadows to green ones in the early breeding season, since the colour is indicative of a poor quality of vegetation which was likely to remain short later in the season. Bare soil, or short vegetation, are preferred for the nest scrape which may be found at any altitude between salt-marsh and rough moorland at 1000 m O.D. Whilst it is easy to write a description of the breeding habitat, it is by no means easy to point to those features of it used in its selection by the bird itself. There are many square kms of apparently suitable Lapwing habitat within the British Isles which are quite unoccupied by Lapwings. Agricultural land on the coastal plane of Lancashire is not so densely populated as apparently similar land in the foothills of the Pennines, in east Lancashire, and it is very difficult to explain the virtual absence of Lapwings in parts of Cornwall, Pembrokeshire and south-west Ireland. A possible explanation for the situation in Lancashire might be found in the behaviour of the birds once the chicks hatch. In east Lancashire Spencer (229) found the majority of families very sedentary, remaining within 100 m of the nest until fledging. On the south Lancashire coast chicks are frequently led quite long distances and often birds take chicks from ploughed land, behind the sea wall, well out onto the salt marsh. It is likely that they are searching for moist areas in which the chicks might feed, and the presence of water might well be a most important factor in habitat selection during the Lapwing's breeding season.

Water is certainly a *sine qua non* of the Redshank's breeding habitat. As soon as Redshank chicks leave the nest, they are led to the nearest suitable wet feeding area and this may involve extremely long and hazardous journeys in years where the rainfall is low. I have one record of colour-ringed chicks and adults moving nearly two kilometres in 24 hours, the journey necessitating the negotiation of four dry walls, two roads, two tall thick hedges and a wide ditch with a rush covered fence at the far side. The journey was made successfully with all four chicks which were carried, one at a time, over the walls by the adult birds holding them between the legs, against the belly. Between obstacles the chicks, only 24 hours old, walked. This journey was exceptional, and in years of normal rainfall Redshank nest near areas where the chicks can feed, although they may wander during the fledging period to other suitable feeding areas. Whilst water is essential in the Redshank's habitat there are other important factors which are more difficult to assess. The distribution of this species is in many ways puzzling. Inland in Britain they nest in an almost semi-colonial state, with perhaps 10 to 20 pairs nesting within a few hundred square metres, and then a distance of 10 to 20 kilometres before another breeding group is encountered. Between these might be several apparently suitable, but deserted, areas. There must be something about these apparently suitable pieces of habitat which makes them unsuitable, or at least less suitable than other areas. It might be purely the traditional absence of the species from such areas, since waders are semi-colonial birds, and are often attracted to sub-optimal habitats by the presence of other birds.

Redshanks persist in nesting on salt marshes which are regularly flooded by the tide, which in some years causes a total loss of eggs and chicks, but in the long run the survival rate in salt marsh habitats must be greater than that of the apparently suitable, but deserted inland areas. It is very easy to describe a bird's habitat but it is often difficult or impossible to pinpoint the factors which determine habitat selection in a particular species. It is very much easier to point out factors which make certain habitats unsuitable to a given species. For example draining fields in which Redshanks nest or planting trees around them within 100–200 metres of the nesting area will cause the desertion of the site.

An examination of the distribution of the Redshank in relation to the distribution of its two nearest relatives, the Greenshank and Spotted Redshank, provides an interesting example of habitat selection which results in the mutual exclusion of each species from the breeding areas of the others over almost the whole of the range (see Fig. 10). Whereas the Redshank lives in grassy marshes, swampy heathlands, river valleys and coastal marshes, the Greenshank habitat is that of more open marshes, bogs, lakes with decaying vegetation and clearings in northern coniferous forests and birch forests. The Spotted Redshank extends into the shrub tundra from the coniferous and birch forests, but again selects marshy or swampy places. Whilst the Greenshank and Redshank overlap geographically in Britain, the habitat selected is different, the Greenshank being clearly associated with the northern coniferous forest.

In North America the Greater Yellowlegs has similar territorial preferences to the Greenshank but the Lesser Yellowlegs occupies a habitat similar to that occupied by both the Redshank and the Spotted Redshank in the Palaearctic. The larger Plovers too have a distribution pattern which is for the most part mutually exclusive. The American (Lesser) Golden Plover has a circumpolar distribution with a gap in the North Atlantic region which is filled by the Golden Plover. The Grey Plover, present in Siberia and North America, is also excluded from this North Atlantic area, and apparently the Golden Plover occupies habitats here which might be suitable to both the other species in question. In the British Isles the Golden Plover occupies a range of breeding habitats from heather moor, wet heath and blanket bog in sub-montane conditions to dwarf shrub heath and lichen heath in montane conditions, whereas in North America the American Golden Plover tends to prefer the drier of these habitats and the Grey Plover the wetter. In this respect the so-called 'Northern' Golden Plover has similar habitat preferences to the American Golden Plover whereas the 'Southern' form appears to prefer a wetter environment. In areas of overlap, for example the British Isles, this is not always the case, but in Scandinavia and Iceland birds of the 'Northern' form often place their nests next to old stumps or logs whereas the 'Southern' form, in more southerly habitats, prefers wetter and more open situations.

The Dotterel occurs altitudinally highest of all the Plovers, above the tree line. In the British Isles it is a bird of the montane *Rhacomitrium* heaths and on the European continent it occurs generally north of the tree line in montane tundra areas. The species clearly selects a habitat unoccupied by other closely related species, as high as possible. At the other altitudinal extreme the Ringed Plover occupies shore habitats, on pebbles and sand mainly near the coast in the southern part of its range, or by coastal tundra pools and lakes in the north. Geographically it is replaced in southern Europe and Asia, by the Little Ringed Plover which is more associated with freshwater and which does not appear to have an ecological replacement in North America.

It is often difficult to pinpoint the factors which cause waders to select a particular habitat, but the choice of the Little Ringed Plover appears to be less complex than others. Water and gravel, or water and the dry bed of a reservoir, appear to be sufficient to support the adults and young of this species. Even if the gravel pit is newly dug, the water apparently attracts sufficient insect life to its edges to support the young, and there seems to be no need for the pool to be colonised by more than the first arrivals at a new aquatic habitat.

In contrast with this apparently simple state of affairs, habitat selection in Sandpipers breeding on the northern tundra, where several species are frequently found together, presents a much more complex picture. Little information is available for this sort of situation with the exception of a careful and interesting study of four species of arctic breeding Sandpipers carried out by Maclean (141) in Alaska, where he studied Dunlins, Baird's Sandpipers, Semipalmated Sandpipers and Pectoral Sandpipers. It is clear from this study that each species reacts to a large number of habitat features, but more interestingly, it demonstrates how the degree of reaction changes throughout the breeding season. For example, interspecific overlap in feeding habitat is greatest in June and least towards the end of July. Habitat overlap is related to food abundance, and when food is abundant the overlap is greatest. This finding is of particular importance when looking at habitat selection outside the breeding season. The factors which cause a bird to select a particular habitat are not necessarily those which aid its survival. Klomp (117) drew the distinction between proximate factors, such as colour of the fields in Lapwings, vegetation length, terrain, and ultimate factors such as food and shelter. Clearly those birds finding the best conditions will survive better so that the selection of the proximate factors requires no explanation. However, exactly what the proximate factors are in different species is often a matter of pure speculation.

The exploitation of a habitat different from that which traditionally a particular species selects occasionally gives rise to the spread of a breeding species into areas previously not occupied, and on occasions to the extension of the range, though generally speaking the range of most species is linked to the presence of suitable habitat. Whilst the spread of the Little Ringed Plover might be cited as an example of a range extension brought about by the creation of artificial habitat (man-made gravel pits) the spread of the Oystercatcher to inland habitats almost certainly resulted from a change in the birds' behaviour.

Oystercatchers were known to nest inland in eastern Scotland, between the Forth and the Great Glen as early as the 18th century, but there can be little doubt that Oystercatchers are ancestrally shore birds. By the turn of the century Oystercatchers had begun to spread up the rivers from the Solway and in the next 50 years the spread continued up the rivers of Cumbria and North Lancashire. Of particular interest in this spread is the fact that it has been entirely from the west, so that the rivers to the east of the Pennines have been colonised from their sources towards the mouth, and the autumn return to the coast of these east-Pennine birds involves a westward movement over the range of hills. Heppleston (85) draws attention to two phases in this inland movement; firstly inland nesting on gravel banks in river valleys over a 200-year period, and, secondly, a spread on to agricultural land. Inland breeding Oystercatchers have a higher survival rate than coastal breeding birds so that it appears that once the step has been taken to select an inland habitat, the birds are at least as successful as in a coastal situation. It is likely that the first step is a behavioural change from mollusc feeding to earthworm feeding on coastal fields, and this may have been brought about, at least in part, by a decline in cockle and mussel populations. There can be little doubt that many Oystercatchers on Morecambe Bay turned to earthworms after the crash in the cockle population following the severe winter of 1962–63. Once earthworm feeding has been established in the coastal situation it is a small step to continuing this diet in inland situations, particularly on agricultural land. The evidence that exists certainly indicates that a change in behaviour of the Oystercatcher has led to a change in habitat selection and to some extent this has been aided by the fact that adult Oystercatchers provide food for their chicks. Inland chicks are fed largely on earthworms caught by the adults and the majority of these would not be available to chicks fending for themselves. Of course this applies equally to large molluscs on the shore, but it may well be this habit of feeding the young which has enabled Oyster-catchers to exploit this new food source and move inland.

Another example of a change in habitat preference has occurred in the Curlew. Both in the British Isles and on the European continent the Curlew has extended its range during this century from its original high moorland habitat into river valleys, low moorland and agricultural land. This extension of its breeding range, which appears to have been made possible entirely by a change in habitat selection, seems to be responsible for a big increase in the total population. In Germany Curlews which originally nested on bogs returned to the same areas once these had been reclaimed and tilled. Follow-ing upon this, tilled land which was previously unoccupied by Curlews was colonised, almost certainly by young birds reared on tilled land. Site tenacity here has probably given rise to a new habitat preference.

During the breeding season wading birds are found in a variety of habitats, ranging from the coast to mountain tops; geographically they occur over most of the land surface free of permanent snow. Whilst it may be an exaggeration to state that they have colonised every suitable habitat, they are, indeed, widespread. Such is not the case outside the breeding season, as they form flocks and move south, often to habitats differing greatly from their summer-ing areas, and congregate on estuaries, shorelines and low-lying wetlands. Outside the breeding season habitat selection is much less precise and many species apparently share the same habitat, whereas in summer they are often geographically or spatially separated. Golden Plovers and Lapwings feed together in the fields. Jack Snipes feed alongside Common Snipes in the boggy areas in which the latter nested; and on the shore Redshanks, Knots, Dunlins, Grey Plovers, Ringed Plovers, Sanderlings, Stints and other less common waders feed together, not only on the same mudflats, but on the same species of invertebrates – mainly *Corophium, Nereis, Macoma* and *Hydrobia*. Godwits, Curlews and Oystercatchers feed and roost with them but their choice of food items extends to other invertebrate inhabitants of the mud, the larger mol-luscs and annelids, such as cockles *Cardium*, mussels *Mytilus* and lugworms *Arenicola*. Winter habitat selection is less precise than the choice of breeding habitat and is based mainly on the location of a food supply capable of sustaining life throughout the winter period. At this time habitat selection is almost certainly influenced by the tendency of birds to join existing flocks.

The choice of habitat clearly influences evolutionary trends. In the main it has a conservative influence in that it tends to prevent new isolated populations being established outside the normal range of the species. If there is a change in habitat selection the species will be better able to extend its range. In some cases, for example the Oystercatcher and Curlew, this may involve no more than occupation of new areas within the old geographical range. But if a species is able to occupy a new habitat outside the limits of its previous geographical range the new population may be both isolated and subject to genetic pressure from the new environment. It might be thought that such a situation would favour rapid speciation, but this is not necessarily the case. Geographical isolation does not always imply genetic isolation. There can be little doubt that the presence in a particular area of birds of the same species acts as an attractant to others and is probably of most importance in habitat selection to birds breeding for the first time. In this connection it is of significance that in most birds, older individuals and established pairs tend to breed earlier. In Redshanks and Lapwings, birds breeding for the first time do so significantly later during the season and thus have the advantage of selecting the type of habitat chosen by the experienced birds. It may be that due to territoriality, or the occupation of the last sites, they do not obtain optimum habitat, but those not doing so would be less successful and thus selected against. The attraction to a habitat of new arrivals by established residents may, therefore, facilitate gene flow between populations and this is probably the case in Dunlins in Finland. There, two populations of the species live in entirely different habitats. The southern population inhabits grassy meadows by the sea shore and lowland eutrophic lakes. In marked contrast, the northern population, which is geographically isolated from the southern population, breeds on high mountain tundra. On morphological grounds the southern population is referable to the so-called 'Southern' Dunlin which has a short bill, whilst the northern population is referable to the 'Northern' Dunlin which has a long bill. However, short billed birds occur in the north Finnish population suggesting some gene flow. Whilst the two populations are clearly ecologically separate, they are almost certainly not genetically separate, so that in this instance it is unlikely that the selection of different habitats will contribute significantly to a possible speciation. Frequently this will be the case, and Mayr's view that geographical isolation (and thus genetic isolation) precedes other kinds of isolation in bird speciation is almost certainly true. It has yet to be demonstrated that habitat preferences play a premier role in speciation.

Nevertheless habitat selection may still play an important part in speciation in that different habitat preferences might evolve in geographically isolated populations to such an extent that, when they come together again, the incipient species might coexist geographically without actually making contact in the same habitats. Species which select a very specific habitat and then occupy a very narrow ecological niche are not so likely as those occupying a broader niche to move outside their normal geographical range and colonise new habitat. It is therefore less likely that they will produce genetically different populations in the form of geographical sub-species, so that intrinsically it is probable that versatile habitat selection contributes towards speciation in this way.

Where a species of bird (or any other organism) is the only one present in that environment, there is no need to specialise, or select a particular habitat; the presence of other species makes it necessary to specialise. The selection of a particular habitat makes more efficient use of the environment and prevents competition between species. It prevents wastage of individuals in unsuitable habitats and may well serve as a reinforcement of geographical barriers. The breeding habitat selected by a particular species is likely to be that in which the greatest number of surviving offspring occur and in other seasons that in which there is the highest survival rate of potential breeding birds.

ADAPTIVE RADIATION

Differences in habitat selection in closely related species are correlated with adaptive differences between them, and survival clearly depends on adaptation to the habitat. As an order the Charadriiformes show a quite remarkable radiation, the auks being aquatic and fish-eating, the gulls feeding largely on carrion and the larger surface animals and the waders feeding on small invertebrates, mainly in wet habitats. Waders occupy a variety of habitats during the breeding season, as has already been described, and possess a wide range of adaptations fitting them for this. Unlike most birds they excel at all three main methods of locomotion, being swift runners, fast flyers and, when necessary, good swimmers. In general, waders are cursorial – adapted to running – but several species, Stilts, Avocets, Godwits and Curlews, have very long legs, at least partially associated with their habit of wading in deep water. These species also have long bills and long necks which are carried outstretched in flight, with the long legs projecting out behind them as a counterbalance.

Waders have, for the most part, lost the power of gripping perches with the feet, and associated with this is the great reduction in size of the hind toe which is absent or elevated, and not in contact with the ground. Most have three clearly separate toes pointing forward, but in some e.g. Semipalmated Sandpiper, there are traces of webbing and others e.g. Avocet, have completely webbed feet associated with the habit of walking in very soft substrates. In the Phalaropes the toes are lobed, providing a larger surface area to form paddles for purposes of swimming.

Plovers are relatively short-legged waders which move rapidly for a short distance and 'freeze'. This also applies to many of the smaller Sandpipers which like the Plovers, are cryptically coloured so that when they stop moving they are often hard to see. The most distinctive group of the Plovers is the Lapwings, so called because of the relatively slow wing beat which contrasts markedly with almost all other waders. The rounded shape of the wing is very characteristic and is probably a consequence of the birds' adaptation to grassland and drier habitats, though the White-tailed Lapwing *Chettusia leucura* occurs in wetter areas, which suggests a reversion from the normal Vannelid habit. Lapwings may possess crests, facial wattles and wing spurs, characters which are not found in other Plovers, and these are associated with display and aggression. In many ways Lapwings have diverged more than other groups from the main wader stock, and they are certainly the most colourful of all waders. They are amongst the most southerly breeding waders, and whilst being colourful are still cryptically coloured in their own habitats.

In marked contrast to the Lapwings are the Golden Plovers, three of which are northern breeders and one, the Red-breasted (New Zealand) Dotterel *Pluviorhynus obscurus*, is restricted to New Zealand. These have a spangled plumage and lack the white nuchal band of other Plovers, but their plumage is marvellously cryptic. They possess long pointed wings typical of waders in general, and they are noted for their extensive migrations, involving long sea crossings, which, normally, Lapwings do not perform.

A third group of Plovers, the Ringed Plovers, are smaller birds than those in the two previous groups. They are characterised by the possession, to a greater or lesser extent of a dark breast band, a black forehead and a black band from the bill through the eye, all of which tend to break up the outline of the bird. The different species occupy habitats from seal level to high altitudes and from dry sandy environments to marshes, and all in all there is a considerable divergence within the group.

Perhaps of particular interest are those Plovers which do not appear to be closely related to the three groups so far described, because these have followed their own lines of evolution to become adapted to particular modes of life. The European Dotterel, which is a mountain species, migrates south in autumn and has a close relative which is found on high ground in the extreme south of South America – the Tawny-throated Dotterel *Oreophilus ruficollis*. The Wrybill *Anarhynchus frontalis* has, as its name suggests, a bill which is curved to the right and which is used for probing under stones for small invertebrates. It is not quite as asymmetrical as it might be because the bill, which is larger than in most Plovers, turns slightly to the left before bending right. The species is restricted to New Zealand and is clearly most closely related to the Ringed Plover. The Sandpiper-Plover or Mitchell's Plover *Phegornis mitchellii* is a solitary, quiet bird found in southern South America associated with mountain streams, and whilst it is almost certainly related to the Plovers it shows convergences with the Sandpipers, particularly in relation to the structure of the bill.

In contrast with the Plovers, the Sandpipers show a greater range of size and morphological variation. Whilst the majority of Plovers are tropical, Sandpipers are generally birds of northerly latitudes and because of this they are a highly migratory group. From a taxonomic point of view they form six sub-families, which broadly give an indication of their overall radiation – Curlews, Godwits and Tringine sandpipers; Turnstones; Woodcocks; Snipes; Calidritine sandpipers and Ruff; and Surf Birds.

Curlews are the largest waders and are characterised by their enormous decurved bill and long legs. Their normal gait is a sedate walk and their breeding habitat often contains deep vegetation such as heathers and willow scrub which other waders normally avoid. The Tringine sandpipers are also associated with vegetation of moderate depth, largely grasses, on their breeding habitat. In general they are smaller birds than the Curlews, but they too have proportionately long legs and bills, though the latter are for the most part straight except in the Terek Sandpiper and Greenshank. These two have slightly upturned bills almost certainly associated with their methods of feeding. Both Curlews and Tringine sandpipers will frequently perch on vantage points such as fences and trees during the breeding season, and this is probably due to the fact that the vegetation in their breeding habitat obscures their view of the area. Green and occasionally Wood Sandpipers nest in disused nests of other birds, in trees, possibly to get a more extensive view over the breeding habitat. The Upland Plover, or Bartram's Sandpiper, shows some convergence with the Plovers, particularly in its feeding behaviour which involves typical Plover-like runs and short pauses.

The Godwits have long straight, or slightly upturned bills and long legs, and like the Curlews and Tringine sandpipers, prefer deeper vegetation during the breeding season, choosing grassland, dwarf willow and heather or sedge tundra in which to nest. When they first arrive at the breeding grounds, they may feed extensively on berries from the previous year, particularly if the ground is frozen or snow covered. On the breeding ground, Godwits feed on terrestrial insects, mainly beetles and caterpillars, and some earthworms and molluscs. Only later in the year after the young have flown do they feed largely on the shore, taking aquatic insects in freshwater habitats and molluscs, crustaceans and marine worms on the coast.

Turnstones have short legs and stout bills and are convergent with the Plovers. They use their stout bills to probe under stones for littoral invertebrates and often for pushing stones aside. The bill is also used for excavation but never for true probing. Turnstones are the most truly littoral species of any wader and even during the breeding season rarely stray more than a few miles from the coast. Where they do so they remain on the moss and lichen tundra, in short vegetation, and whilst the food during the breeding season consists of more insects than at other times, they take marine worms, molluscs and crustaceans (and some insects and insect larvae) all the year round. Occasionally Turnstones will feed on carrion. Birds with relatively short legs move with difficulty in grass or deep vegetation. Bergman (13) showed that this was particularly the case in the Turnstone which takes low steps with spread toes which tend to become caught up in grasses so that normally the species is found in very short vegetation or on the shore. In contrast the Redshank, with its preference for nesting in deeper vegetation, has evolved longer legs and the toes are closed in the high-stepping movement through vegetation so that they are not caught up. A similar comparison was made by Klomp (117) between the Lapwing which prefers short vegetation and the Black-tailed Godwit which nests in higher vegetation.

Woodcocks and Snipes have proportionately the largest bills of all waders. These are quite straight. They are capable of opening the tip of the bill below ground in order to grasp prey for which they probe, and this is facilitated by the great flexibility of the distal parts of the bill. The legs and neck are relatively short. The Woodcocks are unique among the waders in that they are the only group to have colonised woodland to any great extent. They feed extensively on earthworms and insects and prefer woodlands which are not too densely planted and have a wet or damp floor. In this habitat Woodcocks are extremely well camouflaged. Snipe too tend to occupy the sort of habitat often shunned by other waders because of the thick vegetation, and they are not as frequently seen in the open. One of the most interesting adaptations possessed by any wader is the 'drumming' habit or 'bleating' of the Snipe. They twist the outer tail feathers in the fanned tail to make an angle with the other feathers and dive at great speed, until the air passing over them creates a drumming sound when a speed of 40 kph is reached. Drumming occurs mainly at dusk, and whilst both sexes may drum the male performs most commonly in the nesting area.

Dowitchers show a marked similarity to Snipes in that they are relatively long-billed, short-legged birds which often probe for their food, but they differ in feeding in more open situations and the Short-billed Dowitcher feeds largely on the tide-line outside the breeding season.

The true Sandpipers are small waders with relatively short bills and legs, which breed on the tundra of the subarctic or arctic where the vegetation is short. During the breeding season their diet consists almost exclusively of insects and insect larvae and outside the breeding season they feed on the mudflats and the littoral zone. The Spoon-billed Sandpiper has a broadened and flattened tip to both mandibles but the function of this is not clearly understood. The species feeds in a different manner to other Sandpipers, and is more agile, not running from place to place but running forward, moving its bill in semi-circles in front of it, as it progresses, often up to its belly in water. In the breeding season it takes mainly insects, including beetles, Diptera and Hymenoptera. The Broad-billed Sandpiper has a much stronger bill than the other true Sandpipers and in this shows some convergence with the Snipes. The Stilt Sandpiper is longer in the leg than other sandpipers and has a relatively lightly constructed bill with which it takes insect larvae from wet tundra during the breeding season. The Ruff is probably the most striking wader during the breeding season, the male being significantly larger than the female and adopting a neck ruff and ear tufts of varying colours. It is a bird of low-lying grassy marshes and takes a great variety of insects including grasshoppers and water bugs, and some berries.

The Surf Bird was for a long time thought to be related to the Turnstones, but the characteristics of downy chicks indicate a Calidritine relationship, and the short stout bill suggests a convergence with the Plovers. Outside the breeding season it is a bird of rocky shores. It breeds in Alaska above the tree line.

Adaptive radiation in the waders has produced some quite remarkable species. Among them the Oystercatcher has quite the strongest bill in the group. It contrasts markedly with the delicate upturned structure of the Avocet, which is used for collecting larger quantities of small crustaceans and other small invertebrates. These are normally taken in shallow water by sweeping movements of the bill, a method of feeding sometimes used by the Greenshank (and occasionally by the Redshank). Both the Avocet and the Stilt frequent the shores of shallow and brackish pools where, because of the length of the leg, the Stilt is able to wade deeper. Like the Avocet, the Stilt also feeds on small invertebrates, and the slender bill is adapted for rapid mandibular action in picking up small insects, insect larvae, crustaceans and even small fish.

Phalaropes have a way of taking similar aquatic foods in more northern latitudes that involves spinning on the water. Insect larvae and crustaceans are disturbed by the birds' feet, and the prey are obtained by pecking movements of the slender bill combined with movements of the well-developed tongue. Phalaropes usually occur in low-lying coastal regions on freshwater pools on the tundra.

The manner in which Pratincoles obtain their food is very different from that of most other waders. They take insects both on the ground and in the air as swallows do, and will often follow locust swarms or hawk for dragonflies, caddis flies, beetles, Diptera and ants, sometimes long after dusk. They are able to open their bills very widely, which makes this easier. Pratincoles are inhabitants of sandy, open grasslands, steppe regions and savannas, and nest colonially, an adaptation shared by few other waders.

There are many niches into which the waders have not diverged. None are carnivorous or fish-eating, though some species such as Turnstones will take carrion, and Sheathbills will scavenge and rob nests. Some waders take small fish incidentally, but for the most part they take only insects and other small invertebrates. None are plant eaters, leaf eaters or pollen and nectar feeders and whilst some waders will take seed occasionally, it is only in Seed-Snipe that these form the staple diet. Roots, again, are only occasionally taken, by the Godwits, for example, which will take roots and bulbs of pondweed disturbed by ducks.

Waders occupy many of the habitats in which they are found by virtue of the morphological adaptations which they possess and only some of these have been considered here. Adaptations associated with breeding, moulting and geographical distribution will be dealt with in later chapters, and the present review serves to outline the diversity of the group and the variety of general morphology. However, the ability to occupy a particular habitat does not always manifest itself. In the Pectoral Sandpiper body fat is carried at the beginning of the breeding season in Alaska. The species occupies low-lying habitat which is likely to be snow-covered and if this is the case it can reduce or even cease feeding for a period and rely on the body fat for energy. The Dunlin, in contrast, occupies higher habitats less likely to be snow-covered, and does not carry body fat. According to MacLean (141) carrying body fat at this time allows the Pectoral Sandpiper to occupy smaller territories and reach higher densities than the Dunlin. Almost certainly similar subtle adaptations occur in other species and serve to enable some species to occupy habitats which otherwise would remain unoccupied by wading birds. Many such habitats may remain unoccupied by certain species even though they are unsuitable for only a short period of the year. Possibly many of the adaptations which wading birds possess are selected because of stresses at certain times of the year and, particularly in the case of morphological adaptations, it should be possible to examine their use and evolutionary significance.

MORPHOLOGICAL ADAPTATION

From the consideration of habitat selection and adaptive radiation it is quite clear that wading birds occupy a much greater variety of habitats during the breeding season than they do out of it. It is also clear that many of the adaptations that they possess, have been acquired for use in the breeding season. Clearly some characteristics are adapted for use only during the breeding season, and obviously selected for at that time, for example breeding plumage. However other characteristics are used throughout the year and it is less easy to be sure how and under what circumstances they have been selected. Into this category fall those characters associated with feeding. Is the shape, length and general structure of the bill selected for use during the breeding season, the winter season, or both? Do waders that have long legs use this adaptation for feeding or for some other purpose?

In most waders the distal part of the upper mandible is not only pliable but capable of being raised and lowered independently of the rest of the bill, so that only the tip of the bill may be open, or the tips of the two mandibles might be touching whilst there is an open gap in the middle. This property is known as rhynchokinesis and is moderately developed in some waders such as the Plovers and highly developed in the Curlews and Snipes. Whilst the ability to open only the tip of the bill is clearly of value in taking prey by probing, it is equally possible that it has developed in relation to taking small prey items at the end of a long bill. A hinge near the lip of the long bill clearly provides a much more precise tool than one with a hinge at the base.

Again the emergence of a highly developed sense of touch in the bill has been associated with deep probing. Many waders, such as Snipe, do search for their food using the bill tip rather than sight to find their prey, but this does not necessarily involve probing or penetration into the substrate of more than a few millimetres. A sense of touch may be of equal value in manipulating small food particles or in feeding at night. Some support is given to this suggestion by the Oystercatchers. This group feeds by deep probing but lacks the sense of touch of the Sandpipers and Snipes. They take cockles, for example, by sight or by probing. The bill is then inserted below the shell which is levered out of the mud by lateral head movements, and subsequently opened by blows from the powerful, wedge-shaped bill. Mussels are often taken when slightly agape by stubbing the posterior adductor muscle and inserting the bill between the valves of the shell which are then prised apart by the bird opening its bill. It is not surprising that this sort of activity erodes the bill tip which tends to be more pointed in the unworn condition, and chisel-shaped when worn. There is evidence from recurrent measurements taken on individual birds on the Cheshire Dee, during the hard winter of 1962–63, when the birds were unable to feed, that the bills increased in length through growth (250). Clearly it is an advantage to continue growth if there is constant wear, but the Oystercatchers appear to be unique amongst the wading birds in having such bill growth.

Apart from molluscs, Oystercatchers will feed on Crustaceans, Annelid worms and insects. Individuals appear to have their own food preferences, to such an extent that on the Ribble the small mussel beds seem to be regularly occupied by the same individuals, whereas others will feed almost exclusively on *Macoma* and cockles or, on agricultural land, on earthworms and cranefly (*Tipulid*) larvae.

The long legs of some wading birds are clearly used in enabling them to wade in deep water. However, whilst they are used for this purpose they could have evolved for a completely different reason, for example to enable them to take off in, or see over, tall vegetation.

There is a great temptation to assume that if a wader has a long bill it is designed for probing deep into mud. The fact that this bill is used for probing is not to say that it is designed for this purpose. It is quite possible that it has evolved for some quite different purpose and that this design also enables it to be used for probing. In subsequent chapters these possibilities will be examined in the light of the available evidence on feeding ecology (Chapter 9) and the selection of morphological characters (Chapter 11).

CHAPTER 3

GEOGRAPHICAL DISTRIBUTION AND VARIATION

THE present-day distribution of all species of living organisms results from the interplay of several factors, including the ecology of the organism, weather, vegetation cover, altitude and the past history of the species concerned. Whilst some of the parameters involved can be measured with varying degrees of accuracy, an examination of the past history of a species is, to say the least, highly speculative. Even so, any examination of the distribution of wading birds must pay considerable attention to the past history of the group, particularly in view of the fact that many species now breed in arctic or sub-arctic conditions, which have prevailed for only part of their evolutionary history.

The Charadrii evolved during the warm climate of the Tertiary and it is reasonable to assume that waders such as the Calidritine sandpipers, as we know them, could not have existed then. All the species of this group have evolved adaptations to enable them to live in cold environments and the stresses which led to these adaptations were not experienced before the onset of a cold period during the mid-Miocene (Fig. 1). From then on, the cold region moved south until by the end of the Pliocene ($1\frac{1}{2}$ million years B.P.), the climate was similar to that of today and the circumpolar belt of tundra was fully formed. It is likely that, by this time, cold adapted waders occupied the tundra zone during the breeding season and it may well be that the Ringed Plover was one of the first of these species. It is likely that whatever species existed became progressively adapted to the colder environment so that, initially, temperate forms gave rise to cold climate forms which in turn gave

48

rise to forms which could exist on the treeless tundra of the far north. Among these may have been such species as the Turnstone, and the direct ancestors of the Calidritine sandpipers may have evolved by this time, as fossils are known from the end of the Pliocene. It is probable that several different cold climate species evolved as the temperate region was pushed south since pockets of tundra did not link until the end of the Pliocene.

From the end of the Pliocene the climate of the present day Holarctic Region got progressively colder until its climax at the peak of the first Ice Age, some 500,000 years B.P. The extensive tundra zone at the southern edge of the ice sheet provided suitable habitat for the largest populations of arctic waders that had existed until this time but for the next 10,000 years these populations declined as the tundra zone retreated north. The rest of the Pleistocene was a period of fluctuating fortunes for the arctic waders as their habitat increased during the glaciations and contracted in the inter-glacials, in the height of which tundra existed only in three refuges in northern Greenland, Alaska and in the mountains of Verkhoyansk in Siberia. It is widely accepted that Pleistocene events have played an important part in the evolution of our whole avifauna. However, there are few groups of birds which have been affected as much as the waders, and the probable frequent isolation of the arctic breeders, and to some extent the temperate breeders, has led to speciation, sub-speciation and probably extinction on numerous occasions. The history of speciation in wading birds is very complex and difficult to trace. Speciation has been affected greatly by the vicissitudes of the Pleistocene which have also played a large part in determining the present-day distribution. Larson (130) has attempted to trace speciation in waders, and in fact speculates on possible ways in which waders might have evolved since the late Tertiary. On the basis of the known climatic changes during the Pleistocene (four major glaciations and three inter-glacial periods) it is possible to make some assumptions which are very likely to be correct.

1. During the last inter-glacial period tundra species were restricted to refuges in northern Greenland/Ellesmere Island, two areas in Alaska and an area in the Verkhoyansk Mountains in eastern Siberia.
2. Because of the contraction of their ranges any species which had previously given rise to subspecies would no longer have different geographical forms because of the gene flow in the relatively small areas where they were concentrated. An exception might be where one species was present in more than one refuge.
3. During the last glaciation European tundra zones were colonised by birds from the Greenland/Ellesmere Island inter-glacial refuge, Canada was colonised from the Alaskan refuges, and eastern Siberia from the Verkhoyansk refuge (Fig. 2).

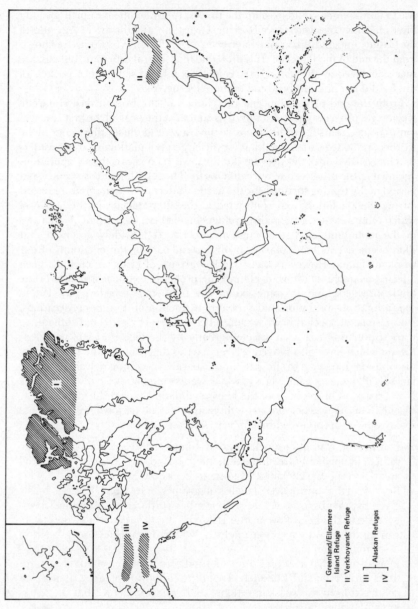

FIG. 2. Tundra vegetation at the height of the last inter-glacial period (after Larson 1957).

I Greenland/Ellesmere
   Island Refuge
II Verkhoyansk Refuge

III ⎫
    ⎬ Alaskan Refuges
IV ⎭

If these assumptions are valid then it is possible that:

1. Subspeciation and the formation of geographically distinct populations of present-day species occurred during and after the last glaciation.
2. Present day species of waders had evolved before the last glaciation.

In the case of the formation of geographically distinct populations, which in some cases are given the status of sub-species, it is possible to examine their distribution in the light of the distribution of glacial refuges. Perhaps the best comparison might be made in species which inhabit tundra areas, and have more than one recognised subspecies.

The distribution of vegetation types during the Pleistocene has received a great deal of attention from botanists. Some disagreement exists concerning the detailed distribution of vegetation during certain periods but there is broad agreement concerning the vegetation during the last glaciation. Fig. 3 shows the distribution of tundra at the height of the last glaciation. This is based on the vegetation map by Frenzel (50) which shows a barrier made up of wood and shrub tundra and the Alpine/Scandinavian ice sheets, which considered together produced a gap between 2000 and 3000 km in extent between the short tundra/steppe vegetation in France and that in western USSR which would be suitable for Dunlins and Golden Plovers. Assuming that any geographical variation which occurs has taken place since the last inter-glacial, a comparison of the known present day geographical variation with the location of these refuges might prove fruitful. Attempts at such a comparison in the past have been hampered by a less than adequate knowledge of the geographical variation in wading birds and because of this a group of my research students and I have carried out detailed studies of the variation in selected species. Selection for study was made on the basis of the species being known to be polytypic (having more than one geographical form) and those chosen were Golden Plover, Ringed Plover, Bar-tailed and Black-tailed Godwits, Redshank, Dunlin and Knot.

Because of the large amount of information which now exists about them they will provide good examples for comparing the localities in which morphologically distinct populations occur with the glacial refugia in which they possibly originated. For the most part geographical variation concerns either the colour of the plumage or the variability in overall size or the size of certain structures such as the bill, tarsus, wing and tail. Consistent variation in any of these characters is regarded as indicative of genetic differences between populations, but it is important to remember that there may be genetic differences between populations which have no obvious morphological expression. It should also be borne in mind that selection for particular characteristics is most likely to be brought about by present day selection pressures, so that geographical variation is, for the most part, an expression of the present rather than the past environment. However, some characteristics of all organisms have existed for very long periods of time and it is often a matter

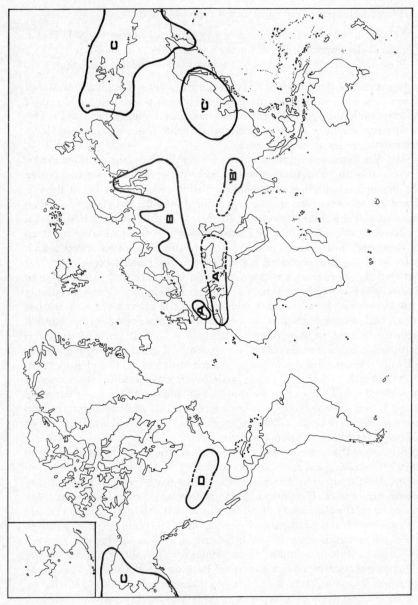

Fig. 3. Refuges at the height of the last glaciation A, B, C, D = Tundra refuges; 'A', 'B', 'C' = Temperate refuges.

of the research worker's judgement whether a particular character is subject to present day selection pressures which might modify it or whether it is a character which has existed for many thousands or millions of years, having resulted from selection in the distant past.

Variation within species of birds has attracted the attention of ornithologists since the time of Linné, and for some time around the turn of the century it was fashionable to provide a sub-specific name for any and every variant collected. It has now become the fashion to weigh and measure nearly every bird trapped for ringing purposes, in order to try to identify the population from which it originates. While scientifically this is much more laudable than merely naming all the forms that occur, it fails to get to the root of the problem of variability which can only be answered by examination of specimens from the breeding grounds of the birds in question. Only where the breeding populations are properly characterised is it justifiable to attribute migrant birds to one of these. It was with this in mind that I got together all the available specimens of breeding Redshank from the museum collections throughout the world, so that breeding populations could be characterised. Subsequently, my research students and I have done the same with other species of wading birds, borrowing specimens from some 170 collections, so that now we have a vast quantity of information which can be subjected to sophisticated forms of analysis, details of which are outside the scope of this book. The broad conclusions of this work are, however, of particular relevance to a consideration of the evolutionary significance of geographical variation in the group.

GEOGRAPHICAL VARIATION

Plumage Differences

Where the breeding range of a species is geographically extensive it is likely that some degree of variability will be found. Among the Plovers this is best exemplified in the Golden Plover where distinct plumage differences occur, and in the Ringed Plover where only very slight plumage differences are found, but body measurements differ in different parts of the range. Both these species can be considered to be tundra forms and in general birds of the cold arctic climate during the breeding season.

East of the Yenesei, and in N. America the Golden Plover (Fig. 4) is replaced by the Lesser Golden Plover. In the western Palaearctic, the Golden Plover has two forms, the boldly marked 'northern' form in Iceland, northern Scandinavia and north-western Russia and the 'southern' form in the British Isles and in the southern Baltic region. The latter is less well marked during the breeding season due to the incomplete assumption of breeding plumage which results from there being only a partial spring moult. The retention of winter feathers is particularly noticeable on the head, breast and belly where

54

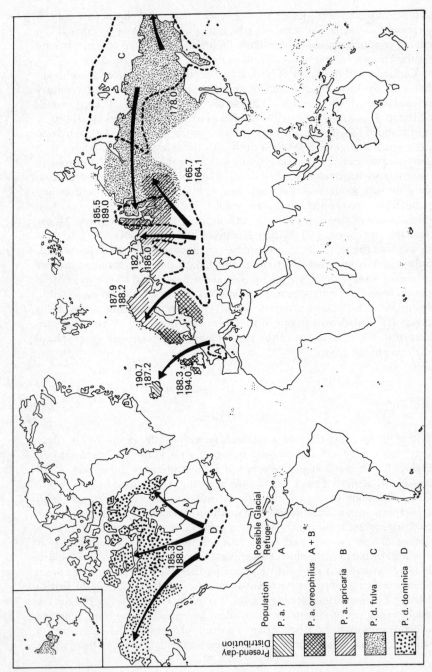

FIG. 4. Distribution and possible refuges of origin of Golden Plover *Pluvialis apricaria* and Lesser Golden Plover *Pluvialis dominica* showing mean wing lengths of male (above) and female (below).

Population

Possible Glacial
Refuge

A

Present-day
Distribution

P. a. ?

P. a. oreophilus   A + B

P. a. apricaria   B

P. d. fulva   C

P. d. dominica   D

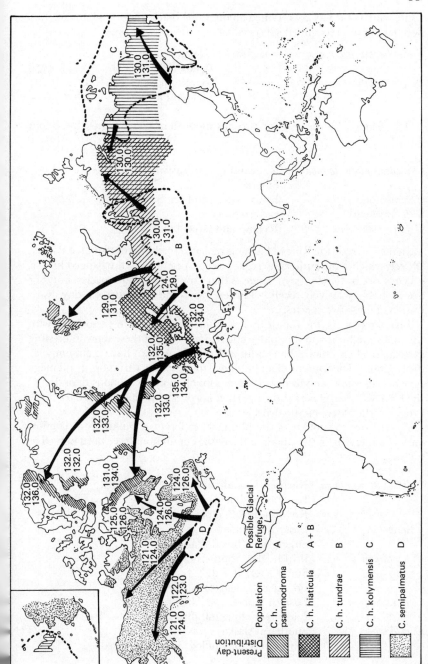

FIG. 5. Distribution and possible refuges of origin of Ringed Plover *Charadrius hiaticula* and Semi-palmated Ringed Plover *Charadrius semipalmatus*, showing mean wing lengths of male (above) and female (below).

white winter feathers are retained amongst the black summer plumage. Two populations are recognised subspecifically at the present time:

Pluvialis apricaria apricaria (=altifrons) 'Northern'
Golden Plover

P. a. oreophilus 'Southern'
Golden Plover

The Ringed Plover (Fig. 5) also has more than one recognisable colour form:

Charadrius hiaticula tundrae N. Scandinavian eastwards to central
Siberia
C. h. hiaticula British Isles, southern Scandinavia
C. h. kolymensis eastern Siberia
C. h. psammodroma Iceland and Greenland

In the Nearctic the Ringed Plover is replaced by the Semipalmated Ringed Plover, which some authorities regard as conspecific with the Ringed Plover; recent work by Taylor (237) suggests that they are separate species, but they are probably relatively recently formed. Fig. 5 shows the present day distribution of these two species.

Like the Plovers, the Calidritine sandpipers in general are associated with the tundra habitat and the cold arctic regions. Two of these show interesting geographical variation, the Dunlin and the Knot. Both have a circumpolar distribution. The Dunlin (Fig. 6) shows the greatest variation in plumage type of any wader and its distribution is much more continuous than that of the Knot which in general breeds further north, so that there is relatively little range overlap between the two species.

Apart from the colour of the plumage, different populations of Dunlins vary considerably in size and in bill length. Populations have been named as follows:

Calidris alpina alpina Northern Scandinavia and N.W. USSR.
Large, long-billed.
Reddish breeding plumage.
C. a. arctica Eastern Greenland.
Small, short-billed. Paler red.
C. a. schinzii British Isles, Southern Scandinavia.
Small, short-billed.
Browner than *alpina* and *arctica*.
C. a. sakhalina Eastern Siberia–N. Alaska.
Large, very long bill. Bright red.
C. a. pacifica Southern Alaska.
Large, very long billed. Very bright red.

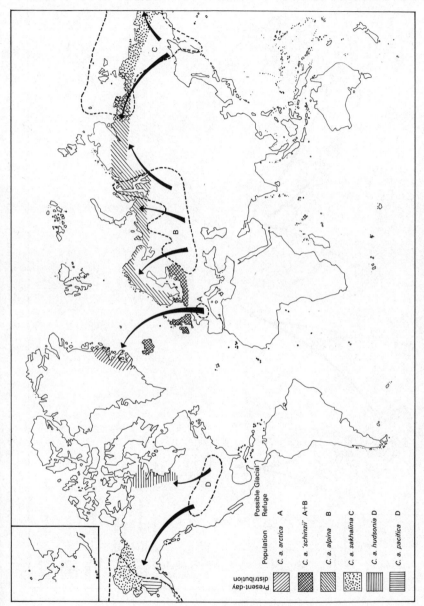

FIG. 6. Distribution and possible refuges of origin of Dunlin *Calidris alpna*.

Population   Possible Glacial
              Refuge

C. a. arctica   A

C. a. 'schinzii'   A+B

C. a. alpina   B

C. a. sakhalina   C

C. a. hudsonia   D

C. a. pacifica   D

Present-day
distribution

58

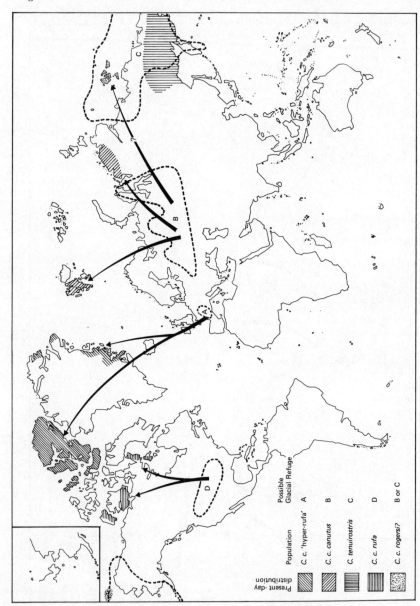

Fig. 7. Distribution and possible refuges of origin of Knot *Calidris canutus* and Greater Knot *Calidris tenuirostris*.

C. a. hudsonia Hudson Bay.
Large, very long billed. Very bright red.
Distinct from 'pacifica' largely on the
basis of completely separate populations
in summer and winter.

In northern Siberia *C. a. centralis* has been described, but this appears to be an intermediate form between *alpina* and *sakhalina*.

The Knot (Fig. 7) has fewer populations with recognisable morphological differences. However, the following have been recognised:

Calidris canutus canutus Ellesmere Island, westward to
New Siberian Islands
C. c. rufa N. Canada south of Ellesmere Island

J. G. Greenwood has found that the Greenland and Ellesmere Island Knots are different in colour from the European Knots, and are identical in colour with the Greenland Dunlin *C. a. arctica*, being paler than the typical form but darker than *rufa*. Verwey (247) also records a difference in this population which he named '*hyper-rufa*'. In breeding plumage there is no difficulty in separating European and Greenland Knot. In eastern Siberia *C. c. rogersi* has been separated because of its slightly larger size and greyer coloration but it is of doubtful validity. In eastern Siberia the Knot is replaced by the Greater Knot, *Calidris tenuirostris*.

The Bar-tailed Godwit is another northern tundra breeder with a range from northern Scandinavia to Alaska (Fig. 8). Two morphologically distinct populations are usually recognised:

Limosa lapponica lapponica Scandinavia, Western USSR.
L. l. baueri Eastern Siberia and Alaska.

The latter has the rump and underwing more spotted. Between the two *L. l. menzbieri* has been recognised but this again is probably merely an intermediate form. In the rest of the Nearctic there is not a closely related replacement for the Bar-tailed Godwit and the Dowitchers apparently replace it ecologically.

Further south the Black-tailed Godwit occurs in a band across Eurasia from Iceland to Kamchatka and Alaska but there is a break in central USSR which clearly separates the breeding populations. Three morphologically distinct populations can be recognised:

Limosa limosa limosa Western central Europe.
Long bill. Reddish plumage.
L. l. islandica Iceland.
Shorter bill. Redder plumage.
L. l. melanuroides Eastern USSR.
Shorter bill. Smaller. Darker.

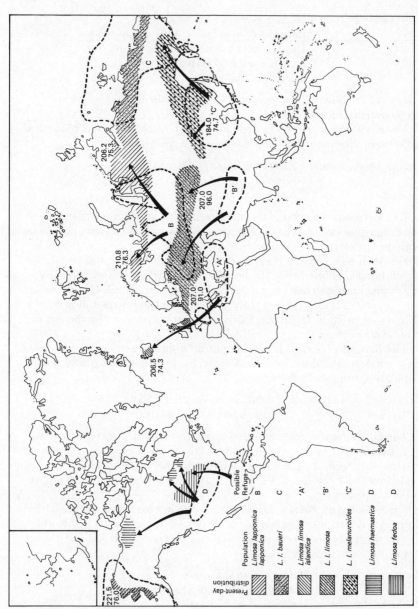

Fig. 8. Distribution and possible origins of populations of Godwits in arctic and temperate areas of isolation showing wing lengths (above) and bill lengths (below) of males.

In the Black-tailed Godwit there is a size cline from east to west. In the Nearctic the Black-tailed Godwit is replaced ecologically by the Marbled Godwit *Limosa fedoa*, which is much larger, but the Hudsonian Godwit is probably its nearest relative. Some authorities regard the Hudsonian and Black-tailed Godwits as conspecific but since the two have different wing patterns and occupy different habitats, this is almost certainly not the case.

There is extensive geographical variation in the Redshank (Fig. 9), and I have recognised the following distinct populations (73):

Tringa totanus totanus	Northern Scandinavia.
	Chocolate brown.
T. t. eurhinus	Himalayas.
	Chocolate brown.
T. t. craggi	Sinkiang.
	Bright red.
T. t. terrignotae	Eastern China.
	Cinnamon.
T. t. ussuriensis	Ussuri Basin to Urals.
	Dark cinnamon.

West of the Urals, *T. t. ussuriensis* adopts less breeding plumage progressively westward, and retains more winter feathers in summer, to a minimum amount of breeding plumage in Hungary and the British Isles.

The same type of breeding plumage is found in Iceland, but there are fewer winter feathers here than in the British Isles. A similar situation occurs north of the Himalayas and there can be little doubt that the reduction of breeding plumage and the retention of winter feathers results from hybridisation between the chocolate brown birds and the dark cinnamon population. In marked contrast to the situation in the Redshank, there is little or no geographical variation in either the Greenshank *T. nebularia* or the Spotted Redshank *T. erythropus* (Fig. 10). In the Nearctic, the Greenshank is replaced by the Greater Yellowlegs and the Redshank and Spotted Redshank are replaced by the Lesser Yellowlegs.

In the arctic and temperate wader species so far examined, most geographical variation has been in the colour of the various forms. In western Europe, however, there is an area where, in several species, the amount of breeding plumage varies and some supposed sub-species are characterised by a deficiency of a full breeding plumage. This is the case in the so-called Southern Dunlin *Calidris alpina schinzii*. The most significant characteristic of this population is the lack of the dark belly found in *C. a. alpina* during the breeding season because of the retention of white winter feathers, which give the belly a patchy appearance. The situation is very similar to that of the so-called 'southern' Golden Plover. However, this characteristic of only a partial assumption of breeding plumage is not limited to these two species; it occurs also in the Redshank and in the Black-tailed Godwit, and there is some

62

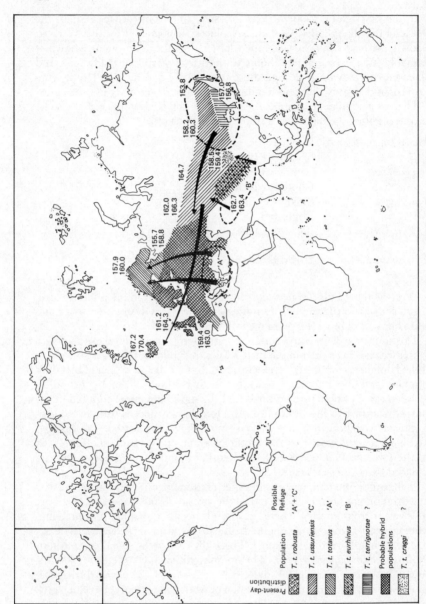

FIG. 9. Distribution and possible origins of populations of the Redshank *Tringa totanus* in temperate areas of isolation showing mean wing lengths of male (above) and female (below).

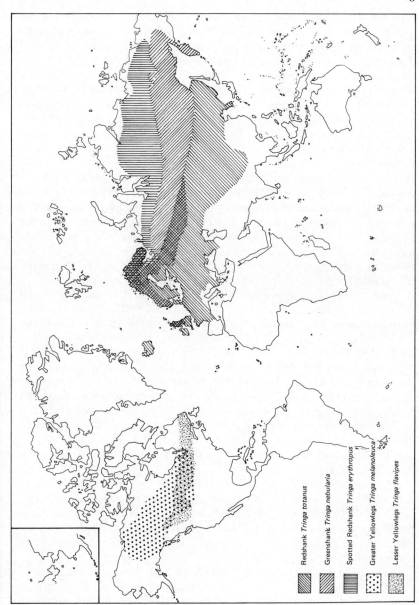

Fig. 10. Present-day distribution of the Redshank *Tringa totanus* and closely related species.

Redshank *Tringa totanus*

Greenshank *Tringa nebularia*

Spotted Redshank *Tringa erythropus*

Greater Yellowlegs *Tringa melanoleuca*

Lesser Yellowlegs *Tringa flavipes*

evidence that Ringed Plovers also retain some winter feathers during the spring and summer. It is of significance that this character occurs in the same geographical region – the British Isles and the European continent as far as the Baltic – in all five species, though in some, e.g. Redshank, the extent is greater. The probable explanation of this is that the populations in this area are hybrid populations. Clearly the normal spring moult has been affected. It is interesting that the same thing happens in hybrid pheasants, bred in captivity, where the normal moulting process is disrupted by the hybridisation. There is other evidence for hybridisation; in the Redshank colour forms which normally exist in other parts of the range occur in western Europe (even the cinnamon form *Tringa totanus terrignotae* found normally only in eastern China) and a great range of individual size occurs; this is typical of a hybrid swarm. Again, the area where only partial breeding plumage is found is in many cases at the point of meeting of the ranges of recognisably distinct populations. The implication is that in western Europe populations of these species have come together after a long period of isolation, and not having evolved quite to the species level, have given rise to secondary hybridisation. Such a hypothesis is difficult to test, but the populations giving rise to the hybrid zones could be as shown opposite.

There is one particularly important piece of evidence, already mentioned briefly, which supports this interpretation. In the Redshank the northern Scandinavian population is of chocolate brown birds *Tringa totanus totanus* and the hypothesis put forward here is based on the hybridisation of this population with a dark cinnamon population from further east *T. t. ussuriensis*. There is a similar chocolate brown population isolated in the Himalayas, and this contacts the dark cinnamon population in the region of Tien Shan, where another hybrid zone exists which has the character of the western European hybrid zone. Again many birds adopt only a partial breeding plumage and several colour forms are found; in other words another typical hybrid swarm exists in Tien Shan. In northern Eurasia the Dunlin *Calidris alpina centralis* has a paler belly colour than either *C. a. alpina* or *C. a. sakhalina* and it is likely that it is a hybrid between the two.

On the basis of the known differences between the various populations in western Europe it is reasonable to postulate geographical isolation during, and possibly for some time after, the last glaciation. An examination of the tundra refuges shown in Fig. 3, is informative in the light of the present-day distribution of genetically different populations of the species of waders under discussion.

Considering first the tundra species isolated in the tundra refuges A, B, C, and D, it is likely that some genetical changes had occurred in separate populations of the same species before the amelioration in the climate which resulted in a northward spread of these populations. With the recession of the ice, tundra species in refuge A probably colonised the areas immediately north, moving through the British Isles, Iceland and into Greenland. In the

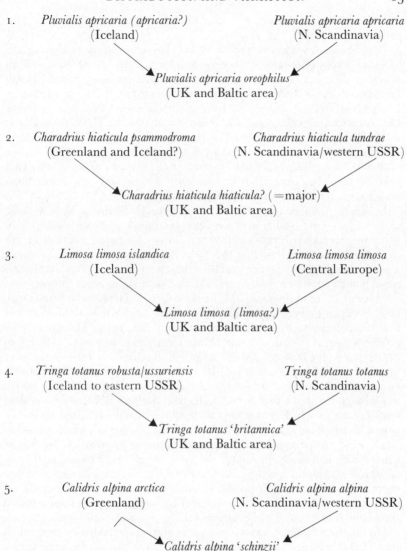

1. *Pluvialis apricaria (apricaria?)*   *Pluvialis apricaria apricaria*
    (Iceland)   (N. Scandinavia)

    Pluvialis apricaria oreophilus
    (UK and Baltic area)

2. *Charadrius hiaticula psammodroma*   *Charadrius hiaticula tundrae*
    (Greenland and Iceland?)   (N. Scandinavia/western USSR)

    Charadrius hiaticula hiaticula? (=major)
    (UK and Baltic area)

3. *Limosa limosa islandica*   *Limosa limosa limosa*
    (Iceland)   (Central Europe)

    Limosa limosa (limosa?)
    (UK and Baltic area)

4. *Tringa totanus robusta/ussuriensis*   *Tringa totanus totanus*
    (Iceland to eastern USSR)   (N. Scandinavia)

    Tringa totanus 'britannica'
    (UK and Baltic area)

5. *Calidris alpina arctica*   *Calidris alpina alpina*
    (Greenland)   (N. Scandinavia/western USSR)

    Calidris alpina 'schinzii'
    (UK and Baltic area)

Dunlin the population concerned would be *C. a. arctica*, in the Knot Verwey's 'hyper-rufa', and in the Ringed Plover, *Charadrius hiaticula psammodroma*. The Golden Plover population would be *Pluvialis apricaria 'x'*, considered earlier, and it is possible that the Bar-tailed Godwit did not occur in refuge A but was limited to refuge B. However, it may have been present and later became extinct.

From refuge B waders moved north to colonise Scandinavia and western Siberia. These populations were of Dunlin *Calidris alpina alpina*, Knot *C. canutus canutus*, Golden Plover *Pluvialis apricarius apricarius*, Ringed Plover *Charadrius hiaticula tundrae* and Bar-tailed Godwit *Limosa lapponica lapponica*. Further east, refuge C may well have given rise to *Calidris alpina sakhalina*, *Charadrius hiaticula kolymensis* and *Limosa lapponica baueri*. The Golden Plover was probably absent from refuge C and replaced by the Lesser Golden Plover *Pluvialis dominica fulva*, and probably Knot were absent, though if *Calidris canutus rogersi* is a discrete population it may well have arisen there, though it is possible that the Great Knot *C. tenuirostris* was the only species of Knot occurring in the area at the height of the last glaciation.

In North America refuge D may well have given rise to *C. a. hudsonia* and/or *C. a. pacifica* which may have become morphologically distinct subsequently, though it is possible that they arose in separate refugia. In this connection it is of interest that the Short-billed Dowitchers were probably separated similarly giving rise to at least two clearly defined populations, and possibly the Solitary Sandpiper and Piping Plover fall into this category, but insufficient information is available on these species. The Knot *C. canutus rufa*, Lesser Golden Plover *Pluvialis dominica dominica*, and Semi-palmated Plover *Calidris semipalmatus* probably also moved north from refuge D.

The temperate refuges during the last glaciation are more difficult to define, but on the basis of Frenzel's maps (50) it is likely that they were fewer than described by Larson (130). In western Europe refuge 'A' probably housed the Icelandic Black-tailed Godwit *Limosa limosa icelandica* which moved up through the British Isles to Iceland. Refuge 'B' housed the typical form *L. l. limosa* which moved up into southern Scandinavia and refuge 'C' housed *L. l. melanuroides*. At the height of the last glaciation a band of wooded tundra and steppe existed right across Eurasia as far west as the Alpine glacier, and it is likely that both the Greenshank and Spotted Redshank occupied this habitat and the latter some of the sub-arctic cold steppe farther north. It is significant that neither of these species shows any geographical variation, probably due to the fact that there was continuous occupation of their habitat (Fig. 10). Further south of this there can be little doubt that the habitat of the Redshank was discontinuous and much smaller in extent than that of the present day. Area 'A' probably gave rise to the present day northern Scandinavian population of the typical form *Tringa totanus totanus* – a small chocolate brown bird with heavy breast markings. It is possible that Area A was further east, as otherwise it is difficult to explain why these chocolate brown birds did not get into Britain and Iceland. Previously I have considered that this form had a refuge in southern Europe and during the retreat of the ice spread up the western European seaboard (73). There are no records of this form from Britain and this is difficult to explain. However, it is

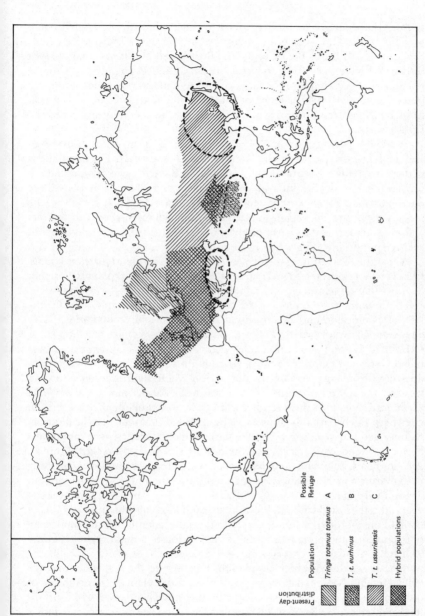

Fig. 11. Spread of Redshank populations with the amelioration of the climate following the last Ice Age.

possible that Spanish records of this form during the breeding season are not of breeding birds, but of migrants which would normally breed in northern Scandinavia. If this is the case, the original spread of this chocolate brown bird could have been from south of the Black and Caspian Seas, without reaching the coast south of Denmark. This hypothesis now seems the more likely, particularly in the light of the breeding Redshank from southern France lacking a full breeding plumage and being generally similar to the British birds.

A second population of chocolate brown birds probably existed in Refuge B and this persists in the Himalayas as *T. t. eurhinus*. The populations of these two refuges were probably derived from a single population occurring further north in the last inter-glacial period. Refuge C probably housed the dark cinnamon *T. t. ussuriensis* which spread westwards on the recession of the ice, giving rise to the regions of secondary hybridisation shown in Fig. 11. Table 1 summarises the distribution of present-day sub-species populations in relation to possible refuges of origin.

Whilst the derivation of the present day colour morphs of all these species from probable glacial refuges is rather speculative, it does explain the present day distribution of different populations.

The hypothesis accounts for the occurrence of hybrid zones and for the lack of assumption of a full breeding plumage in many populations. This phenomenon arises where a north Scandinavian population contacts a Greenland/Iceland population, and where one or other is absent e.g. in Bar-tailed Godwit, Temminck's Stint, Greenshank, Spotted Redshank, Ruff, it does not arise. Furthermore, in this region where hybridisation occurs in western Europe e.g. Iceland, Britain/southern Baltic, populations of cold arctic forms occur at their southern limits, considerably further south than elsewhere. Such a situation might well be expected as a result of hybridisation. Salomonsen (213) draws attention to the fact that the occurrence of organisms normally found in the arctic, at the latitudes of Britain on the European Atlantic coast, is not limited to birds but is widespread amongst invertebrates, both marine and fresh-water. He suggests that as the glaciers pushed south in Scandinavia during the Younger Dryas (11,000–10,400 B.P.), some 4000 years after the last glaciation, the animal populations moved south too. As the climate ameliorated, some organisms gradually adapted to the increasing temperatures, and remained south of the previously normal range. It could well have been the recovery from the Younger Dryas which brought the previously separated wader populations together for the first time since the glacial refuges A and B had separated. This would explain the rather different outcome of secondary hybridisation in this area compared with the in-tergradation occurring between populations which had been separated for a shorter time. It would also provide the genetical make-up which would be the more amenable to climatic adaptation – the hybrid swarm.

Whilst the exact way in which populations were separated and came

TABLE I. Present day distribution of named sub-species populations in relation to possible glacial refugia of origin

Species	Alaska	N. Canada	Ellesmere Island / W. Greenland	Eastern Greenland	Iceland	UK/Baltic	N. Scandinavia / W. Siberia	Central Siberia	Eastern Siberia
Golden Plover	P. dominica fulva C	P. dominica dominica D	—	—	P. apricaria apricaria? A	P. apricaria oreophilus Partial B.P.	P. apricaria apricaria B	P. apricaria apricaria B	P. dominica fulva C
Ringed Plover	C. hiaticula kolymensis C + C. semipalmatus D	C. semipalmatus D	C. hiaticula psammodroma A	C. hiaticula psammodroma A	C. hiaticula psammodroma A	C. hiaticula hiaticula Partial B.P.	C. hiaticula tundrae B	C. hiaticula tundrae B	C. hiaticula kolymensis C
Black-tailed Godwit	—	—	—	—	L. limosa islandica 'A'	L. limosa ? Partial B.P.	L. limosa limosa 'B'	—	L. limosa melanuroides 'C'
Bar-tailed Godwit							L. lapponica lapponica B		L. lapponica baueri C
Redshank					T. totanus robusta Partial B.P.	T. totanus 'britannica' Partial B.P.	T. totanus totanus 'A' or 'B'	—	T. totanus ussuriensis 'C'
Dunlin	C. alpina sakhalina C + C. alpina pacifica D?	C. alpina hudsonia D?	—	C. alpina arctica A	C. alpina 'schinzii' Partial B.P.	C. alpina 'schinzii' Partial B.P.	C. alpina alpina B	C. alpina centralis? Partial B.P.?	C. alpina sakhalina C
Knot	—	C. canutus rufa D	C. canutus canutus? (hyper-rufa?) A	C. canutus canutus? (hyper-rufa?) A	—	—		C. canutus canutus B	C. tenuirostris C
Glacial Refugia	Eastern Asiatic Refuge C	Central N. American Refuge(s) D	Western European Refuge A	Western European Refuge A	Zone of Hybridisation		Eastern European Refuge B	Eastern European Refuge B	Eastern Asiatic Refuge C

together again is very speculative, there can be no doubt that these processes occurred during and after the last glaciation. It follows, then, that most speciation occurred prior to the last glaciation, though Ringed Plover and Semi-palmated Ringed Plover may well be examples of speciation resulting from the last glaciation. Here a further 10,000 years of separation compared with Dunlin, Godwit and Redshank populations appears to have been enough for speciation which some 20–30 thousand years of separation had failed to achieve.

It is possible that some populations were separated during the last inter-glacial period, as they were pushed south, but later waves of colonising birds from the refuges probably maintained a gene flow and prevented genetical and geographical isolation. It is likely then that all the tundra species as we know them today were isolated during the last inter-glacial period in the four main refuges, the largest of which was Greenland/Ellesmere Island (F ig. 2). Refuge I probably housed the Golden Plover, whilst the Asiatic (Lesser) Golden Plover was in II and the American (Lesser) Golden Plover in III and IV. Refuges II, III and IV probably also accommodated the Grey Plover. Probably Dunlin, Knot and Ringed Plover occupied refuge I though the latter may well have occupied regions on the coast of northern Scandinavia. Refuge I probably held the Bar-tailed Godwit too, with the Long-billed Dowitcher and Short-billed Dowitcher in refuges III and IV, and the Asiatic Dowitcher in II, and it is clearly possible that the Greater Knot was isolated in refuge II during the inter-glacial.

There can be little doubt that at the onset of the first Ice Age cold climate forms were pushed south, populations separated and sub-species formed. During the first inter-glacial period the ice retreated and the cold climate forms moved north into relatively small refuges, almost certainly with the total loss of the sub-species formed. This process was repeated twice more and at the present time we may well be only partially along the way to another inter-glacial maximum. It is likely that on each occasion similar isolated populations formed sub-species in more or less the same areas, only for them to be eliminated with the onset of the interglacials. Some might have survived as species and Larson (130) has attempted to allocate all present day species to areas and times of origin. He allocates Sanderling, the Phalaropes, the Marbled Godwit, the Stilt Sandpiper and Buff-breasted Sandpiper exclusively to the Greenland/Ellesmere Island refuge (I), whilst suggesting that the Surf Bird, Great Knot, Grey-rumped Sandpiper and Spoon-billed Sandpiper were limited to the refuges (II, III and IV) on either side of the Bering Straits (Beringia). Where glacial sub-species have become isolated in different inter-glacial refuges, new closely related species pairs, of recent origin are suggested, as follows:

Beringia species	*Greenland/Ellesmere species*
Lesser Golden Plover	Golden Plover
Red-necked Stint	Little Stint
Rock Sandpiper	Purple Sandpiper
Western Sandpiper	Semi-palmated Sandpiper
Long-billed Dowitcher	Short-billed Dowitcher

All these species could easily have been formed as late as the third glaciation and there can be little doubt that other species were formed (and possibly some of these) by the earlier glaciations. It is therefore very much an act of faith to accept Larson's suggestion that species pairs such as Curlew–Sandpiper/Dunlin and Sharp-tailed Sandpiper/Pectoral Sandpiper are of Tertiary origin. It is outside the scope of this discussion to consider species formation, except in as far as this affects present day distribution. A more detailed consideration of the likely distribution of species, in the light of the best available vegetation maps and climatological knowledge of the Pleistocene and late Tertiary, may well provide further information on distribution, but at present this is only at the stage of promising to be an interesting future line of research. For the present it must be sufficient to speculate on the origins of morphologically distinct populations and recently formed species.

All the cold climate waders, and many of the temperate forms, migrate south in autumn and in order to maintain the existing degree of geographical variation, most species must return to the same geographical area the following breeding season. Many populations must have their own discrete wintering areas where they do not meet other populations of the same species (and thus minimise gene flow), and most individuals must be faithful to their own areas of origin. There are some species which do not behave in this way, and perhaps the best example is the Lapwing. Ringing recoveries have shown that individuals of this species may nest very large distances from their places of origin and this certainly increases the gene flow within the population. There is no geographical variation in this species and probably this is as much associated with the vagrancy of the species as with the continuity of the distribution. Geographical variation is associated with geographical isolation only in that the latter ensures a minimum of gene flow; it is important to maintain this isolation by a minimum of mixing with other populations outside the breeding season to ensure the return of birds to their original breeding areas.

Measurements

Throughout the breeding range of many species of waders there is great variability in the length of different structures. Wing length, bill length and tarsus length are all measured as a matter of course in studies of variation, and

TABLE 2. Variation in measurements of the same population of Redshank in different seasons compared with measurements of museum specimens from the same area (N.W. England)

MALES

	Weight	Wing	Tail	Bill	Tarsus Length	Tarsus Width
1973		165.11 ±0.93	63.41 ±0.72	41.88 ±0.55	47.79 ±0.59	2.41 ±0.02
1974	127.60 ±1.16	162.14 ±0.53	62.65 ±0.49	41.24 ±0.27	48.00 ±0.33	2.40 ±0.01
1975	127.37 ±1.08	164.33 ±0.40	64.98 ±0.31	41.45 ±0.30	48.28 ±0.36	2.42 ±0.01
Measurements from museum specimens		158.70 ±1.20	64.50 ±0.70	41.30 ±0.56	48.70 ±0.46	2.18 ±0.02

FEMALES

	Weight	Wing	Tail	Bill	Tarsus Length	Tarsus Width
1973		170.52 ±0.70	65.17 ±0.62	42.41 ±0.52	48.14 ±0.46	2.40 ±0.02
1974	137.06 ±1.05	166.12 ±0.50	64.62 ±0.53	41.97 ±0.24	48.58 ±0.30	2.42 ±0.01
1975	133.84 ±1.05	166.83 ±0.42	65.16 ±0.34	41.66 ±0.18	49.23 ±0.22	2.44 ±0.01
Measurements from museum specimens		162.10 ±1.33	65.80 ±1.03	41.70 ±0.50	47.60 ±0.63	2.19 ±0.03

often tarsus width and tail length are also measured. In most waders wing length generally gives an overall indication of the size (weight) of a bird, but since the weight varies greatly with the season (Chapter 5) care must be taken in examining this relationship. In addition wing length measurements are subject to inaccuracies due to wear, and although it might be thought sufficient to compare measurements taken from the same time of the year where relative wear might be thought to be the same from year to year, my work on a breeding population of Redshank has shown that a single population might vary in mean wing length from year to year. Table 2 shows measurements taken in three separate breeding seasons, and clearly the 1974 season showed a significant difference in wing length, whereas measurements of the bill and tarsus showed no differences from season to season. Care has also to be taken in comparing field measurements with measurements of museum skins and the differences for the same population of Redshank can

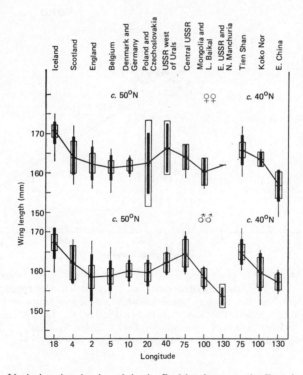

FIG. 12. Variations in wing length in the Redshank, across the Eurasian continent. The thin black line shows the range of measurements, the thick line one standard deviation on either side of the mean, the horizontal line the mean, and the box two standard errors on each side of the mean (after Hale 1971).

also be seen in Table 2. There is a significant shrinkage of the wing and also of the tarsus in respect to width.

Despite such problems measurements often show a pattern. In the Redshank, for example, there is an east-west cline in wing measurement across Asia at 50°N and at 40°N (Fig. 12). West of the Urals the wing length falls to rise again in Iceland. There seems to be no obvious reason why there should be a reduction in wing length in central Europe, but if the wing length is plotted against the mean minimum May temperatures (those to which the birds would be subjected on the breeding ground) then a clear relationship is seen to exist (Fig. 13). This is a good example of Bergmann's Rule (see Chapter 11), where in colder climates the bird is larger, so reducing the surface area/volume ratio.

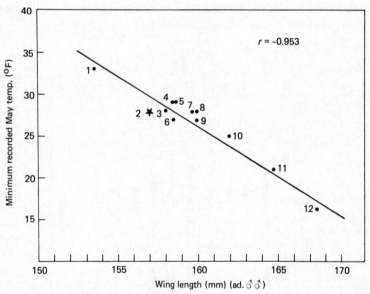

FIG. 13. The relationship between wing length and the minimum recorded May temperature in the Redshank in Europe and Asia.   1, Mukden, Manchuria; 2, mean of 22 stations in Northern Norway, Sweden and Finland (June minimum); 3, Salamanca, Spain; 4, Oxford, England; 5, Brussels, Belgium; 6, Chiu-Ch'uan, China; 7, Wroclaw, Poland; 8, Kassel, Germany; 9, Fort William, Scotland; 10, Moscow, USSR; 11, Semipalatinsk, USSR; 12, Akureyri, Iceland (after Hale 1973).

The northern Scandinavian (chocolate brown) population of Redshank is significantly smaller (mean wing length of males = 157 mm) so that if this population is plotted in Fig. 13 the point falls well below the regression line;

however, it is known that this population lays eggs some four weeks later than birds further south, and if the data for northern Scandinavia are plotted using the June minimum temperature the point then falls on the regression line. From this it seems clear that wing length, and overall size, are selected for by present day influences.

In northern Asia, the cline in wing length is reversed in other species of waders, and there appears to be an increase from west to east in Grey Plover, Lesser Golden Plover, Dunlin, Knot, Bar-tailed Godwit, Greenshank and Spotted Redshank. In species having a breeding range between that of the Redshank and the northerly breeders, for example Curlew, there is apparently no variation in wing length across Eurasia.

As in the Redshank, the smallest Ringed Plovers occur in Northern Scandinavia and they breed significantly later than more southerly populations.

Bill length varies considerably in most wading birds, but it is not an overall reflection of size as is wing length. In Redshank, for example, some of the largest birds (from Iceland) have the shortest bills, and indeed several species of waders have short bills in Iceland, for example, Dunlin, Black-tailed Godwit and even Golden Plover. This is clearly an example of Allen's Rule (1) which states that the extremities of warm blooded animals are shorter in colder climates than in the same species in warmer regions – a defence against heat loss. In the male Dunlin the bill length may vary from a mean of 21.8 mm in *Calidris alpina arctica* to a mean of 28.5 mm in *C. a. sakhalina*, and again the northern Scandinavian population is anomalous in having a very long bill – mean of 25.7 mm. For the most part, tarsus length is a reflection of bill length, and tail length of wing length. However, because of the variability in different parts of the breeding range it is possible to characterise a population on the basis of a series of measurements of the various limbs and appendage (see Chapter 5). Variations between populations in the measurements of various structures is almost always clinal during the breeding season where populations are continuous but the direction of the cline might well be reversed more than once.

SUB-SPECIATION

Whilst populations can be characterised on the basis of measurements, there is little point or justification in attributing sub-specific names to these populations, where clines occur. It is justifiable to name the extremes of a cline as in the Redshank, *Tringa totanus ussuriensis* ⟶ *T. t. robusta*. Because the so-called British Redshank *T. t. britannica* falls within this cline, and because the character on which it was originally separated, the lack of assumption of a full breeding plumage, also applies to other populations and characterises the hybrid population, I recommended that this should be referred to as *T. t. totanus* × *robusta* (73). It can also be argued that there is good reason to refer to discrete populations which have evolved in glacial refuges by a trinomial, so long as they retain characteristics by which they might be distinguished. In the Redshank (Fig. 9), apart from the *T. t. ussuriensis/robusta* cline, *T. t. totanus* (Northern Scandinavia), *T. t. eurhinus* (Northern India), *T. t. terrignotae* (Eastern China) and *T. t. craggi* (Sinkiang) can be substantiated. No other sub-species, including the British Redshank *T. t. britannica* can be upheld. In the Dunlin *Calidris alpina arctica* (Fig. 6), (Greenland), *C. a. alpina* (Northern Scandinavia/Western USSR), *C. a. sakhalina* (Eastern Siberia), *C. a. hudsonia* (Northern Canada) and *C. a. pacifica* (Southern Alaska) can be substantiated, but not *C. a. schinzii* which should probably be referred to as *C. a. artica* × *alpina*. The Knot (Fig. 7) has an un-named but recognisable form in Greenland, *C. canutus canutus* (Northern Eurasia), *C. c. rufa* (Northern Canada) and a doubtful form in *C. c. rogersi* (on the Bering Straits). Amongst the Godwits (Fig. 8) two forms are recognisable in the Bar-tailed Godwit, *Limosa lapponica lapponica* (Northern Scandinavia and Western Siberia) and *L. l. baueri* (Eastern Siberia and Alaska); in the Black-tailed Godwit *L. l. islandica* (Iceland), *L. l. limosa* (Europe) and *L. l. melanuroides* (Asia) can be substantiated. The Plovers provide a more difficult situation in that the probability is that the Icelandic and Northern Scandinavian populations are genetically but not morphologically distinct. In the Golden Plover (Fig. 4) the 'southern' population is probably a hybrid of the Icelandic and Scandinavian populations. The latter bears the trinomial *Pluvialis apricarius apricarius* (=*altifrons*), but the Icelandic population probably should be re-named which would make the so-called 'southern' Golden Plover *P. a. oreophilus* properly referred to as *P. a. apricarius* × *X*. The same problem arises with the Ringed Plover (Fig. 5). *Charadrius hiaticula psammodroma* (Greenland) and *C. h. tundrae* (Northern Scandinavia and Western USSR) are probably genetically different populations which have given rise to a hybrid Icelandic/British/Southern Scandinavian population, at present referred to as *C. h. hiaticula* but probably more properly named *C. h. psammodroma* × *tundrae*. In the east of Siberia *C. h. kolymensis* should probably be recognised, and in the Nearctic the species is replaced by *C. semipalmatus*.

It might well prove possible to test the hypothesis on which this proposed nomenclature is based using techniques involving protein patterns obtained by the electrophoresis of proteins from egg white or blood. The main problem will lie in obtaining the material, but it is a line of research which might well provide evidence on relationships at different levels within the Charadrii, and a possible insight into the timing of formation of species during the Pleistocene and earlier.

PRESENT DAY DISTRIBUTION CHANGES

The breeding ranges of birds are not fixed, but in a dynamic state of flux. Climatic changes combine with topographic changes which together with genetic modification in the organisms themselves all contribute towards the

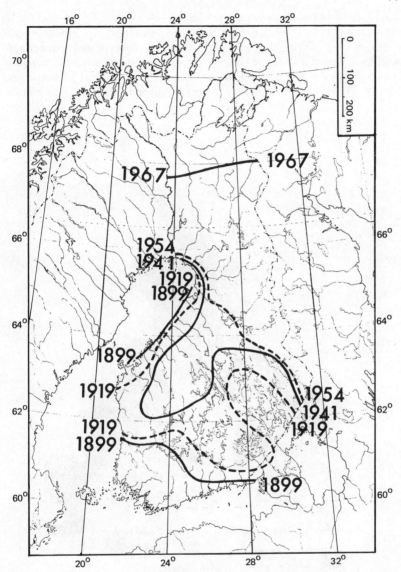

FIG. 14. Expansion of the breeding area of the Lapwing *Vanellus vanellus* in Finland.
The limits of 1899–1954 according to Kalela (1955), the limit of 1967 on the basis of an
oral report by Komonon (after Väisänen 1969).

dynamics of populations which are for ever fluctuating in numbers, frequently only on a small scale, but regularly resulting in the expansion and contraction of the breeding area. Whilst records have existed, Avocet and Ruff have deserted Britain as breeding species, and returned, and there has been an increase in the Redshank population and a decrease in Lapwings. Golden Plover and Ringed Plover are declining in numbers, the former

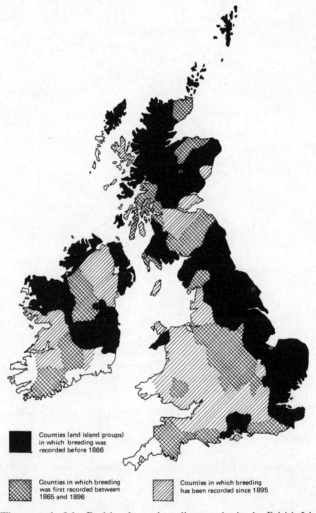

Counties (and island groups) in which breeding was recorded before 1866

Counties in which breeding was first recorded between 1865 and 1896

Counties in which breeding has been recorded since 1895

FIG. 15. The spread of the Redshank as a breeding species in the British Isles (after Thomas 1942).

probably due to climatic change, the latter probably due to the activities of Man in its littoral breeding area. The Lapwing is expanding its range in Scandinavia, and during the past 75 years there has been a gradual northerly expansion of the breeding range in Finland (Fig. 14) probably associated with the increasing spring temperatures during this period. In Britain the spread of the Little Ringed Plover, discussed in Chapter 2, is one of the more obvious changes in distribution that has gone on record and the BTO Redshank Enquiry (240) provided information on the possible spread of that species in Britain during the past hundred years (Fig. 15).

Whilst changes in the distribution of different species can normally be readily appreciated, changes within populations which do not alter the overall distribution of the same species are less obvious. In a study of the Ringed Plover, Väisänen (245) found that during the past 100 years the egg volume of birds breeding in Northern Scandinavia (*C. h. tundrae*) had increased significantly (Fig. 16). This was clearly due to an increase in the size of the birds, and this I checked by measurement of skins. It appears that during this period there had been a northward movement of the larger Ringed Plover and the small birds (*tundrae*) previously occupying large areas of Scandinavia were pushed back into Lapland. The Redshank showed a similar change with an increase in the size of the bird (73) and of its eggs

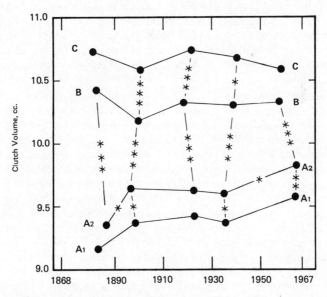

FIG. 16. Mean clutch volume in the Ringed Plover in Northwestern Europe, 1868–1967. A1, Northern Fennoscandia; A2, Northern Baltic; B, Southern Scandinavia; C, British Isles (after Väisänen 1969).

recorded. Furthermore in the Redshank it was possible to show that the small chocolate brown birds *Tringa totanus totanus* were decreasing in Northern Scandinavia, though the sample was small. 11 out of 12 Redshanks taken before 1900 were of the dark phase, chocolate brown birds, but in the period since 1900, only 16 of the 27 birds were of the original dark phase. Table 3

TABLE 3. Mean wing lengths in Redshank in Norway and Sweden before and after 1910 (after Hale 1971).

	Northern Scandinavia		Southern Scandinavia	
	Males	Females	Males	Females
Wing length prior to 1910	155.6	159.3	155.8	160.4
S.D.	3.2	3.7	2.8	2.8
n	11	8	11	8
Wing length post 1910	156.6	160.3	158.0	164.0
S.D.	3.8	3.9	3.2	6.3
n	13	7	17	7

shows the increase in mean size of Redshanks in the same periods. In both the Ringed Plover and Redshank the hybrid zone has spread north during the past 100 years, probably due to an amelioration of the climate. If the spread north continues it is likely that the dark chocolate brown Redshank *T. t. totanus* will be absorbed into the hybrid zone and cease to exist in the not too far distant future.

It is clear that the spread of the hybrid population into Scandinavia has taken place only during the past 100 years, and in the Ringed Plover where medium sized birds have resulted from the hybridisation between the large British population and the small Scandinavian birds, these lay some 15 days earlier than the small and large birds within the same populations. In the Redshank similar heterosis may well have been responsible for the extended breeding range within the British Isles in the last 100 years (Fig. 15) which cannot be attributed to climatic amelioration as can the northward spread in Scandinavia. In the hybrid populations of both Redshank and Ringed Plover the spread of the laying period is much greater than in the original popu-lations of small-sized birds in Scandinavia, and the earlier laying will certainly allow the production of replacement clutches more frequently than in the northern population. This may well be the advantage which the hybrid populations have over the previous populations of small birds, and the comparative lack of breeding plumage in the hybrid Redshanks does not appear to be a disadvantage.

Changes in distribution have happened frequently in the evolution of the

Charadrii and geographical forms of different species must have been wiped out on numerous occasions by processes such as those which threaten the small chocolate brown Redshank in northern Scandinavia. Populations must frequently have approached the species level only to be swamped by the gene flow from other populations whilst on other occasions new species have been formed which in their turn have gone through the same evolutionary processes. Too often we view populations only in the context of an unchanging species in a single time quantum; in reality populations are constantly changing, and geographical variation, well illustrated in the waders, is a clear demonstration of the potential for such change.

In waders the various colour forms (morphs) are only in evidence during the breeding season and it is clear that this plumage is selected for during the breeding season. Whilst clear patterns exist in the dimensions of various parts during the breeding season Salomonsen (211, 212) has argued, at least in the Redshank and Ringed Plover, that selection for overall size takes place in the winter range. The evidence for such claims will be examined in subsequent chapters.

CHAPTER 4

BREEDING BIOLOGY

The breeding season of waders begins with the return to the breeding grounds in spring and normally ends with the departure from the breeding grounds in autumn. For waders outside the arctic circle this may be a large part of the year but for arctic waders the stay on the breeding grounds is often short, lasting only long enough to lay, incubate and rear the young to fledging. In some cases the period on the breeding ground may be even shorter as often one bird of a pair may move south before the fledging of the young, or if a bird is unsuccessful in either mating or in breeding, the southerly autumn movement may occur early.

At the beginning of the breeding season the population of a species is at its lowest numerically, and at its highest after the hatch. Initially, on the return to the breeding area, the food supply need cater for only the breeding birds, but within a month that same area must be capable of supporting a population, in many cases nearly three times the initial size in most wading birds. In temperate regions, waders arrive at their breeding areas relatively early. Oystercatchers are on their Scottish breeding grounds in February and by the end of that month, Lapwings are back on the high fields of the Pennines. In March, Redshank and Curlew move inland and during the past 25 years their return to their breeding haunts in northern England has become progressively earlier. Common Sandpipers do not arrive in force until April and so escape the spring snowfalls and frosts that at times affect other British breeding waders. However, spring cold spells rarely last long in the British Isles and most waders are affected but little once they are back on their breeding grounds. Initially there is, in some species, e.g. Lapwing, Curlew, a tendency to remain in groups, at least for some part of the day but as pairs become established on their breeding areas, flocking tendencies decrease.

The return to the arctic takes place much later, and in the extreme north, Knot arrive back on their breeding areas in the last few days of May, or in early June. In some instances, arctic waders may arrive before the melt of the snows and find difficulty in feeding. Mention has already been made of the fat provision in the Pectoral Sandpiper, which enables birds to exist for a short time in very unfavourable conditions and it may well be that other species of arctic waders possess the same adaptation. In the arctic this may be a time of high mortality as, in years where there is a late melt and there has been a difficult northward journey, fat reserves may be so depleted that there are none available on arrival to sustain birds until the melt. At the time of arrival of arctic waders on the breeding ground, relatively little of the tundra is exposed. In Alaska, MacLean (141) shows that over 90% of the tundra is still snow-covered at this time and that the melt in most years occurs at the end of the second, and beginning of the third week of June. Not until the end of the third week of June is exposure more or less complete, and in bad years this may be a week or more later. It is quite possible that for a period of between two and three weeks, waders are finding their food supply on significantly less than 20% of the tundra so it is likely that heavy predation of the invertebrates takes place on the small part of the tundra which is exposed. Whilst this may be of advantage later in the season when young can then exploit an almost untouched source of food, it must be a difficult time for the breeding adults which rely on areas blown free of snow on which to feed.

COURTSHIP AND DISPLAY

There can be little doubt that in some cases birds arrive back on the breeding area already paired; usually these are pairs maintained from previous years and they tend to remain close together when feeding and often can be easily recognised as pairs in flight over the breeding area. Many birds arrive unpaired; these consist of those birds whose mates have died, those that have become separated from their mates during the winter and those who are breeding for the first time.

In temperate regions there appears to be a drift back to the breeding areas rather than the relatively concentrated arrival which occurs in the arctic. Nethersole-Thompson (163) suggests that male Greenshank tend to arrive at the nesting areas before females, whereas in the Red-necked Phalarope, Bannerman (8) concludes that females arrive first. In arctic breeding Red-necked Phalaropes, this is also generally the case (31, 91), as it is in the Grey Phalarope (92) and Wilson's Phalarope (90, 110). In Redshank, like Greenshank, there is a tendency for males to arrive first, but it is only where populations are colour-marked that certain sex-identification can take place in most waders; Phalaropes are, of course, exceptions since the sexes can be identified. Grosskopf (68) shows the return of Redshank to the German breeding grounds as taking a period of seven weeks (Fig. 17). In contrast,

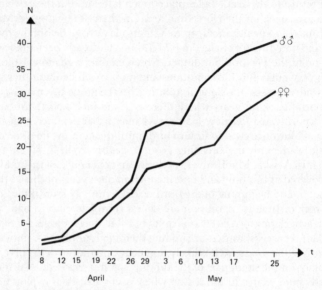

FIG. 17. Numbers of Redshank (n) returning to breeding area on Wangerooge, West Germany during April and May (after Grosskopf 1958).

Soikkeli (227) records that in Finland, 75% of the Dunlin population arrived within a period of five to six days after the first arrivals, in two years; in two other years the period was 15 days. In Finland, both sexes of Dunlin arrive together but both Heldt (81) and Holmes (93) record males arriving first.

In the arctic, if the snow melt is late, the arrival of the majority of breeding waders is delayed. When this occurs, Dunlin mainly arrive paired (93). Others pair within a few days (two to ten), as do most arctic waders; the time spent on the breeding area before breeding is short. In contrast, Oyster-catchers and Redshank may be present on their breeding areas for four to five weeks or more before laying in temperate areas. Colour-markings has shown that where birds of a pair arrive on the breeding area at different times, they actively seek a mate immediately on arrival and obtain a new mate as soon as possible, so that birds forming a pair one year may have different mates the next.

Temperate waders do not face the problems of food shortage encountered by arctic waders on reaching their breeding areas, and spend more time in display, often with very incomplete ceremonies at the beginning of the season. Most waders perform a song flight, the main function of which is almost certainly to attract a mate, and in territorial species this may be performed by the male over his territory; in species such as the Redshank and Curlew the male performs anywhere over the breeding area. The object in this display is to attract an unmated female into the air, and occasionally the display flight takes place between paired birds, when the female may also perform, and possibly this plays some part in the maintenance of the pair. During the song flight the normal wing beat is not used and the wings are quivered, in some species below the horizontal, e.g. Redshank and Greenshank, and in others in a V-shape above the horizontal, e.g. Knot and Curlew. The wing quivering is alternated with a glide and in many species gives rise to a characteristic switchback flight. A song flight performed by one male often stimulates others to behave similarly and at the end of the display, when the birds glide down to the ground, they may pause with their wings stretched up above their back. This final glide and wing-lifting may well act as a separate ceremony in pair maintenance and later in the season it often gives rise to the full courtship display. In Phalaropes the sexual rôles are reversed, and in some species the display flight has different characteristics, e.g. Oystercatchers, and in others it is absent, e.g. Ruff. Occasionally the display flight occurs later in the season, probably as a displacement activity in the presence of predators, but its main function, and its usual time of performance, is in the early breeding season.

The early breeding season is a time of incomplete displays, largely because females are unco-operative. This applies more in temperate breeding areas, since usually both male and female are in breeding condition by the time of arrival on the arctic breeding areas. Further south, males in general come into breeding condition before females and initial attempts at courtship display usually come to grief because of the females' lack of co-operation. In many waders, e.g. Redshank, males experience difficulty in the initial stages in recognising females, and males will court, and attempt to copulate with other males of the same species. Ground and air chases are also a feature of this time of the breeding season and it is very easy to mistake the sexes at this time, as often the chasing bird is a female and she is as likely to pursue a male or another female as to be herself pursued by a male. However, once pairs are formed, recognition of the sexes is better, but even then the pursuer in chases is not always the male, as a female will often chase away another male. Much of this chasing arises because one bird approaches too close to another of a pair, or because a female does not want to copulate, and much of it is not territorial in essence. Chases and incomplete displays occupy considerable time in the early breeding season in temperate regions, and seem to serve little purpose. Waders also spend a large proportion of daylight hours sleeping and preening.

In many waders the defence of territory takes a proportion of their energy, though some species tend to be much less territorial than others. In general, Plovers can be said to defend a territory and boundary clashes between male Lapwings from adjoining territories are a very common feature of the spring. In contrast, some species, e.g. Redshank, appear to be almost semi-colonial and tend to nest in groups. In these circumstances it is not easy to see how dispersion over the nesting area is achieved.

The dispersion of waders over the breeding area varies greatly. In the Knot it can be as low as 1.09 pairs per km^2 (166), or with Western Sandpipers as high as 750 pairs per km^2 (96, 97). These are extreme figures and the normal breeding density of most waders lies between them. In Orkney, Lapwings nest at a density of 77 pairs per km^2 (229) and Redshank may reach a similar density on saltmarsh in northern England; Golden Plover reach their highest densities in the British Isles of 16 pairs per km^2 on Pennine limestone grassland, though 5.7 pairs per km^2 is more usual (204).

In the Golden Plover, Ratcliffe suggests that the density decreases where the food supply is poor; territories appear to be smaller in areas of good food supply. There is a surprising regularity in the dispersion of nest sites as shown in Table 4 where in each of three different breeding areas the nests are evenly spaced. Fig. 18 shows the distribution of Golden Plover nests on Mallerstang limestone grassland and it is clear that territoriality has resulted in an even

TABLE 4. Nest spacing of Golden Plover in different breeding areas

	Mallerstang limestone grassland	Alston Moor blanket bog	Moorfoot Hills blanket bog
1963	—	—	434± 47
1964	—	—	423± 56
1965	—	445± 56	453± 99
1966	—	—	463± 80
1967	—	—	452± 80
1968	—	—	387± 77
1969	—	—	422± 68
1970	—	—	—
1971	—	—	—
1972	—	—	—
1973	205± 28	—	433± 72
1974	210± 18	446± 72	—
1975	206± 33	—	—
1976	207	445	433

Figures are mean distances in metres between each nest and its nearest neighbour, with standard errors (95% confidence limits). Distances are estimated in the field by measured paces (after Ratcliffe 1976).

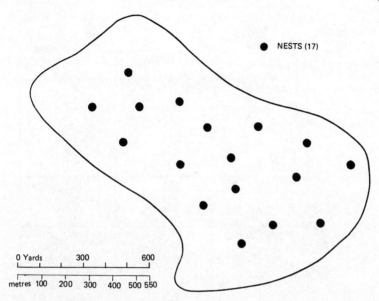

FIG. 18. Dispersion of Golden Plover nests on Mallerstang limestone grassland in 1974 (after Ratcliffe 1976).

spacing of nests. This can be compared with a similar even spacing in the Western Sandpipers in western Alaska (Fig. 19), where again, territoriality in the early breeding season results in the dispersion of the nests over the available habitat. In both these cases the territory apparently ceases to have a useful function after hatching. In the case of the Western Sandpiper the young are led from the nesting area on heath tundra to lowland feeding areas, and territory defence wanes as incubation proceeds; families wander freely after the hatch. Golden Plover tend to remain on the nesting areas after the hatch but again territoriality has waned by this time. It may well be that territoriality has served its purpose in restricting the overall numbers on a particular piece of ground to those which it can support when the young have hatched, and the fact that the adults of both species tend to feed away from the territory in the early breeding season goes some way to suggest that the food supply is being deliberately conserved.

Generally speaking, most waders are actively territorial in the early breeding season and usually it is the male who defends the territory, though in some cases, e.g. Phalaropes, it is the female. Plovers, many Sandpipers, Oyster-catchers and Snipe all begin the breeding season by establishing breeding territories and these vary in size according to the habitat. Since many species do not feed within their breeding territories it is difficult, at this time, to see the

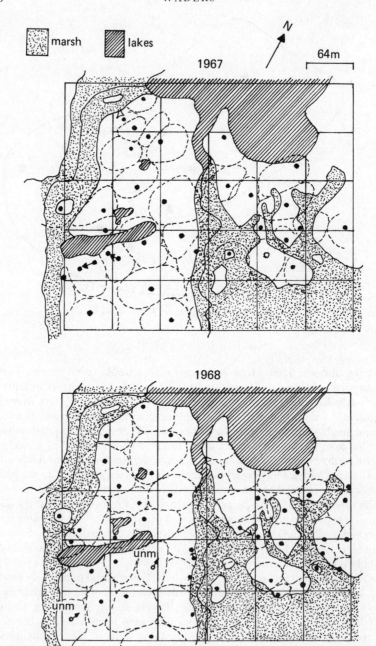

marsh   lakes

N

64m

1967

1968

unm

unm

link, if any, with food. The size of territories varies regionally, but within a region there is a remarkable consistency in size, as has been shown in the case of the Golden Plover and Western Sandpiper. This also applies to Snipe (243), Lapwing (229), Dunlin (93, 94) and Oystercatcher (85). As the season progresses, territory defence is less in evidence and by the time chicks have hatched, most waders' behaviour has changed from a defence of territory against others of the same species to the defence of an area around the chicks against potential predators. It appears, then, that just at the time when territories would appear to have their maximum value in terms of a feeding area, territoriality breaks down. At the time of the hatch the food supply required of the breeding area is greater than at any other time and it does seem likely that there is some mechanism to prevent over-exploitation. The probability is that the early season territory-holding ensures a breeding density which is unlikely to exceed the potential food supply. Having achieved a suitable breeding density, unless led to specific good feeding areas by the parents, chicks probably wander randomly feeding unless a particularly good food supply is encountered. Under such circumstances the parent birds need not spend time in intra-specific territorial defence, particularly as they are frequently involved in defending the 'chick areas' against potential predators.

At the beginning of the breeding season the time involved with activities associated with breeding is much greater in the males of most species of wading birds than in the females. This probably reflects the fact that males come into breeding condition before females. For the most part, female waders preen, feed and sleep on their potential breeding areas, and only occasionally become involved in excessive activity when chased by a male or when chasing a bird of another pair. In the meantime her mate is involved in display flights, territory defence and in early courtship displays. A significant proportion of the energy output of males is used in this way at this time of the year, whilst females are relatively inactive. In arctic regions this activity in the males lasts, at the most, for a few days, but in temperate regions it may last five or six weeks. Redshanks seldom lay much before the last week in April, whereas their initial displays can be seen in the second week of March.

Ground nesting waders normally excavate a scrape for the nest and this is usually initiated by the male bird. Scraping is a form of display, and whilst it

FIG. 19. Spacing of male Western Sandpipers in two summers on the main study area, Kolomak River, Alaska. Paired lines represent observed territory boundary contact points between adjacent males; broken lines approximate territorial boundaries. Solid dots represent location of nests found; open circles indicate nests not actually found but known to be present in that general vicinity. Arrows between two nests indicate sites of second nesting following failure of the first. Each square of the grid equals 0.4 ha (1 ac). 'Unm' refers to the territory of an unmarked and unmated female (after Holmes 1971).

may take place in the absence of the female, usually she is present. The male normally rotates on his breast in the area chosen, and kicks out vegetation and soil with his feet, calling, fanning his tail and attracting his mate to his activities. During the course of the early spring, several scrapes (10–15) may be made, but often only a single one for replacement clutches. The female selects the scrape in which she will lay, and often the first egg is laid on bare soil and the scrape lined during subsequent layings and during incubation. In Plovers, and those waders nesting in the open, scraping is easy to observe, but in Sandpipers and other waders nesting in vegetation it is very difficult to see, and the performance is more frequently heard than seen; usually it is accompanied by a characteristic call, a 'soft, husky "skrr, skrr"' in the Lapwing (229) and a quiet 'too-too . . . too-too' in the Redshank. Often the attention paid to the scrape is the first indication that a female is approaching the stage where she is prepared to tolerate the advances of her mate, and the initial incomplete courtship displays of the male give rise to the full courtship ceremony. These displays are, in many waders, amongst the most elaborate of any birds.

Perhaps the best known courtship display of any wader is that of the Redshank which was so beautifully described by Selous (218) and Huxley (105). In the full display the long chases of the early breeding season are gone, and after a short chase with the male moving crab-wise, with the head out to one side at some 20° to the line of the body, and tail fanned, the female stops and the male opens his wings and holds them almost vertically above his back, displaying the white undersides to the female. The male then begins to flutter his wings through a few degrees, giving the impression that they are vibrating, whilst at the same time singing the disyllabic 'tloo-tloo' song. Continuing the song the male approaches the female slowly with exaggerated high steps and fanned tail. Usually the male's head is bowed and the bill points towards the ground. If the female remains still the male approaches until he is immediately behind her, when he pauses and the song changes to a vibrant trill as he flutters from the ground and mounts the female. Often the female will sing if she is willing to copulate, but only immediately prior to egg laying is the full ceremony performed successfully.

Occasionally copulation takes place without a full courtship display, and whilst this is unusual in the Redshank it occurs more commonly in other species, such as the Oystercatcher. Most waders have a courtship display which involves wing lifting. Godwits, Curlews, Calidritine Sandpipers, Tringine Sandpipers and Plovers all have courtship displays of this type, but in many species of waders courtship displays have not been observed to any great extent. Each species has a characteristic display, often with the emphasis placed on particular plumage characteristics, such as the black and white tail in the Black-tailed Godwit, and often the chases and display flights play a greater part than in the Redshank and Curlew. In the Oystercatcher the 'butterfly flight' is an exaggerated form of display flight, and communal piping ceremonies play a part in the early displays of the breeding season, but copulation often takes place without preliminaries. The Woodcock's display flight, which is known as 'roding' occurs mainly at dusk, and the owl-like flight is much more frequently observed than the ground display of courtship, leading to coition, where the male struts round the female with drooping wings and raised and spread tail. This ground display is very similar to that of the Common Snipe, but the Great Snipe has a communal display at a lek, as has the Ruff.

At leks, the performing males are apparently in competition, as frequently they clash. The Great Snipe leks at dusk and into the night and there is evidence that males display at leks as far apart as 10 km (48). Ruffs lek mainly early in the morning and it is possible that here again males perform at leks several kilometres apart. The behaviour at the lek is very complex and has been well described by Hogan-Warburg (89) and van Rhijn (206). In both the Great Snipe and the Ruff, a single male may copulate with several females within a short space of time (a few minutes) and in the case of the Ruff, three nests in which the eggs hatched during the space of six hours, in Lancashire in 1976, could well have resulted from a single male. Females are attracted to leks where copulation takes place, but in the Ruff not all males are involved in copulation. Two groups can be distinguished, independent males and satellite males. The former are generally dark-coloured and can be sub-divided into resident males which defend territories (residences) and marginal males which do not. The satellite males are mostly white and do not defend territories, but unlike marginal males are allowed access to the residences; satellite males are not involved in aggressive behaviour whereas independent males are, and the satellites serve mainly in the attraction of females to the lek. The evolution of communal displays of this sort has far-reaching consequences. After copulation the entire breeding effort falls upon the female; the whole of the incubation and tending of young are her responsibility. It is difficult to see the advantage of this. Possibly the conspicuous plumage of the male might draw too much attention from potential predators to the presence of a nest or chicks were he to be involved with incubation and chick rearing, and it may be that through the male's absence from the feeding areas of the rest of the family, more food is available to them. Certainly this seems to be the case in some arctic waders where one parent deserts the family after the hatch. There is clearly no pair formation in birds with such communal displays, and whilst they are atypical as far as the waders as a whole are concerned they provide examples that show one parent can tend both eggs and young with a survival to fledging sufficient to maintain the population. This in itself is interesting.

EGG LAYING AND INCUBATION

The laying of the first egg normally occurs within 24–48 hours of successful copulation, and subsequent eggs are laid at intervals of 30–36 hours in most species of wader. With few exceptions the clutch size is four, and MacLean (140) suggests that this number is ancestral. In species which feed their young (Burhinidae, Haematopodidae, Dromadidae, Chionididae and Glareolidae) the clutch size is often reduced to two or three and this may well be related to the energetics of this habit. In species which lay four eggs and also feed their young, e.g. Common Snipe, feeding takes place for only a short period of some seven days. It is surprising that so many species normally lay a clutch of four eggs; many species are capable of laying more (some Sanderling in the Canadian arctic lay eight eggs – two clutches of four (183)) and an individual female Redshank is capable of laying twelve or more eggs in one season; in fact most species are capable of producing one or more replacement clutches. There can, therefore, be little reason to doubt that clutch size in waders is adaptive, as has been well demonstrated in most other groups of birds (128).

In many waders the eggs are laid in the open, with little nest material, and when they are not covered by the bird they rely entirely on their cryptic coloration for protection; this is the case in most Plovers, Oystercatchers, Stone Curlews, Pratincoles, Godwits and Curlews. Sandpipers tend to nest in vegetation where their eggs are usually at least partially covered, but they still retain their cryptic coloration. Incubation normally begins with the last egg, which is to be expected where a synchronous hatch is necessary. Within the group all possible incubation schedules occur; perhaps the most common is the shared schedule, where male and female take turns at the incubation and cover the eggs for the majority of the incubation period. This is the case in many Plovers, Snipe, Tringine Sandpipers and Calidritine Sandpipers such as Dunlin and Baird's Sandpiper, where Norton (174) records birds sitting for 96–98% of the incubation period. Where only one sex incubates, the time during which the eggs are covered is significantly less. In arctic Canada where Parmelee (182) records female Sanderlings laying two clutches, one of which she incubates whilst her mate covers the other, the daily range of egg covering is from 67–89% of the available time. A similar situation occurs in Temminck's Stint, where each bird of a pair incubates a separate clutch (87). This is of the same order as in the Pectoral Sandpiper where only the female incubates, covering the eggs for about 85% of the time (174). In Phalaropes the male incubates and this is also the case in most Dotterel (164).

There is clear evidence that different populations of the same species may adopt different strategies. Parmelee & Payne (183) showed that Canadian Sanderling from the high arctic laid two clutches in quick succession and that each was reared independently by one of the parents. In contrast, Pienkowski & Green (192) showed that in Sanderling in Greenland the two adults shared incubation at one nest and here the eggs were covered for a time (96%) of the same order as that in other species with a similar schedule. In some cases, waders may be double brooded in the more conventional fashion, with a second clutch being laid when the young of the first clutch have just hatched, or even fledged.

In Ringed Plover, Laven (132) and Bub (19) have recorded two broods in one season, in non-Arctic conditions, as has Soikkeli (227) in the Dunlin. Snipe and Woodcock commonly have two broods in which the female attends both. This is relatively unusual in most Sandpipers, but I have two records of this occurring in Redshank. It is usual for waders to replace lost clutches, perhaps twice, but there is a tendency for replacement clutches to contain fewer than the normal full clutches; where three eggs occur in species which normally lay four eggs, it is likely that this is a replacement clutch.

The incubation period varies from about 17 days in the Red-necked Phalarope to about 30 days in the Curlew, but the majority of species incubate for a period of 22–24 days. If the eggs are addled or infertile they will sit for much longer periods, and I have recorded a Redshank still sitting after 42 days on addled eggs; the normal incubation period is 22–23 days in Redshank.

The onset of egg-laying is correlated with differences in spring temperature, and a rise in temperature brings about egg-laying between four and six days later in most species. When the temperature rises above about 8°C, Red-necked Phalarope lay three to four days later (88) and this same period of three to four days usually elapses in producing a replacement clutch should the first be lost. This seems an unusually short period for the growth of oocytes but other waders replace their lost clutches in similar short periods; Dunlin take three (81), or four days (227), Redshank six days, Kentish Plover four days (208), Ringed Plover five days (132); these are minimum estimates and often replacement clutches take longer to produce.

In most waders the complete clutch is 50–70% of the weight of the female, but in Stints it reaches 90%, so that in Temminck's Stint, which produces two clutches in a short period of time, the total weight is of the order of 180% of the weight of the female. In the European Curlew the clutch weight is only 40% of the weight of the female and in the Oystercatcher, laying three eggs, 20%.

Generally speaking, the eggs of waders are large for the size of the bird, and there is a significant fall in weight in the female from the time immediately before laying to the beginning of incubation, presumably related to egg production. Holmes (93) recorded one individual female Dunlin weighing 92.1 g immediately before egg-laying compared with 60–65 g for the mean weight of a female at this time. On returning to the breeding ground Dunlin have little, if any, body fat and their weights are close to the lowest recorded; increase in weight takes place immediately prior to laying. In the Oystercatcher, too, there is a fall in weight from a pre-breeding mean of 616 g to a mean of 520 g on the first day of incubation (155). This is approximately 16% of the body weight. In Dunlin there appears to be a slight gain in weight early in incubation and a slight fall during the rest of the incubation period (Fig. 20).

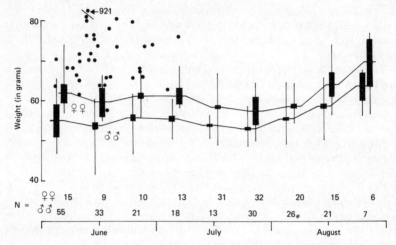

FIG. 20. Body weight of adult Dunlin at Barrow, Alaska, in the summers 1959 to 1963. Mean weights for each 10 day time interval are connected by the horizontal line; the vertical lines represent range and the bars a distance twice the standard error on each side of the mean. Weights of egg-laying females are shown individually by dots (after Holmes 1966).

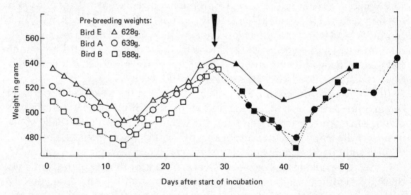

FIG. 21. The pattern of weight change in three female Oystercatchers from the start of incubation to the time of fledging. Open symbols = incubation period; solid symbols = fledging period; the arrow shows time of hatch. Pre-breeding weights were obtained 20–30 days before laying (after Mercer 1968).

In Oystercatchers, where females take the larger share of the incubation, there is a loss in weight for the first part of the incubation period in females, followed by an increase in the second part (Fig. 21); there is then a fall again during the first part of the fledging period, followed by an increase in the second half. In general there is no significant difference between the weight of incubating birds at the beginning and end of the incubation period, or between the initiation of incubation and the fledging of the young. However, in Oystercatchers there are two periods during this time when a loss in weight of about 7% occurs; no such weight loss normally occurs during winter and it does appear that, at least in adult females, Oystercatchers only have difficulty in maintaining weight during the breeding period.

The young normally hatch within a period of less than 24 hours and most leave the nest shortly after they are dry, unless it is late afternoon when they may spend the first night in the nest. If hatching is delayed in one egg it is frequently deserted as the adults generally lead the chicks from the vicinity of the nest to a suitable feeding area. Oystercatcher chicks often remain in the nest for a day or two but they are exceptional. The chicks are tended by one or both parents, and normally they crouch when danger threatens. Distraction displays by the adults are common around the time of the hatch and when the chicks are young these vary from a repetition of the display flight to injury-feigning, and in some cases adults will attack a potential predator; sheep and cattle are often driven away from the nest site by Lapwings, but Redshank seldom attempt this. In some cases, waders sit extremely close during the final period of incubation and at this time even Redshank may occasionally be picked from the nest by hand.

Egg losses during incubation vary enormously. In the Ringed Plover, analysis of BTO nest record cards shows that 5.3% of eggs are lost and a further 6.4% are infertile (196). In addition, some pulli fail to emerge successfully so that between 11.7% and 14.9% of eggs fail to hatch. This is a relatively high success rate with between 3.23 and 3.35 chicks per successful nest. Similar high rates of hatching success occur in other waders; in the Western Sandpiper, Holmes (98) gives hatching success as 72.5%, 85.5% and 91.7% in three successive years; in the Dunlin in Finland, Soikkeli (227) records 73%, 58%, 78%, 84% and 55% success in five consecutive years, and in the same species in Alaska, Holmes (93) estimated losses of less than 50% and probably about 20–25% overall. In Turnstone, Nettleship (165) gives a 33% loss in Turnstone eggs during incubation. All these figures fall within the overall estimate for Charadrii of 66–96% hatch (15). However, in some circumstances, such as waders nesting on salt marshes hatching success can be much lower as a result of losses to tides and grazing cattle; under these circumstances losses can exceed 75%, and over a period of four years, hatching success on a Lancashire salt marsh was 48%, 34%, 47% and 18% in the Redshank. Despite such low hatching success there was no indication that the population was affected and no decrease was observed.

Fledging and mortality

There are two main difficulties in assessing fledging success in waders. Firstly, the young are hard to find even when their approximate location is known, and it is very difficult to be certain that all the brood have been discovered even after searching for a long period. Secondly, the parent birds take less interest in the chicks towards the end of the fledging period, and in these circumstances it is often difficult to find their approximate location, and frequently the young are some distance apart. Probably the best way to obtain an estimation of fledging success is to see the young very soon after they have flown for the first time, together with their parents. Even then it is necessary to have colour-marked birds to be sure of identification.

Boyd (15) points out that fledging success (survival from hatching to fledging) varies from year to year, but that survival from hatching to fledging typically averages 40–80%. Keighley (113) found a fledging success of 86% in Oystercatchers on Skokholm and Nordberg (173) 78% in the same species in Finland; these estimates contrast markedly with a fledging success of only 4.6% in German Oystercatchers (34). Nordberg (173) in Ringed Plover and Rittinghaus (208) in Kentish Plover, found fledging successes of the order of 50%, whereas Laven (132) recorded 60% in Ringed Plover. Bergman (13) found a fledging success of nearer 60% in Turnstone, a figure similar to that of Nettleship (165) for the same species, and RSPB estimates for Avocets in the early days of the Suffolk colony were less than 30% fledging success. In all these estimates there is a high degree of possible error and it is likely that most estimates are under-estimates since it is highly probable that some surviving young were overlooked.

Early in the fledging period one or both parent birds remain in the vicinity of the young and defend an area around them against potential predators. The size of the area defended depends to some extent on the topography. In an inland Redshank population nesting on rough moorland this is usually between 4–6 hectares; on flat, salt marsh habitat, the 'chick areas' are usually 3–4 hectares in area. The size of the defended area is larger in bigger birds, and in the Whimbrel on which I worked in arctic Norway the 'chick area' varied in size between 6 and 30 hectares in heathland with some scrub birch. Curlews will defend an even larger area, up to 40 hectares, on occasions. The 'chick areas' tend to be larger when both adults are present with the young, probably because of the greater likelihood of the potential predator being sighted earlier when two adults are present.

In some wader species only the females tend the chicks, e.g. Pectoral and Curlew Sandpipers, whereas in others only the male normally is present, e.g. Phalaropes and Dotterel. During the first few days after hatching the young are brooded regularly, but thereafter normally only at night. In cases where broods feed close together an adult will brood young from another pair, and in Phalaropes (88) a male having lost its young may adopt another brood. This

PLATE I. *Above*, female Lapwing uncovering brood patches before incubation, at nest on rough grassland. *Below*, female Kentish Plover about to settle on eggs.

PLATE 2. *Above left*, Curlew; *right*, Avocet in flight. *Below left*, immature Curlew Sandpiper; *right*, adult Spotted Redshank searching for food.

PLATE 3.
Turnstone in flight.

Dunlin and a
Curlew Sandpiper
showing its white
rump in flight.

Sanderling in
winter plumage.

PLATE 4. *Above*, migrant Purple Sandpipers. *Below*, Common Sandpiper about to brood.

PLATE 5. *Above*, Golden Plover at nest in Scotland; an intermediate bird between normal 'southern' and 'northern' plumage. Some winter feathers can be seen on the breast.   *Below*, a Scottish breeding Dunlin, a relatively dark individual of the so-called *C. a. schinzii*.

PLATE 6. *Above*, Black-tailed Godwit at nest, showing the relatively small amount of summer plumage and the retained winter plumage feathers on the mantle and scapulars.   *Below*, Ringed Plover at nest, showing retained worn winter feathers on coverts, mantle and back.

PLATE 7. British nesting Redshank. *Above*, a well marked bird incubating. *Below*, a poorly marked individual showing retained winter plumage, approaching the nest.

PLATE 8. Black-tailed Godwits displaying. *Above left*, display flight; *right*, ground display showing rhynchokinesis in bill. *Below*, well marked male Redshank performing the wing lifting ceremony of the courtship display.

has also been recorded in Dunlin (227), Kentish Plover (209), Dotterel (202) and probably both brooding and adoption of strange young occurs commonly in waders, particularly those which nest colonially or semi-colonially.

Where both adult birds remain with the brood, often one is more attentive than the other. In the Dunlin the female broods for a few days but then apparently loses interest and does not even mob predators. This usually indicates that the female is about to leave the breeding area, but the male usually remains until the young are capable of flying at 20–22 days after hatching (227). Frequently only one adult remains with the chicks at the end of the fledging period and this is usually the male. In Phalaropes even the male deserts the young after some two weeks, that is before they can fly, and even before this he has stopped giving alarm calls in the presence of potential predators.

Chicks put on weight rapidly after hatching and Phalaropes almost treble their weight in the first five days, whereas Dunlin double their weight in this period and Snipe double their weight in a week. At fledging, most young weigh considerably less than their parents and the primaries and bill have not usually reached maximum length.

Fledging periods vary greatly from about 18–19 days in Phalaropes and Turnstone to 5–6 weeks in Oystercatcher and Curlew. With the few exceptions already mentioned the young feed themselves throughout this period, during which the breeding grounds must support between two and three times the number of birds present at the beginning of the breeding season. In some cases approximately half the adult population leaves the breeding area (e.g. Pectoral Sandpiper) and it seems likely that this strategy makes more food available to those birds remaining (141).

In arctic areas the eggs hatch at the time when the maximum invertebrate food supply is available, but even so there does appear to be a higher degree of habitat specialisation between closely related species at this time than in the earlier part of the breeding season, presumably to prevent, as far as possible, competition for the same food supply (141). It is important for breeding birds to be able to obtain their food quickly and easily, as during the breeding season there are numerous other activities, such as display, incubation and the tending of young, which occupy a large part of their time.

Studies of breeding biology of waders have probably provided us with the most accurate estimates of mortality which are available. Estimates of mortality derived from ringing recoveries are far too high, and involve errors caused by ring loss. Boyd (15) reviews mortality and fertility in the Charadrii mainly based on the recoveries of ringed birds and uses the method of Lack (121) supplemented by that of Haldane (71) to calculate mortality. It has been shown that these estimates, based on long distance recoveries, are much greater than those derived from recoveries at the site of ringing or those derived from the return of marked breeding birds (70); furthermore, it has been shown that mortality rates based on long distance ringing recoveries would not maintain the numerical stability of the populations concerned. Colour-marked populations of breeding waders therefore provide important data on mortality.

TABLE 5. Comparison of mortalities based on ringing recoveries and returns to breeding areas.

Species	Annual mortality (%) from		(b) Ringing recoveries
	(a) Returns to breeding area		
Oystercatcher	7.5	(Jungfer, 1954)	15.9–30
Ringed Plover	25–30	(Bub, 1962)	42
Kentish Plover	25	(Rittinghaus, 1956)	41
Turnstone	22.2	(Bergman, 1946)	33.6
Redshank	25	(Grosskopf, 1964)	31.5–56.9
Dunlin	27	(Soikkeli, 1967)	37.7

Grosskopf (69, 70) has shown that the annual mortality in a German population of Redshank is approximately 25%, and this compares with 31.5–56.9% quoted by Boyd (15) from ringing recoveries. British ringing recoveries give an annual mortality of 42%, but the returns to my own breeding population in the north of England are even lower than Grosskopf's estimate, between 17% and 20%. In the Dunlin, Soikkeli (227) found an annual mortality of 27% in his colour-ringed population and in the breeding Dunlin in Alaska, Holmes (93) found first-year breeders replacing an annual mortality of 28.6–30%; these estimates compare with a figure of nearly 40% from ringing returns. In all cases where comparison has been possible, returns to the breeding ground have shown lower mortalities than ringing recoveries (Table 5). It may well be that even these estimates are too high, as the assumption is made that the live birds all return to their original breeding area; this is largely true, but some Redshank certainly may nest 2 km away from the previous year's nest, and occasionally marked birds may well be overlooked.

It has already been shown that the population densities of a species during the breeding season vary from place to place, and there is some evidence that this might be related to food supply, particularly in the Golden Plover. In many species the territory size determines the density of breeding birds, and thereafter little difficulty seems to be experienced in obtaining sufficient food. It may well be that at the first arrival at the breeding grounds, difficulty is experienced in finding food and there can be little doubt that this is the case in some arctic breeders, and this in itself may determine territory size. Birds attempting to breed for the first time may do so only if there are vacant territories available, and the tendency of young birds to breed later may well result in their breeding for the first time only when obvious opportunities occur due to previous mortality of adults. It is possible to see how territoriality can act in a density-dependent manner to limit the population size, but it is less easy to understand how those waders which do not behave territorially, e.g. Redshank (72) are limited in numbers. There is some evidence to suggest that high density populations produce fewer fledged young per pair than lower density populations, and this might well be the density-dependent factor which has an over-riding effect. However, in these circumstances it is difficult to see why high density populations occur in the first place when, in the case of the Redshank, there are apparently perfectly suitable nesting areas entirely unpopulated. It may be that a comparative study of high density and low density populations, involving experimental recolonisation of cleared areas within the high density population, may shed some light on this problem as may closer studies of feeding during the breeding season. Lack (123, 127) put forward the proposal that bird populations in general are limited by density-dependent mortality of young, and that the most likely density-dependent factor was the food supply. No-one familiar with the autumn flocks of arctic waders can doubt that there are very good and very bad breeding seasons in the arctic, reflected by the numbers of juvenile birds in the flocks. Certainly more information is required concerning the reasons for the variable breeding success, and the causes of mortality on the breeding grounds. Only when detailed population studies have been carried out on the breeding grounds will there be evidence on which to base conclusions. A great deal of attention has been paid to the feeding biology of wading birds in winter; some of this attention should be transferred to similar studies on the breeding grounds, when it is possible that this period of the life cycle might be shown to be of over-riding importance.

CHAPTER 5

MIGRATION

Populations of birds migrate if the survival rate is greater than if they remained on the breeding ground. Within a species some populations may be migratory and others non-migratory, and migratory populations may carry out journeys over very different distances. Many individuals must die during the migration. In each case, however, it is likely that the population has a survival rate greater than would be the case if a different strategy was adopted. Most wading birds migrate south at the end of the breeding season as in many cases the breeding grounds could not support the population in winter. The spring return to the breeding grounds is carried out because these areas are capable of supporting the population better than the areas further south during the breeding season. During the course of evolution of wader species, breeding and wintering areas have been subject to frequent climatic changes which have undoubtedly affected the patterns of migration, and there can be little doubt that migration as a behaviour pattern has arisen independently on several occasions.

It is likely that seasonal changes in food supply make some areas better than others for breeding and wintering, and food supply and breeding requirements are the ultimate causative factors of migration. Distinct from these are the proximate factors which stimulate the movement south in autumn and north in spring; these may be temperature changes, changes in photoperiod (daylight/darkness ratio) or the onset of anticyclonic weather, but whatever factor(s) is effective, it takes effect before shortage of food actually occurs, and these proximate factors act through the rhythm of the sexual cycle and ensure movement towards or away from the breeding ground. Light is an accelerator of the sexual cycle in many birds, and cold an inhibitor. During the spring migration a sudden fall in temperature may result in reverse migration

('Ruckzug'), particularly amongst early migrants, but this does not happen in autumn, and southward flights are merely delayed.

In many waders the young separate into small flocks at the end of the breeding season, and in most species, e.g. Dunlin and Curlew, either adults or young predominate in autumn flocks. In those species in which adult moult precedes the autumn migration, juveniles move south well before the adults. In the British Isles, most breeding waders make their way to the coast or coastal lowlands at the end of the breeding season. In the Redshank and Curlew these movements often take place in family parties, and large flocks are formed only on the coast. In the Lapwing and Golden Plover, small travelling parties come together to form larger flocks before moving on to the coastal lowlands, and in mild weather some flocks remain on the higher ground. In the arctic, small parties form larger groups as they move south, particularly where stops are made on the coast or in feeding areas inland. Many waders move south in small groups, e.g. Dotterel, Common Sandpiper, or even singly and often it is only on the wintering grounds that they form large parties; some species remain singly or in small groups even in winter, e.g. Solitary Sandpiper and Greenshank.

Not only do juveniles form separate flocks on occasions, but in the adults one sex may begin the southward movement before the other. In many waders, e.g. Redshank, if only one parent is left with the chicks, it is the male which remains and the female which leaves. The early departure of one parent may well have a considerable survival value when food is in short supply and in Alaska (141) the female Semi-palmated Sandpiper and the male Pectoral Sandpiper leave the breeding area soon after the hatch. In the Semi-palmated Sandpiper, early adult migrants tend therefore to be female and in the Pectoral Sandpiper, male. It is also possible that early migrant Dunlin are predominantly female (86).

Our present state of knowledge of migration comes from three main sources, observation of visible migration, data from the ringing schemes and radar studies of bird movement. Each of these sources gives information of a different type but taken together they provide an overall picture of migration. Visible migration enables individual species to be identified, but since only a small part of migration is visible (much is carried out at night and outside the range of vision), the amount of data derived from this source is limited. Ringing has provided a vast amount of information on bird movements, but most waders are ringed away from the breeding grounds, so that information on the migration of birds of known origin is limited. Radar studies have greatly increased our knowledge of this field of ornithology, but here there are difficulties of species recognition. However, additional information on night migration, times of departures and arrivals, heights and speed of movement, has been obtained using radar techniques but, as in studies of visible migration, quantification has proved to be difficult because low flying birds do not appear on the screens.

Wader movements occur in all months of the year, and the autumn return movement in southern breeding species such as Lapwings has often begun before the northward spring movement has been completed in arctic species. Autumn migration in western Europe brings in birds from two main sources. From northern Scandinavia and eastern Siberia, birds arrive from the east, and from Iceland, Greenland and arctic Canada the passage is from the north-west. There is also a significant influx of Lapwings from the east. Generally speaking waders migrate in small parties, but there are exceptions to this. The Eskimo Curlew used to migrate in large flocks in both autumn and spring, before its decline, and migrating Lapwing flocks may contain several thousand individuals. However, radar studies of migration have shown that most movement is in small parties, from one or two to several hundred birds. Again, this has proved difficult to quantify because single echoes on radar screens may involve individuals or large groups.

In June and July, Lapwings arrive on the east coast of England from Germany and Holland. At this time of the year they wait for favourable winds, probably because westerlies are associated with rain and generally unfavourable conditions. Departures from the European coast normally take place about three hours before sunset. This means that when darkness falls the birds are midway across the North Sea and it is significant that radar observations have shown that there is no deviation from the heading originally chosen at this time. Presumably under these circumstances a switch to stellar orientation is made as darkness falls. Radar studies have also shown that whilst over the North Sea, birds will maintain their sense of direction but apparently not their sense of position (124).

In August and September it is possible to recognise wader flocks on radar screens since their well spaced echoes with an air speed of 30–40 knots (35–46 mph) contrast markedly with the 'misty' mass of echoes travelling at 20 knots (Passerines). In October and November, larger thrushes and starlings are easily confused with waders. Throughout autumn, Lapwings move into the east coast of England in increasing numbers and the flock sizes are bigger at this time. While in early autumn Lapwings will only cross the North Sea with a following wind, when they tend to fly high (above 3000 ft), by September they will migrate into a headwind, but under these circumstances they fly low, just above the waves, as they do in rain. Fig. 22 shows a diagram of a radar display showing Lapwing type echoes SSW from Denmark and waders moving SW off the Dutch coast. Behind the westerly moving clouds of hail or rain the birds have descended below the radar horizon.

In good weather conditions, waders arrive at the east coast of England at a height at which they are generally not observable by eye, but in poor weather conditions they come in low, circle over the shoreline, perhaps feed for a few minutes and then move on in a westerly direction. The direction of arrival is difficult to see but radar tracking has shown that arctic waders arrive in a SSW direction, presumably from Norway. Lack (125) points out that eastern

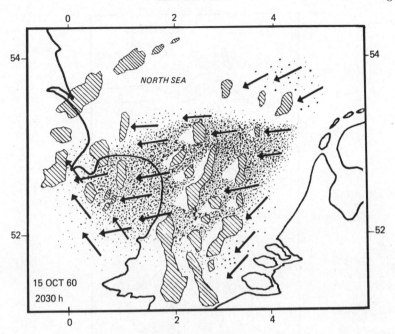

FIG. 22. Radar display in East Anglia at 20.30hrs. on 15 October 1960, with N.E. wind. The echoes are shown in black on a white background instead of the other way about. The main movement is W. from Holland, continuing over East Anglia. Note the absence of bird-echoes behind each hail or rain cloud, due to the birds descending, but rising again later. To the northeast there is also a W.S.W. immigration from Denmark, at this time of Lapwing-type echoes, but later in the night including passerines. Off the Dutch coast there is a S.W. movement of shore-birds. Over the land to the west there is a small N.W. movement, presumably of winter visitors and not a reversed migration. Re-drawn from his notebook by J. L. F. Parslow (after Lack, 1963).

breeding species such as Knot, Bar-tailed Godwit, Curlew-Sandpiper and Little Stint presumably change direction during the migration, but the likelihood is that they travel on a great circle from east of the Taimyr, which would bring them down the peninsula of Scandinavia to arrive in England from the NNE. On crossing the north Norfolk coast, waders tend to turn west into the Wash rather than coasting south, possibly because this direction is nearer to their heading. The speed of flight of these migrating arctic waders is greater than that of Lapwings and Lack estimated the average air speed (of 16 echoes) to be 38.4 knots (44.25 mph). Arrivals at the east coast of England in autumn occur mainly in early morning.

The southward movement of migrant waders in autumn can be detected as

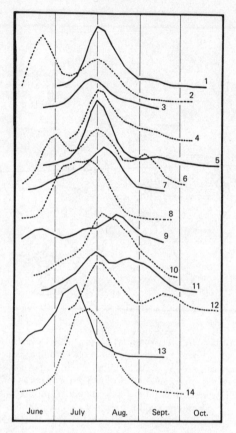

FIG. 23. Average daily passage of some wader species at Ottenby bird observatory, Sweden, from five years' observations. 1, Bar-tailed Godwit; 2, Curlew; 3, Whimbrel; 4, Knot; 5, Dunlin; 6, Ruff; 7, Wood Sandpiper; 8, Redshank; 9, Spotted Redshank; 10, Greenshank; 11, Ringed Plover; 12, Grey Plover; 13, Lapwing; 14, Oystercatcher (after Svardson 1952).

early as mid-June, and different species have peak passages at different times. Fig. 23 shows the average daily passage of some wader species through the Swedish observatory at Ottenby, on the island of Oland. Curlew, Ruff and Lapwing are the earliest migrants and show peaks in June and July. The Ruff shows a three peaked curve largely because some adult birds move south at the end of June. In the Curlew, females tend to move south first. By the end of May these three species and Redshanks, Spotted Redshanks and Oystercatchers are beginning their southward movement and might be regarded as early migrants, whilst Bar-tailed Godwits, Knots, Dunlins and Grey Plovers might be termed late migrants. According to Svardson (235) the bulk of the diurnal passage of these 'later' migrants is of adults, the young of the year either travelling later, or nocturnally. Fig. 23 does not show absolute numbers, but merely peak occurrences. Dunlins are by far the commonest wader migrants at Ottenby in autumn and more than ten times as many Dunlins pass through as Knots. Most Siberian Knots probably pass further east into Africa, but small numbers cross the North Sea and are found on the Wash in autumn. Lack (125) records Knots arriving with other arctic waders from the NNE at Cley, on the north coast of Norfolk though the possibility exists that these could be from Greenland. Probably most birds passing through Ottenby stop off at the mud flats of the Waddenzee for a time whereas birds arriving directly at the Wash fly in a great circle north of Oland. Both the Wash and the Waddenzee form important moulting and feeding areas in autumn and

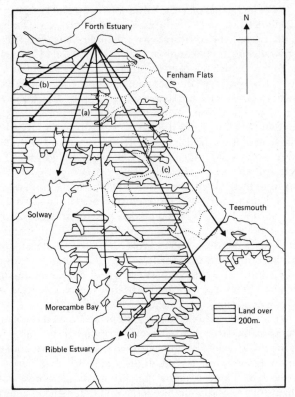

FIG. 24. Overland movement of waders seen by radar in relation to important feeding areas (after Evans 1968).

many wading birds interrupt their southward movement there. There is also some movement between the two areas as ringing results have shown, and wader type radar echoes moving east in September could well indicate a movement of waders from the Wash to the Waddenzee or the delta region of Holland and Belgium. On all the major estuaries of Britain and north-western Europe, waders pause to refuel and many pause long enough to put on significant weight before moving further south. Whilst many birds remain on particular estuaries all winter there is significant movement between estuaries and this is shown very well by the radar studies of Evans (45) in north-east England. Fig. 24 shows four important autumn overland movements between (a) the Forth and the Solway and Morecambe Bay, (b) the Forth and the Ayrshire coast, (c) the Forth and the Wash and Teesmouth and (d) the Ribble estuary. In addition there is an ESE movement of waders which begins inland, probably of birds making for the Waddenzee. The movement from the Forth to the Solway (a) is, initially, likely to be an overland movement of Oystercatchers which takes place in July and August and latterly, in September, movement of Curlews, Whimbrels, Ringed Plovers and Dunlins. Flights between the Forth and the Ayrshire coast (c) might well be a concentration of the southerly movement of Scandinavian waders, mainly Curlews and Golden Plovers (207) – which has been recorded mainly in September. The SSW movement (b) from July well into September is probably composed of Icelandic and possibly Greenland birds, and there is also a coastal movement of waders, in the same direction, of birds from the same sources (43). These are probably mainly Dunlins, Ringed Plovers, Turnstones and Redshanks. The overland movement from the Tees to the Ribble occurs mainly in September and probably consists of Golden Plovers, Bar-tailed Godwits, Curlews and Dunlins from Scandinavia.

It is clear from these observations that waders readily move overland, and whilst most of them are relatively short journeys of some 60–70 miles, the SSE movement from the Forth is of some 200–250 miles. A coastal movement would increase the length of journey only slightly so that it seems clear that overland flights are not deliberately avoided. Of equal interest are the findings that waders compensated for drift by the wind, following the same tracks nightly under different weather conditions, and not merely maintaining a constant heading. They also appeared to be able to navigate accurately under totally overcast conditions.

In autumn the estuaries of western Europe accommodate waders which have bred in Canada, Greenland, Iceland, Scandinavia and Siberia. Waders arriving in the British Isles from the north-west spread down both coasts and the majority of Knots occurring on all the major British estuaries are of the Canadian and Greenland breeding populations. Some Knots from Siberia reach the British Isles, as ringing recoveries and radar studies combined with field observations, have shown. Similarly, nearly all Redshanks occurring on the British estuaries are from Iceland or the British Isles, though there are ringing recoveries in the British Isles of birds bred in the Low Countries. Redshanks from northern Scandinavia do not normally pass through the British Isles, which is surprising since the majority of Dunlins on the Wash in autumn are from northern Scandinavia and eastern USSR, and many of the Curlews are Scandinavian in origin. Sanderlings and Ringed Plovers occur from both Greenland/Iceland and Northern Scandinavia/USSR populations and Turnstones behave similarly with the exception that no Russian birds have yet been recorded on the Wash, suggesting that the Siberian population of this species moves south-west of the British Isles. Obviously, autumn passage Bar-tailed Godwits and Grey Plovers are of the Siberian population and both these species occur on both east and west coasts of the British Isles. In the Oystercatcher, however, the west coast populations are largely of Iceland/Scotland origins, though some are Scandinavian, whereas east coast birds are largely from Scandinavia and European USSR, with smaller numbers from the local breeding populations and from Holland, Scotland and the Faeroes.

Many of the waders to be found on the estuaries of western Europe, in the autumn, do not remain there for the winter. They use the estuaries merely as 'staging posts' on which to gain weight before proceeding further south,

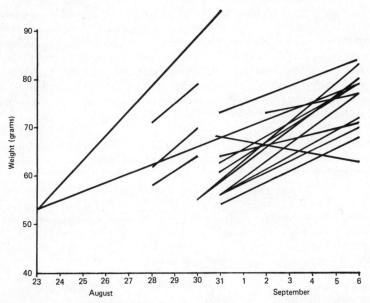

FIG. 25. Weight changes of Curlew Sandpipers retrapped on the Wash and at Wisbech sewage farm, Lincolnshire/Norfolk, during the 1969 influx (after Stanley and Minton 1972).

though some species also moult. Ringed Plovers from both the Iceland/Greenland population and the Scandinavian/USSR population, together with Sanderlings from Greenland, pause on our estuaries for two to three weeks, gain weight and move on. The Dunlins from the north Scandinavian/eastern USSR population, *Calidris alpina alpina*, remain to moult for a longer period of some ten weeks and then move on, and many of the Sanderlings from Siberia moult on the Wash. These birds do not gain as much weight as those that pause only to refuel. Fig. 25 shows the increase in weight of individual Curlew Sandpipers marked in East Anglia (231). During August, birds gained an average of 3.9 g per day compared with 2.6 g per day in September and attained a weight of some 75 g before continuing migration, an addition of more than 55% of the lean body weight given by Pearson *et al* (185).

It is likely that waders storing up fat reserves at staging posts do so in order to complete their migratory journey in continuous flight, rather than by a series of short flights, and it is also likely that direct routes are taken into Africa, in some cases directly across the Sahara Desert. Waders are well-known to be capable of long sea crossings and their presence outside the breeding season on Hawaii and other Pacific islands shows that they are well capable of oceanic journeys in excess of two thousand miles.

Several methods for estimating the potential flight ranges of birds have been suggested (152, 153, 172, 178, 187, 244), but all involve assumptions of one sort or another, particularly in connection with the respiratory rates of migratory birds which, so far, it has proved impossible to measure accurately. All methods involve calculating ranges in still air, but on migration it is the distance covered in relation to the ground which is important. Winds clearly have a smaller effect on the flight range of birds travelling fast than on slow flyers and waders travel at above average speeds (see page 114). Waders are thus less affected than many migrants by adverse winds.

TABLE 6. Flight range capabilities (in miles) of migrant waders on the Atlantic coast of the USA (after McNeil and Cadieux, 1972).

	Autumn		Spring	
	Mean	Max	Mean	Max
Greater Yellowlegs	861	1790	c. 850	—
Lesser Yellowlegs	1300	2100	850	1400
Knot	1800	2900	—	—
White-rumped Sandpiper	1950	2600	1000	—
Least Sandpiper	1800	2600	1135	1650
Short-billed Dowitcher	1800	2700	—	—
Semi-palmated Sandpiper	1500	2000+	1300	—
Hudsonian Godwit	2115	2820		—

Flight ranges have been estimated for several species of North American waders during their autumn and spring migrations on the Atlantic coasts between Nova Scotia and the New England States and South America (152). These are shown in Table 6. With the exception of the Greater Yellowlegs, the flight range in spring appears to be smaller than that in autumn and it is likely that the autumn journey requires a much longer sea crossing. This is because the autumn migration route lies to the east of the spring route, a fact which has been recognised in the Lesser Golden Plover for many years. Fig. 26 shows this for the Lesser Golden Plover, and radar studies (9) have shown that other waders also follow this elliptical route. It appears to be an adaptation to take advantage of the prevailing winds, so that migrants have a following wind at least for the first part of both the autumn and spring journeys.

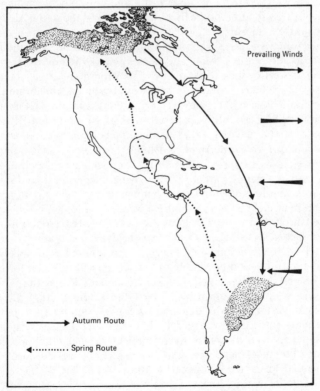

FIG. 26. Migrations of the American Golden Plover (*Pluvialis d. dominica*) (after Lincoln 1935).

Table 6 indicates that the maximum calculated flight range is significantly greater than the mean, which is probably an underestimate. Greater Yellowlegs reach Wake Island in the Pacific (111) and it is believed that this journey is unbroken and even greater than the maximum calculated (153) for this species. It is probable that many waders complete their journeys using only a part of their fat reserves. Lesser Golden Plovers arriving at Wake Island from the north contained, on average, 22 g of fat, which was more than that used on the journey if a continuous flight of 2400 miles was assumed. It has also been shown that some individuals of the White-rumped Sandpiper arriving in South America still have sufficient fat reserves to travel a further 800–1300 miles (149, 151).

In contrast to the data shown in Table 6, Johnston and MacFarlane (111) have shown that in spring the fattest Lesser Golden Plovers are capable of a journey at least as long as the autumn migration. The estimated flight range in April is 6200 miles for the largest birds compared with 5900 miles in the autumn. They suggest that only birds weighing 150 g, and having fat reserves in excess of 18 g will attempt the flight from Wake Island to the Aleutians or the Kamchatka peninsula.

In most wader species, spring migration appears to be carried out more quickly than autumn migration, and possibly more directly. In Europe the prevailing westerly winds will aid birds following great circle routes from Africa, and much more fat is put on before migration than in autumn. Again 'staging posts' are used, but it may well be that migrants remain for a time on the more northerly estuaries as a result of reversed migration ('Ruckzug') which radar studies have shown to be much more common than was at one time thought (40). In North America, Dunlins have been recorded putting on as much weight as 12 g in $1\frac{1}{2}$ days on the Copper River Delta, in Alaska, which is used as a staging post for birds moving further north and it is likely that, as in the autumn, the rates of weight increase at staging posts are much faster than the weight gain prior to the start of migration.

In the Curlew–Sandpiper, Elliott et al (41) show that from a mean lean weight of 53.0 g, at the Cape, South Africa, there is a gradual increase in weight of 0.1 g/day from mid-February to mid-March, followed by 0.57 g/day until the end of March and 0.73 g/day for the first fortnight of April. This gives a migration take-off weight of about 80 g, with a fat store of 27 g. Using the formula given by McNeil and Cadieux (152) this gives a theoretical migratory range of 2020 miles. It is likely that this is a considerable underestimate of the flight range if the Lesser Golden Plover is capable of a flight of 2400 miles on 18 g of fat. Even so, the Curlew–Sandpipers wintering in the Cape Province, must employ staging posts in their northward journey.

Very similar spring weight changes to those in the Curlew–Sandpiper are shown by Dunlins on the Cheshire Dee. Eades and Okill (39) showed a weight increase of 0.57 g/day during the first half of May, to a migration take-off weight of 75–80 g, which compares with a maximum breeding weight of 53 g

(228). In one individual, thought to be *C. alpina arctica*, there was a rate of increase of 1.4 g/day. On the Wash, Dunlins show an increase in mean weight from below 50 g in March to 75 g in May (158) and generally speaking arctic-breeding species put on more fat in spring than other waders. There can be little doubt that the fat is mainly used as fuel for the migratory flight, but it is clearly of advantage to spring migrants to arrive at the breeding ground with some reserves as a food supply may not be readily available on arrival. MacLean (141) has shown that this is particularly important in the Pectoral Sandpiper.

It may be for this reason that some species use staging posts well short of their maximum flying ranges. This is the case in the Knot returning to Greenland and Ellesmere Island as many use Iceland as a staging post. It has been claimed that Knot could not reach Greenland under normal weather conditions from the Wash, but since Wash birds put on 40 g in weight between March and May, and Morecambe Bay birds up to 80 g during this same period, this is almost certainly not true. Even at the most pessimistic estimates, this weight increase would allow birds theoretically to reach the east coast, and probably the west coast of Greenland, though it must be recognised that the birds would be heading into the prevailing winds. McNeil and Cadieux (153) have estimated that individual Knot had ranges up to 2900 miles in the second week of August.

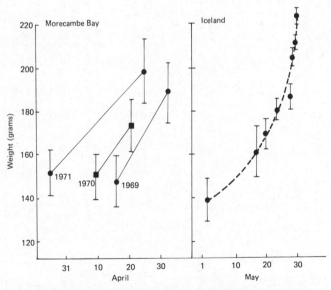

FIG. 27. Premigratory spring increase in weight of Knot (after Prater 1974).

TABLE 7. Theoretical flight ranges of European waders on spring migration based on curves calculated by Berger and Hart (1974).

Species	Age/Sex	Fat-free wt (estimated)	Mean Spring wt.	Fat wt	Authority for data	% fat	Potential flight duration (hrs)	Approx. range in miles	Locality	Possible maximum destination
Oystercatcher	Ad	480	600	120	Minton (1975)	20	42	1890	Wash	Kolguyev
	Ad ♂	520?	585	60(105)	Dare (1977)	10(17)	18(30)	810(1350)	Morecambe Bay	S.W. Iceland (Greenland)
	Ad ♀	535?	620	85(140)	Dare (1977)	14(23)	27(48)	1215(2160)	Morecambe Bay	Iceland (N. Greenland)
Grey Plover		210	310	100	Minton (1975)	32	55	2750	Wash	Taimyr Peninsula
Ringed Plover		60	75.21	15-21	Eades & Okill (1976)	20	24	840	Dee (Cheshire)	S.W. Iceland
Redshank		140	152(174.2)	12(34.2)	Minton (1975)	8(20)	10(28)	450(1260)	Wash	Orkney (Iceland)
		147.3 (140)	174.2	26.9 (34.2)	Boer (in Glutz 1977)	15(20)	20(28)	900(1260)	Holland	Faeroes (Iceland)
		105	130	25	Minton (1975)	19	27	1215	Wash	Iceland Lofoten Island and S. Finland
Knot		130	175	45	Minton (1975)	26	35	1575	Wash	W. Greenland
		130	210	80	Prater (1972 & 1974)	38	65	2925	Morecambe Bay	Ellesmere Island
Sanderling		51	81	30	Minton (1975)	37	45	1800	Wash	Arkangel W. Greenland
Dunlin		47	77.5	30.5	Eades & Okill (1977)	39	53	2650	Dee (Cheshire)	Yamal Peninsula
		47	75	28	Minton (1975)	37	49	2450	Wash	Yamal Peninsula

Figures in brackets are from other sources than those indicated and likely to be nearer the true levels.

Prater (197) records a mean May weight of 150 g for Knot in Iceland in 1971 and on the basis of a mean weight of *c.* 220 g in early May of the same year in Morecambe Bay, suggests a weight loss of 70 g+ for the 800-mile flight. This seems excessive and it may well be that the heavier Morecambe Bay birds make the flight directly to Greenland whereas the lighter birds use Iceland as a staging post. A similar percentage weight loss is not indicated by the 1970 data (Fig. 27). Of particular interest is the weight gain in Iceland in 1971, where a mean increase of 41.9 g was recorded in 14 days, equivalent to 3 g/day. For a flight with a maximum range of 1650 miles it is likely that considerable reserves would be still available on arrival on Ellesmere Island, particularly since these birds weighed in excess of 200 g in Iceland, before the final stage of migration.

Different species of waders carry different amounts of fat (Table 7) and it is surprising that the Bar-tailed Godwit apparently carries very little pre-migratory fat in spring in north-east England (47); on the Wash there is little spring data on this species, but here again the indications are of little or no spring weight gain. Conversely, the Sanderling may double its fat free weight in spring (158). Berger and Hart (12) have constructed curves (Fig. 28) to estimate potential flight duration knowing the body weight and fat content. Using this information and the flight speeds shown in Table 8 it is possible to

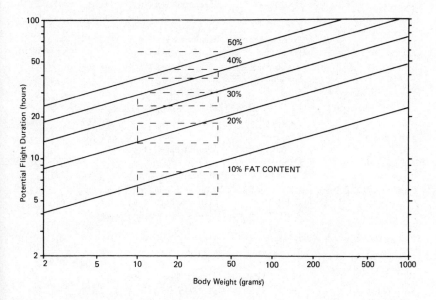

FIG. 28. Potential flight duration in relation to fat content and body weight. Rectangles and dashed line include ranges given by Odum et al. (1961) (after Berger and Hart 1974).

TABLE 8. Flight speeds of wading birds

	Location	Authority	Speed (mph) of Normal Flight	Migration
Stone Curlew	UK	Meinertzhagen (1955)	30	
Oystercatcher	Tanganyika	Meinertzhagen (1955)	45–49	
	UK	Meinertzhagen (1955)	32, 35	
Ringed Plover	UK	Meinertzhagen (1955)	36	
Semi-palmated	California	Meinertzhagen (1955)	28–55	
Ringed Plover	USA	Longstreet (1930)	32	
	USA	McNeil (1969, 1970)	30, 35	
Kentish Plover	Israel	Meinertzhagen (1955)	34–39	
Sand Plover	Israel	Meinertzhagen (1955)	34–39	
Caspian Plover	Kenya	Meinertzhagen (1955)		47–51
Dotterel	UK	Meinertzhagen (1955)		45–50
	Israel	Meinertzhagen (1955)		45, 50.5
Golden Plover	UK	Meinertzhagen (1955)		60
American Golden Plover	Illinois, USA	Meinertzhagen (1955)	62	
Grey Plover	USA	McNeil (1969, 1970)	45, 50	
	Florida, USA	Meinertzhagen (1955)	24	
Lapwing	UK	Meinertzhagen (1955)	28, 37, 30–40	
	UK	Lack 1963a		35.1 (radar)
	Europe	Meinertzhagen (1955)		30, 40–45
	Israel	Meinertzhagen (1955)		37 (HW)
Greenshank	Tanganyika	Meinertzhagen (1955)	46, 49	
	Somaliland	Meinertzhagen (1955)	44	
Lesser Yellowlegs	USA	McNeil (1969, 1970)	40, 45	
Greater Yellowlegs	USA	McNeil (1969, 1970)	40, 45, 45	
Marsh Sandpiper	Tanganyika	Meinertzhagen (1955)	48, 51, 51.5	
Terek Sandpiper	Tanganyika	Meinertzhagen (1955)	48–51	
	Somaliland	Meinertzhagen (1955)	44	
Turnstone	USA	Longstreet (1930)	27	
		McNeil (1969, 1970)	35, 40	
Curlew	UK	Meinertzhagen (1955)	20	
	Ireland	Meinertzhagen (1955)	60	
	Tanganyika	Meinertzhagen (1955)	42–48.25 (17 counts)	
Whimbrel	Ireland	Meinertzhagen (1955)		40–45 (HW)
	Tanganyika	Meinertzhagen (1955)	43–52 (19 counts)	
	Florida, USA	Meinertzhagen (1955)	34	
Long-billed Curlew	USA	Meinertzhagen (1955)	35 (HW)	
Willet	Florida, USA	Meinertzhagen (1955)	27 (HW)	

Location	Authority	Speed (mph) of Normal Flight	Migration
Short-billed Dowitcher	California, USA	Meinertzhagen (1955)	43	
Common Snipe	UK	Meinertzhagen (1955)	25, 34.7, 25–50 (Drumming)	
Hudsonian Godwit	USA	Cadieux (1970)	45	
Pin-tailed Snipe	Bengal, India	Meinertzhagen (1955)	26–31	
Woodcock	UK	Meinertzhagen (1955)	44.6	
American Woodcock	Cumberland, USA	Meinertzhagen (1955)	27.2, 13, 35	
Little Stint	Tanganyika	Meinertzhagen (1955)	49	
Sanderling	Florida, USA	Meinertzhagen (1955)	41 (TW)	
Western Sandpiper	California, USA	Meinertzhagen (1955)	45, 52	
Knot	USA	Longstreet (1930)	38	
Dunlin	USA	McCabe (1942)	45, 55	
White-rumped Sandpiper	USA	McNeil (1969, 1970)	45, 50	
Least Sandpiper	USA	McCabe (1942) McNeil (1969, 1970)	45, 55 45, 50, 50	
Semi-palmated Sandpiper	USA	Longstreet (1930) McNeil (1969, 1970)	32 40, 50, 50	

HW = Head wind
TW = Tail wind

estimate theoretical flight ranges for other wading birds, and Table 7 shows this for common European spring migrants.

It may well be that all estimates of flight range capabilities of wading birds are well in excess of those distances over which the birds migrate in a single flight. Evans and Smith (47) found that in the Bar-tailed Godwit, fat reserves accumulated before migration were usually more than sufficient for the flight but that muscle weights after migration were lower than the lowest recorded in non-migrants. Clearly, muscles may be drawn upon as protein reserves during migration and this may limit the potential range. If this is the case, excess fat may be carried to provide a source of energy which on some occasions is not available until the end of the journey, or alternatively it may be provided as a reserve for unusually bad journeys. It is likely that on occasions both these alternatives may apply, but there can be little doubt that most waders complete each stage of their migratory journey with ample fat reserves, and this is of particular importance in the return to the possibly initially inhospitable breeding grounds in spring.

Theoretical flight ranges are affected by winds and migrating birds often wait for favourable wind conditions before embarking upon a long flight. Radar studies have made it possible to quantify wind effect and other factors influencing migration. Table 9 shows the effect of factors influencing westward migration of waders in the autumn in East Anglia, after Lack (125). Density of migration was greater with following winds, as would be expected, intermediate with cross winds and lowest with opposing winds. The stronger the opposing wind the lower was the density of migration. Density was also higher in anticyclonic conditions and when the weather was clear, as opposed to cloudy. Temperature appeared to have no influence, but it is known that birds flying at normal or high temperatures lose more water than is available from metabolic processes. It is therefore clearly beneficial to reduce water loss

TABLE 9. Factors influencing the westward wader passage observed by radar from East Anglia, 26 August – 27 September (after Lack 1963a).

	FOLLOWING WIND		OPPOSED WIND		CROSS-WIND	
	Number of days	Mean density of migration	Number of days	Mean density of migration	Number of days	Mean density of migration
General situation						
anticyclonic	59	1.2	25	0.20	17	0.5
transitional	18	0.7	26	0.15	10	0.2
disturbed	11	0.5	53	0.04	14	0.04
Surface wind-speed in knots						
2–7	33	1.0	20	0.39	15	0.5
10	27	1.0	15	0.08	15	0.2
15	20	1.0	33	0.02	4	0.3
Over 20	8	1.1	36	0.03	7	0.1
Cloud						
0/8–4/8	50	1.3	22	0.16	13	0.5
5/8–7/8	25	0.7	48	0.14	13	0.2
8/8	12	0.6	34	0.03	14	0.1
Temperature in °F						
Below 54	4	0.4	9	0.19	3	(0.8)
55–59	23	1.1	49	0.14	24	0.3
60–64	45	1.0	43	0.06	14	0.2
Over 65	16	1.0	3	—	0	—
Total Diurnal	39	0.81	44	0.14	22	0.32
Total Nocturnal	49	1.17	60	0.08	19	0.25

Note: Following winds were from between N.E. and S.E., opposed from between S.W. and N.W. and cross-winds from N. or S. The cloud record was missing for one morning with a N. wind and one morning with an E. wind.

Density is measured on an arbitrary increasing scale from 0–3 where 3 is much more than 3 times as much migration as 1.

to a minimum and this can be brought about by flying at low temperatures, at night or at high altitudes, particularly where deserts have to be crossed. Flying at high altitudes may reduce the capability of oxygen uptake, but apart from the lower temperatures at high altitudes there is also the advantage of lower air density and thus increased speed (18). Radar studies have shown that speed of flight is increased by greater height up to 3000 m, and it may be that below such heights, altitude has little effect on oxygen uptake (12).

The heights at which migratory birds fly was a source of much speculation until the advent of radar studies. Prior to this the only reliable information had been collected by Meinertzhagen (154), largely from aeroplane observations; these data are shown in Table 10. For Lapwings on spring migration,

TABLE 10. Altitudes of migratory flights in wading birds (after Meinertzhagen, 1955).

Species	Season	Location	Dir.	Height
Lapwing	Spring	France		6500
		France		5500
		Germany		1300–1800
		Egypt		8400
		Irish Sea		8400
	Autumn	France		2000–8500
		France	N	6000
				8000
Whimbrel	Spring	France	NE	4000
		France		4000
Godwit and Curlew	Autumn	Himalayas	S	20,000
Woodcock	Autumn	Ireland		3000
Sandpipers	Spring	France	E	12,000
Waders	December	France		9500–10,000
Small Waders	Spring	California		1500

heights ranged between 5500 ft and 8500 ft, and in autumn between 2000 ft and 8500 ft, but it is clear from Table 10 that this height is largely determined by the topography of the land. For example, in the Himalayas, Godwit and Curlew have been recorded flying south at a height of 20,000 ft, and there is a record of a skeleton of a Black-tailed Godwit taken from a glacier at 16,000 ft in the Himalayas. From a theoretical point of view, migrating at this height should present a physiological problem to the birds, but certainly they seem capable of such flights. Height also seems to vary with the meteorological conditions and Lack (125) found that the height at which Lapwings migrated was constant on any one evening, but varied significantly between evenings. On a particular September night the heights at which different flocks were recorded varied within 2000 ft, but on different nights the mean height was between 3000 ft and 6000 ft. In June and July, heights varied between very low (below radar horizon) and 6000 ft.

Often waders migrate at very low altitudes, just above the sea, and this particularly happens in rain. Probably most waders migrate at relatively low altitudes, but it is likely that they will seek altitudes which provide the most favourable wind conditions (35).

The fact that many waders have been recorded at high altitudes brings into question the extent to which mountain ranges constitute physical barriers. Baird's Sandpipers follow mountain chains in both the Andes and the Rocky Mountains and have been recorded at a height of 13,000 ft. The Pectoral Sandpiper has also been recorded in Colorado at this height, and in the Argentine at 12,000 ft (233).

It has been suggested that the speed at which migrating birds travel is probably greater than that of normal flight (35), and it is likely that the spring journey is accomplished more rapidly than the autumn migration through the stimulus of the onset of breeding. The record of 110 mph for a northbound Dunlin in spring (147) is more than twice as fast as its normal speed and like many earlier records (Godwits 140 mph, and Curlew 240 mph) an exaggeration. Meinertzhagen (155) provides data for flight speeds of many species of birds and Table 8 shows those given for wading birds together with some data taken from other sources. Comparison of measurements taken in 'normal flight' with those taken on migrating birds, suggests no significant difference in flight speeds, but it is possible that the methods used for measurement are not sufficiently accurate to indicate differences. Perhaps the best indication of the speeds achieved by migrating birds comes from radar studies and Lack (125) describes wader migration on radar screens as being characterised by 'well spaced echoes with an air speed of 30–40 knots', and showed that migrating Lapwings, in September, moved with an air speed of 30.5 knots (35 mph), a figure based on the average air speed of 31 echoes. Given a following wind, such speeds could be very much increased. The upper limits of speeds measured from radar observation could well apply to Sandpipers as the flight speeds given in Table 8 tend to be in excess of Lapwing flight speeds.

Since it appears that both the speed and height of migration are optimised, it would be surprising if the route of the journey itself was not as direct as possible. However, some populations move southward in short stages in autumn and tend to move slowly north again in spring. This applies particularly to short-distance migrants, such as the Redshank population of the British Isles and the Ringed Plover population of Denmark. Such movements are clearly shown by ringing recoveries which have provided a great deal of information on the movements and wintering areas of wading birds. There are two particular areas, however, in which ringing recoveries have not

provided a great deal of information on wading birds, firstly for birds of
known breeding areas (as few adults are ringed on the breeding ground), and
secondly for the routes that long-distance migrants follow, largely because
they make flights where there is little or no chance of recoveries occurring en

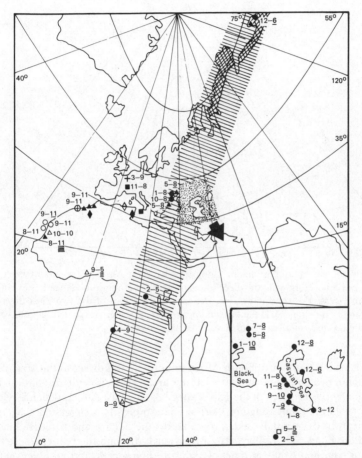

FIG. 29. Gnomonic projection showing recoveries of Curlew-Sandpipers, excluding
local recoveries within Southern Africa. The symbols give the country of ringing as
follows: South Africa = ● ; Morocco = ○ ; Mauritania = ■ ; Kenya = □ ; Sweden
= ▲ ; Tunisia = △ ; Ivory Coast = + ; Finland =   ; Britain = ♦ ; France = ◊ .
Ringing and recovery months and the number of elapsed seasons are shown. The
hatched area marks the main breeding grounds of the species (Vaurie 1965). Data
obtained up to 1976 have been included (after Elliott et al 1976).

route. There are exceptions to this. Twelve Curlew–Sandpipers ringed in South
Africa have been recorded in the area of the Black and Caspian Seas on a
direct great circle between the wintering ground in South Africa and the
breeding area in the Taimyr in northern Siberia (Fig. 29). It is suggested that

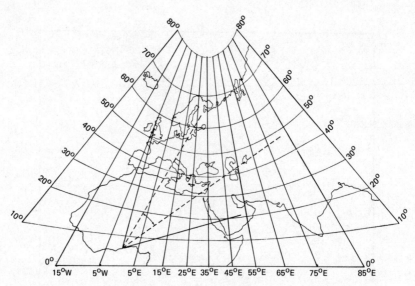

FIG. 30. An oblique gnomonic projection of West Africa, Europe and West and
Central Siberia showing the direction of initial spring migration of waders in Ghana.
From Accra, the continuous lines denote the directions of the two most divergent
departure headings, and the broken lines represent the great circle directions within
which lay 76% of all departures (after Grimes 1974).

birds which summer in South Africa migrate inland direct to the area of the
Caspian Sea and then on to the Taimyr area. There is evidence that the first
major stop is the area of the Rift Valley lakes in East Africa, which is within
the probable flight range of Curlew–Sandpiper. It is suggested that West
African birds normally take a route across the Sahara and through Tunisia
and the Black Sea, rather than further north through the Baltic, where they
occur commonly only at times of high breeding success and suitable weather
conditions. Radar studies of Grimes (67) have shown that waders take great
circle routes directly inland in Ghana, in spring (Fig. 30), and it is most likely
that they cross the Sahara towards the region of the Black Sea. Such a route
back towards northern Siberia avoids all the major mountain ranges, and
Elliott et al (41) concluded that Curlew–Sandpipers migrate directly to the
breeding grounds even if this necessitates crossing inhospitable areas such as

the Sahara and Arabian deserts, the Congo forests or major mountain ranges. This almost certainly also applies to other waders. Grimes (67) found that as the season progressed, waders take a more easterly heading returning first to the westerly parts of the breeding range. This fits in well with the European breeding grounds thawing before those in west and central Siberia. The spring flight from West Africa is aided by favourable winds above 2000 m as birds fly from south-west to north-east, and Moreau (161) regards the trans-Sahara flight, often with the addition of the crossing of the Mediterranean Sea, as commonplace. This view is supported by radar studies in the eastern Mediterranean (21) where overflying of the coastal areas, from further south in spring, occurred frequently. This work also showed that the crossing of the Mediterranean during migration occurred on a broad front both in spring and autumn (Fig. 31) and that in all likelihood the birds were maintaining directions which allowed for drift.

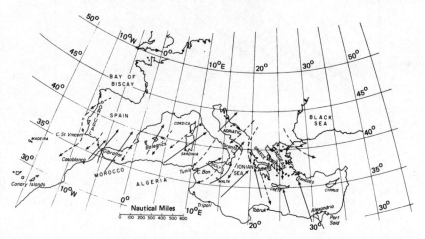

FIG. 31. Radar patterns of Migration across the Mediterranean Spring ————————— Autumn ————————— (after Casement, 1966).

The work of Dick *et al* (33) on the migration of the Knot also suggests that this species follows great circle routes on migration. Certainly Knot migrating from Siberia to Mauretania do not follow a single compass direction and either move from one suitable feeding area to another or follow direct, great circle routes. The latter would seem to be the most likely, particularly in the light of the observation that certain waders, including Knot, arrived on a SSW course on the eastern coast of the British Isles (125). Fig. 32 shows the likely great circle routes for the Greenland/Ellesmere Island Knot and the Siberian Knot bound for Mauretania; it also shows the probable great circle

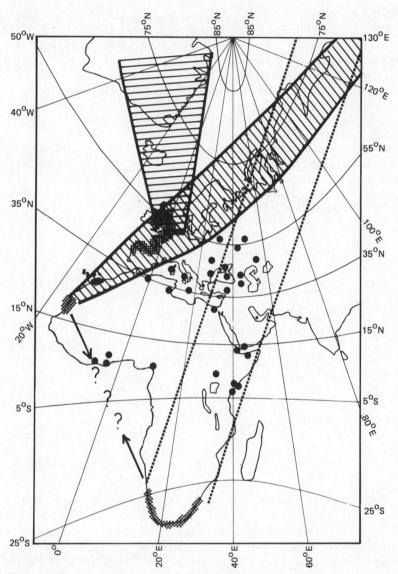

FIG. 32. Gnomonic projection showing the main (hatched) and tentative (dashed) migration routes of Knots from the breeding grounds to the known wintering areas (stippled). Arrows with '?' indicate movement by an unknown route. Solid dots refer to observations of Knot away from the main migration route (after Dick et al 1976).

route from Siberia to South Africa via the East African Rift Valley lakes, but only a relatively small number of Knot winter in South Africa. There is, however, evidence that other species use this last route, for example Little Stint, Curlew–Sandpiper and Ruff (185, 41), and the probability is that most waders use direct routes (great circles) to and from the breeding grounds in spring and autumn. There is not yet sufficient evidence to indicate whether the same routes are followed in spring and autumn, but it may well be that these may differ slightly as in the case of the overland spring route in the USA compared with the autumn sea route (Fig. 26).

Different populations of the same species differ in their migratory habits. In those species which have populations probably derived from secondary hybridisation, for example Redshank, Dunlin, Golden Plover and Ringed Plover, the hybrid populations tend to migrate much shorter distances than non-hybrid populations breeding further north and give rise to the so-called 'leap-frog' migration (212). It may well be that these hybrids are capable of wintering further north and so do not undertake a long migratory journey. More northerly breeding populations migrate at later dates than more southerly populations of the same species and this is illustrated for the Redshank in Table 11. From this it can be seen that the northerly populations of Scandinavia return north mainly in May, whereas British, Danish and Dutch birds move north earlier. Danish and Dutch pulli appear to move south later than British Redshank pulli and the more northerly populations spend more time on the wintering ground and less on the breeding ground than more southerly populations, as suitable conditions prevail for shorter periods in the north.

The number of stages during journeys between breeding and wintering grounds in wading birds may well be fewer than has been suggested in this short review. As Moreau (161) points out, birds which migrate from Siberia to the tropics may well, according to current theory, require to refuel, but no suitable area has so far been suggested for waders migrating, say, over three thousand miles, from Tomsk to Khartoum; therefore, it may be that estimates of fat consumption in flight are wrong. The data given for the Lesser Golden Plover by Johnston and MacFarlane (111) suggest that this is so. There is also some evidence to suggest that birds making a shorter over-all journey take on less fat than those making a longer journey, e.g. Curlew–Sandpiper in South Africa (41) and Kenya (185), and whilst this could be for the first stage only, why do the Kenya birds not take on more fat initially so that less need be acquired at the staging posts?

At the end of the breeding season most waders move south, and it can be accepted that this is because food is likely to be better where they intend to winter than on the breeding ground. At the time of departure, in fact, this may not be so: for example, they have little difficulty putting on fat at the southerly staging posts for further journeys, and in autumn, when the invertebrate foods are at their highest biomass in the northern hemisphere, stays

TABLE 11. Comparison of migration times in different populations of Redshanks. Numbers recaptured (excluding those recaptured in country of ringing) in percentages for each month of migration period (after Hale 1973).

Area of recovery	Month of recovery					
	Jul.	Aug.	Sep.	Mar.	Apr.	May
Sweden (N) (pulli)	8	51	17	2	6	16
	11%	67%	22%	8%	25%	67%
Sweden (N) (adults)	2	6	6	3	6	9
	14%	43%	43%	17%	33%	50%
Sweden (N) (total)	10	57	23	5	12	25
	11%	63%	26%	12%	29%	59%
Sweden (Scania)	5	15	8			
	18%	54%	28%			
Finland (total)†	3	40	17		3	9
	5%	61%	28%		25%	75%
Norway (total)†	3	3	6			4
	25%	25%	50%			100%
Denmark (pulli)	3	19	6	3	2	
	11%	68%	21%	60%	40%	
Denmark (juv.)	34	128	95	49	13	9
	13%	50%	37%	69%	18%	13%
Denmark (adults)	9	16	7	53	20	16
	28%	50%	22%	60%	22%	18%
Denmark (total)*	45	179	109	111	37	25
	13%	54%	33%	64%	21%	15%
Holland (pulli)	1	2	3	1	5	3
	17%	33%	50%	11%	55%	34%
Holland (adults)	1	2	2	4	5	1
	20%	40%	40%	40%	50%	10%
Holland (total)	2	4	5	5	10	4
	9%	36%	45%	26%	53%	21%
British Isles (pulli) >50 m	6	7	9	7	3	
	27%	32%	41%	70%	30%	
British Isles (adults) >50 m	6	2	1	5	3	6
	67%	22%	11%	36%	21%	43%
British Isles (total) >50 m	12	9	10	12	6	6
	39%	29%	32%	50%	25%	25%
Iceland	1	1	1	1	1	
	33%	33%	33%	50%	50%	

* Includes birds of unknown age.
† Not possible to separate into age groups from data given.

for this purpose may be quite protracted. Strangely enough, waders moving northwards under pressure of their breeding cycle, may remain at these posts for shorter periods in spring, when the total invertebrate biomass is at its lowest, and even so they put on weight more rapidly than at any other time. There can be little doubt that some of this is an insurance against an initially sparse food supply on the breeding ground. From these facts, it is difficult to see how shortage of food could be a factor in motivating the waders to migrate from the southern winter range, unless of course the supply should become inaccessible because of snow or frost cover – both of which are rare in the estuarine environments in which they feed. Clearly there are other factors involved in the northerly migration, and these will be considered in subsequent chapters.

CHAPTER 6

WINTERING POPULATIONS

FOR many waders the breeding grounds are inhospitable places outside the short breeding season: for other, more southerly populations (even of the same species) the breeding and wintering grounds are the same. This clearly implies that different populations of the same species have evolved different strategies in order to occupy breeding areas which at other times of the year do not always provide a suitable habitat; in other words, whilst some populations are relatively sedentary, others carry out extensive migrations to reach their wintering areas. It is likely that, in order to avoid competition, waders of a particular species spread out over an extensive wintering area. It does not follow that if this wintering area was smaller competition would result in an increased mortality; probably the result would be that food was obtained less easily and the availability of other areas, where food was more easily obtained, would clearly result in the colonisation of these areas. The areas occupied by wintering waders are probably those in which food can be obtained with least energy output in terms of feeding effort and migration. Both Lack (122) and Salomonsen (210) regard the wide dispersal of birds during the winter, and the occupation of different wintering areas by different populations as being adaptations to combat competition for food.

Salomonsen (212) has considered the winter distribution of bird species in general in some detail and has proposed the terms 'synhiemic' and 'allo-hiemic' to describe populations which have the same winter quarters, and different winter quarters, respectively. No doubt most wader species can be said to be partially allohiemic, though some, like the Eurasian and Greenland/Ellesmere Island populations of Knot, might be said to be completely allohiemic, wintering in Africa and western Europe respectively (Fig. 32). Where such populations exist, two factors are of prime importance in the evolution of the species. Firstly, if populations are geographically separated in both the breeding and non-breeding seasons, then no gene flow is possible between the populations, and a situation exists in which speciation might take place. Secondly, in both breeding and non-breeding seasons, the separate populations are subject to different environmental factors which might play a part in the selection of morphological structures such as wing length (an indication of overall size), bill length and tarsus length. Where populations are synheimic the possibility clearly exists of birds from different breeding populations mixing, and birds from one breeding population returning north with the other population in the following spring, resulting in gene flow between the populations. Even in circumstances such as this, where partial alloheimy exists it can affect the evolution of the populations, but, as Salomonsen (212) rightly points out, selection is the only genetic factor involved in winter.

In considering evolutionary effects on wintering populations it is necessary to know in what areas different breeding populations overwinter, and if, during the course of the winter, there is much movement of birds about the wintering range. In other words, it is necessary to know if birds are faithful to their wintering areas to the extent that they are faithful to their breeding areas. What evidence exists suggests that many are. Table 12 which is taken from Moreau (161) shows that many wading birds return in subsequent winters to the original ringing site, and Elliott et al (41) quote six records of Curlew–Sandpipers made up of groups of 2, 2, 3, 3, 3, and 4 retrapped together after original trapping at the same time; in five cases a full season had elapsed and in the sixth, two seasons. These data clearly suggest that the birds had nested in the same area and migrated together in both directions, so that at least in some species small groups tend to remain together and as Isakov (106) suggests, form small fixed populations which can be considered as examples of alloheimy on a small scale.

In other species too, the incidence of return to the same wintering area is very high. Bainbridge & Minton (6) record that of 269 winter recoveries of Curlews in the British Isles, 81% were within 30 km of their ringing site. Even within an area such as the Wash, the attachment of wading birds to one particular part is evident between seasons (158), and Dunlin on the south shore of the Wash show few retraps more than 2 km from the place of ringing. In Morocco, Peinkowski (190) has shown that Ringed Plovers, Redshanks, Little Stints, Dunlins and Curlew–Sandpipers show high return rates to the site of ringing despite the fact that most of these birds subsequently move on to winter further south in West Africa.

TABLE 12. Recurrence of wading birds in subsequent winters at site of ringing in Africa (after Moreau 1972).

		Number of birds	
Species	Area and year of ringing	trapped	retrapped in next or subsequent seasons
Curlew Sandpiper	Cape Province	?	1
	Kenya Nak. 1968/69	14	1
Little Stint	Cape Province	1292	89
	Kenya Naiv. 1967/68	32	1
	Kenya Naiv. 1968/69	310	7
	Kenya Nak. 1966/67	115	6
	Kenya Nak. 1967/68	502	7
	Kenya Nak. 1968/69	361	3
Ringed Plover	Kenya Naiv. 1967/68	21	2
Common Snipe	Kenya Naiv. 1967/68	2	1
	Kenya Naiv. 1968/69	16	1
Ruff	Kenya Nak. 1966/67	145	4
	Kenya Nak. 1967/68	360	9
	Kenya Nak. 1968/69	830	5
Wood Sandpiper	Zambia	?	6
	Kenya Naiv. 1967/68	28	1
	Kenya Naiv. 1968/69	67	1
Common Sandpiper	Transvaal	?	1
Green Sandpiper	Zambia	?	6
Marsh Sandpiper	Kenya Nak. 1966/67	49	2
	Kenya Nak. 1967/68	126	2
	Kenya Nak. 1968/69	139	2
	Cape Province	?	2

Note: Naiv. = Lake Naivasha.   Nak. = Lake Nakuru.

It seems that many waders follow the same route each year to and from the same wintering grounds and breeding grounds and use the same staging posts. However, the fact that many maintain small population groups and are faithful to their summer and winter haunts provides no information about the birds which are not recovered; do these move elsewhere or do they die? This is important from an evolutionary point of view as movement may result in gene flow in subsequent breeding seasons. Some wintering waders seem more subject to movement than others and Minton (158) has shown by means of ringing recoveries that the Knot falls into this category, and some individuals

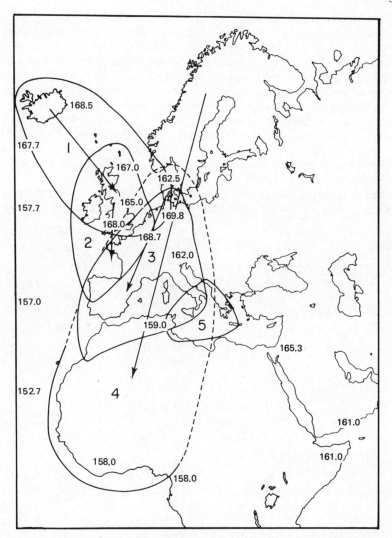

FIG. 33. Winter ranges of Redshanks from 1, Iceland; 2, United Kingdom; 3, Denmark, Germany, Holland and Belgium; 4, Sweden, Norway; 5, Hungary. Breeding areas and corresponding winter quarters are connected by arrows. Figures inserted at left give average wing lengths (measured on the breeding range) of the population wintering in the area in question. Measurements on the map show actual means of wing length (♂) for wintering birds in that area (after Hale 1973).

select different estuaries for moulting and wintering in different seasons, either in Britain or on the continent of Europe. However, over much of the wintering areas of waders, particularly in Africa, there are few ringing recoveries, and while wintering areas can be mapped for different species with a fair degree of accuracy (161), this is done largely on the basis of sight records in winter and gives little information about the movement of individual birds. Very little of the information we possess is derived from ringing recoveries, and even where they exist the breeding grounds of the ringed bird are seldom known, since most birds are ringed actually on migration. Wintering grounds in western Europe are much easier to establish by means of ringing recoveries than those further south or east where there are few successful ringing schemes and few recoveries are made.

In the Redshank the breeding populations of Iceland, the British Isles, Denmark, Germany, Holland and Belgium winter mainly within Europe

Region	No.	Sex	Age	Allocate to regions			Date (month)
7	1	0	0	29+	13	21	9
7	2	0	0	(22)	5+	21	3
7	3	0	0	14+	15	24	2
7	4	0	0	14+	15	16	2
7	5	0	0	14+	15	24	2
7	6	0	0	14+	24	15	2
7	7	0	0	14+	16	15	6
7	8	0	0	14+	15	28	6
7	9	0	0	14+	28	15	1
7	10	1	0	14+	20	9	2
7	11	1	0	14+	9	15	2
7	12	1	0	14+	15	25	2
7	13	1	0	14+	9	28	2
7	14	1	0	14+	15	25	1
7	15	1	0	14+	15	25	1
7	16	1	0	14+	15	25	1
7	17	1	0	14+	25	15	1
7	18	1	0	14+	25	15	1
7	19	1	0	14+	25	15	1
7	20	1	0	14+	15	25	1
7	21	1	0	14+	25	15	1
7	22	1	0	14+	15	25	1
7	23	1	0	14+	25	24	2
7	26	0	2	10+	4	20	3

Region	No.	Sex	Age	Allocate to regions			Date (month)
7	27	0	2	28+	26	12	2
7	28	0	2	14+	15	24	2
7	29	0	2	(15)	24+	25	2
7	30	0	2	(30)	6+	23	7
7	31	0	2	8+	22	12	9
7	32	0	2	10+	28	25	8
7	33	0	2	28+	1	3	8
7	34	0	2	10+	28	1	6
7	35	0	2	9+	5	26	8
7	36	0	2	8+	12	27	8
7	37	0	2	4+	1	7	9
7	38	0	2	(22)	29+	23	7
7	39	0	2	12+	13	26	9
7	40	0	2	(1)	28+	3	10
7	41	0	2	7+	2	4	10
7	42	0	2	4+	7	1	8
7	43	1	2	(17)	(15)	14+	3
7	44	1	2	14+	20	4	1
7	45	1	2	(17)	14+	15	2
7	46	1	2	28+	27	4	2
7	47	1	2	28+	4	27	2
7	48	1	2	14+	17	15	2
7	49	1	2	14+	15	28	2
7	50	1	0	14+	15	25	6
7	51	1	0	14+	15	25	1
7	52	1	2	(15)	(17)	14+	2
7	53	1	2	14+	15	28	2
7	54	1	2	(15)	28+	27	11
7	55	1	2	(15)	(24)	(25)	8*
7	56	1	2	(22)	(11)	(23)	9*
7	57	1	2	29+	9	5	9
7	58	1	2	13+	5	1	8
7	59	1	2	8+	23	11	7
7	60	1	2	9+	5	26	8

FIG. 34. Print-out of results for 'allocate to regions program' from analysis of data concerning Redshanks collected in Holland outside the breeding season (after Hale 1973).

(Fig. 33). Northern Scandinavian populations winter largely in Africa and this is brought about by a 'leapfrog' migration, though some birds winter as far north as southern Norway and Sweden. In these western European populations of the Redshank there is a partial allohiemy, although it is likely to be small in the case of the northern Scandinavian population.

In order to overcome the relative scarcity of ringing schemes outside Europe, I developed a method of using a computer to determine wintering areas by comparing measurements taken from breeding populations with those taken from wintering birds. Redshank breeding populations were labelled using five measurements: wing length, tail length, tarsus length, tarsus width and bill length. Individual wintering birds were thus allocated to one of the breeding areas according to which population its measurements fitted best. The three most likely areas were given in order of best fit, and if best fit occurred outside a distance of twice the largest recorded ringing return, it was discounted and the next best fit taken. The print-out for Holland (Region 7) is shown in Fig. 34 and from this it can be seen that the majority of wintering birds were allocated to Iceland (Region 14). Fig. 35 shows the computer recoveries of all Redshank allocated to Iceland and from this and Fig. 33 it can be seen that all occur in the region of ringing recoveries. Table 13 shows computer recoveries in relation to ringing recoveries. Similar comparisons

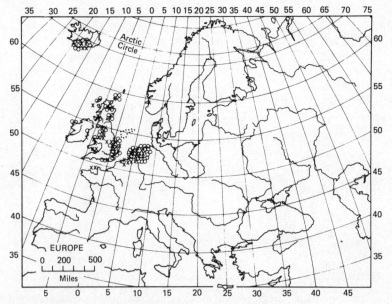

FIG. 35. Computer recoveries of Redshanks allocated to Iceland; **x** = winter recoveries; **o** = recoveries outside the winter season (after Hale 1973).

TABLE 13. Recoveries of Redshank of Icelandic origin from November–January inclusive (after Hale 1973).

Area of recovery	Iceland	British Isles	Belgium/ Holland	Norway	Elsewhere
1. Ringing recoveries	Some number not known	8	2	0	1
2. Computer 'recoveries'	4	33	18	1	0

were made between computer 'recoveries' and ringing recoveries for other areas in western Europe and reasonably good agreement was obtained. For the British Isles only one of nineteen allocated 'recoveries' occurred in countries where there were no ringing recoveries, and this was for Denmark where undoubtedly some of our birds find their way. Of particular significance is the lack of computer 'recoveries' outside the ringing area (Table 14). The same procedure for obtaining computer 'recoveries' was then carried out for the rest of the range of the Redshank where ringing recoveries do not occur, and the wintering areas shown in Fig. 36 were drawn up. It is likely that this shows a reasonably accurate picture of wintering quarters of the different Eurasian breeding populations. Since these results were originally published, a Redshank ringed in the Philippines was recovered in the Ussuri Valley in eastern USSR (148), which is the area predicted by the computer programme.

It is not claimed that such computer 'recoveries' are accurate in allocating individuals, but it is likely that the wintering ranges of populations can be mapped using such a technique, possibly more accurately than when using ringing recoveries, as in many cases there are vast areas from which no ringing recoveries have so far been obtained; of course the technique involves collect-

TABLE 14. Recoveries of Redshank of British origin from November–January inclusive (after Hale 1973).

Areas of recovery	Brit. Isles <100 m from place of ringing	Brit. Isles >100 m from place of ringing	France	Spain/Portugal	Belgium/Holland	Denmark	Elsewhere
1. Ringing recoveries	100	26	19	1	2	0	0
2. Computer 'recoveries'	14	2	0	1	1	1	0

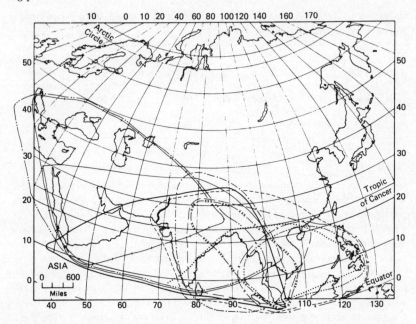

FIG 36. Winter ranges of different breeding populations of the Redshank from computer 'recoveries' (after Hale 1973).

Western USSR —+———+———+—	North-east India ——— ——— ———
Central USSR ——·· ——·· —	Tibet ———xxx———xxx———
Tien Shan ————————	Koko Nor ··
North-west India ————————	Eastern USSR ———x———x
Mongolia/	Lop Nor
Lake Baikal —————————	(Erythristic) ———·———·———
Inner Mongolia/	
Eastern China ——···———···———···—	

ing together museum specimens that cover the entire wintering range of the species in question. Also, in the case of Africa, the relatively small chance of recovery of ringed birds has the consequence that the mean distance of recovered wintering birds from the place of ringing is likely to be an under-estimate, so that it is not surprising that computer recoveries generally show wintering areas to be further south than ringing recoveries (Table 15).

The possibility exists of improving upon the statistical treatment in comparing breeding and wintering measurements in the Redshank. In the Dunlin, Ringed Plover, other Tringine Sandpipers and Godwits a more sophisticated statistical approach by my students has provided interesting results.

In the Ringed Plover, most populations probably winter further south than

TABLE 15. Distances* at which Redshanks were recovered during the winter months November to January (after Hale 1973).

| | First year birds | | Adults | |
	Ringing recoveries (ringed as pulli)	Computer 'recoveries'	Ringing recoveries (ringed as pulli)	Computer 'recoveries'
Iceland	1060	939	870	1070
British Isles	218	224	128	375
Holland	1013		837	1006
Denmark	1087	1056	1039	—
Norway	923 (adult + 1st year)	2575	923 (adult + 1st year)	796
Sweden	1308	2457	985	1869
Finland	1782	3150	1950	2205
Hungary	632 (adult + 1st year)	840 (adult + 1st year)	—	—

*Distances are calculated to the centre of the allocated breeding area.

ringing records suggest (237). Salomonsen (212) suggests an allohiemic distribution of some of the wintering populations of Ringed Plover (Fig. 37). Other wintering populations, from the Nearctic, are superimposed on Salomonsen's map, and it is clear that the north European and Siberian populations are largely synhiemic with the Nearctic birds which are, in fact, significantly larger. The wing measurements of wintering populations given by Salomonsen (212) are transposed from the breeding areas and take no account of populations from other breeding areas which might winter there; the marginal wing measurements, therefore, do not necessarily refer to the total wintering population, wing measurements of which are given in various places on the map together with an indication of the mean overall size of birds from different areas.

Salomonsen (211, 212) used data from the Ringed Plover and the Redshank to show that in winter smaller birds (with smaller wing measurements) wintered further south, and larger birds wintered in the north of the range. As in the case of the Ringed Plover, measurements from breeding areas were transposed to wintering areas, so that again they were not real measurements of the wintering Redshank populations. Fig. 33 shows actual winter measurements on the map and Salomonsen's measurements marginally. Whilst there is a large discrepancy in the figures, in general larger birds do winter further north in the west of the area shown, but in the east large Redshanks from western USSR move into Africa for the winter. Generally speaking larger birds do winter further north, but this is a long way from demonstrating that selection for size takes place in the winter range as was suggested by Salomonsen (212); this question is discussed in Chapter 11.

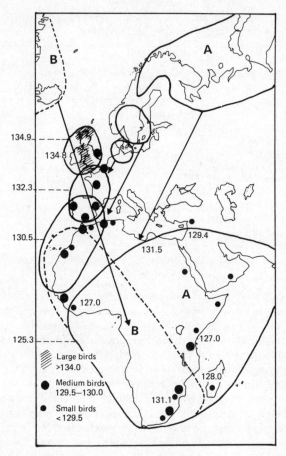

FIG. 37. Breeding areas and winter-quarters of a number of populations of the Ringed Plover. Breeding areas and corresponding winter-quarters are connected by arrows; the British population is resident. Figures inserted at left give average wing-length (measured on the breeding area) of the population wintering on the area in question. (Based on Salomonsen 1955). Measurements on the map show actual mean of wing length for wintering birds in that area (after Taylor 1978). Dotted wintering areas (after Taylor 1978).

Whilst many wader populations move great distances to their wintering grounds, some British breeding waders are almost sedentary. Most British Redshanks, Dunlins, Golden Plovers and Ringed Plovers move only relatively short distances south, whereas populations of similar sized birds from Denmark make much more extensive journeys to more southerly wintering grounds. It has been suggested in Chapter 3 that in the case of the four species in question, the British populations are hybrid populations. It is possible that hybridisation has enabled these birds to winter further north and carry out shorter migrations. However, there are other British species of wader that also move only short distances; some Oystercatchers and Curlews will move as far south as southern Spain and possibly Morocco, but many are almost sedentary, as are British breeding Snipes. The Dotterel, Common Sandpiper and Greenshank, on the other hand, perform extensive migrations into the African continent.

The distances which different populations of the same species are prepared to cover in order to find suitable wintering grounds varies enormously. In the Redshank some British birds winter on the estuaries on which they breed, while other non-British birds perform migrations in excess of 3000 miles. Fig. 38 shows mean distances between breeding and wintering grounds in different populations of this species and it is interesting to see that the smallest birds, from the east of the range, perform the largest migrations.

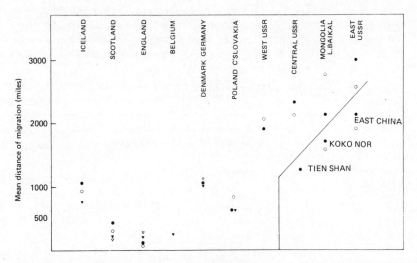

FIG. 38. Mean distances of migration by the more northerly Redshank populations: (●) adults computer data, (O) first year birds computer area, (▼) adults ringing recoveries, (▽) first year birds ringing recoveries (after Hale 1973).

It is evident from what has been said above that even within the same species, wading birds experience a wide variety of conditions in their wintering range. In the north birds may have to contend with severe winters, on occasions, when a large part of their feeding areas might be frozen over, and even during the mildest winter there will be cold spells which could be avoided by migrating further south. There must be some advantage in remaining north; presumably, on average, there is a higher survival rate than would be achieved by moving south, even taking into account mortality in bad winters. Nearer the equator winter conditions must be much easier and south of the equator wintering waders will experience a second summer. The requirements for wintering in these very dissimilar conditions will be different and it may well be that populations have adaptations selected from these different conditions. Amongst several possible adaptations are two which have already been considered. Firstly, overall size may well be important in that the surface area/volume ratio is smaller in large birds, and this helps to reduce heat loss. Secondly, the ability to deposit fat may be more important in the north of the wintering range as an 'insurance' against conditions which may hinder or prevent feeding. It is certainly true that in general the more northerly wintering populations are of larger birds and this is well illustrated in the Redshank (Fig. 33) and Ringed Plover (Fig. 37). Further consideration will be given to this in Chapter 11. It is known that some birds respond to cold by putting on weight (115, 169) and in this connection the fact that waders on the Wash have a mid-winter (December) peak in weight is of importance. The peak involves a fat addition to the fat-free weight of the order of at least 20%, and the data (158) for eight species of waders on the Wash are shown in Table 16. It is likely that the estimated fat-free weights are

TABLE 16. Wintering weights of adult waders wintering in Britain (after Minton, 1975).

Species	Estimated fat-free weight (g)	Midwinter peak weight (g)	% fat
Oystercatcher	48	590	23
Ringed Plover	60	78	30
Grey Plover	210	276	31
Turnstone	105	123	17
Redshank	140	162	16
Knot	130	159	22
Dunlin	47	57	21
Sanderling	51	59	16

too high in most cases. Mascher (145) gives a figure of 34–35 g for Dunlin on migration in southern Sweden, and it is likely that this is the same population occurring on the Wash where a figure of 47 g is given (158) as the fat-free weight. Also, a December peak in weight has been recorded for Bar-tailed Godwit on Lindisfarne (N.E. England) with fat at 12.8% of the total body weight (47). The early winter increase in weight is not limited to waders wintering in estuarine conditions and at Sevenoaks, in Kent, similar peak

December/January weights have been found in Common Snipe wintering inland, where September weights (average 102.3 g) increased to 114.0 g (9%), in December.

In the African continent, there are small increases in weights in the northern winter (December) in Curlew Sandpiper at the Cape and at Lake Magadi, Kenya (41). These are of the order of less than 10% of the body weight, but throughout the year the fluctuations in weight at both sites reflect the changes experienced on the northern breeding ranges, which suggests an internally controlled rhythm in fat deposition. Again in Kenya, winter (December) fat weights are much lower than in northern Europe and of the order of 3–10% of the body weight. Whereas on the Wash waders tend to put on weight in this period from September to December, in Kenya a loss in weight occurs. Waders arriving with surplus fat tend to lose it and in the Little Stint (156) the weight decrease continues from October until April, in the Cape, when there is a dramatic, pre-migratory increase.

Weights of autumn waders in Morocco are significantly lower than those on the Wash (193), and whilst this is to be expected after such a flight, weight levels did not show a tendency to increase after the moult, as they do further north. Knot and Whimbrel proved to be exceptions to this, but in general weight levels in Morocco were 10% or more below Wash weights. However, as was the case on the Wash, weights of juvenile waders were significantly below those of adults, and it was clear that this could not be through shortage of food in either adults or young since the moult proceeded rapidly and normally. A similar situation was found in Mauretania in 1973 (32) where weight levels were only 70–90% of the weights of the same species in Britain. Of particular interest in this work was the fact that Bar-tailed Godwits had weight levels below those of the fat-free British weights, which suggests that protein levels may well be maintained below those in Britain. If this is the case in other waders, it is an observation of some significance; in the north of the wintering range protein, as well as fat, may be used as a food reserve and it is possible that estimates of body fat may be affected by assuming an unvarying fat free weight. It is also of some importance that the energy requirements for maintenance are lower at lower weights, and therefore there can be little doubt that heavier birds in the north are able to obtain the additional food, as compared with Moroccan/Mauretanian birds. If this was not usually the case presumably they would be lighter, or fatter birds would winter further south.

From the December peak the weights of waders in northern Europe decline to a March minimum and this is clearly shown by data collected on the Wash (158) and on Morecambe Bay (198). Table 17 shows the decline in weight in Knots, Dunlins and Redshanks on Morecambe Bay related to the utilisation of fat. At present there is no evidence to suggest that fat is used up because of an insufficient food supply, or that it dwindles as its main purpose has been served in December. Fat reserves seem to fall with the decreasing temperature and increasing day length and it is quite possible that this has little to do with

TABLE 17. Fat score and total body weight (in gms) of waders wintering on Morecambe Bay: all adults (after Prater 1975).

		Average	Dec.	Jan.	Feb.	Mar.
Knot	score		4.05	4.22	2.78	2.42
	wt		155.5	156.5	147.0	144.1
Dunlin	score		4.14	3.10	3.00	—
	wt		61.2	53.7	52.9	—
Redshank	score		4.80	3.50	4.33	2.80
	wt		178.9	158.7	163.1	139.4

(5) very fat: interclavicular gap filled, subcutaneous fat covering the entire ventral area, significant amount of peritoneal fat.

(4) fat: interclavicular fat body well developed, subcutaneous fat present in distinct although separated bodies on each pectoral muscle. Some peritoneal fat.

(3) average: interclavicular fat body well developed, little subcutaneous or peritoneal fat.

(2) fairly thin: some interclavicular fat present, very little subcutaneous, no peritoneal fat.

(1) thin: no fat present although atrophied fat body tissue may remain especially in the interclavicular area.

the food supply. In April the gain in weight is not clearly linked with an increasing food supply and the likelihood is that the whole annual cycle of fat deposition is controlled, as already suggested, by some internal mechanism. The matter will be discussed further in relation to winter food supplies in Chapter 9.

It appears then that in waders wintering in the tropics where the stresses of the climate are less than in northern Europe, fat deposits are smaller and birds are relatively lean. It is likely that winter fat deposits serve two purposes; firstly as an additional insulating layer, and secondly as a food reserve during periods when food may be difficult to obtain.

There is some evidence that in waders older birds are more capable of maintaining winter fat deposits than younger birds. On the Wash juvenile birds of most species tend to be lighter than adults at the mid-winter peak. This also applies to Bar-tailed Godwit on Lindisfarne and Curlew-Sandpiper in South Africa.

From December, peak weights generally fall gradually until the spring, but the Oystercatcher presents an exception. Throughout the period from August to April adult Oystercatchers increase in weight, due to the deposition of fat with a slight pause in December (27). This occurs in both mussel-feeding birds, and cockle-feeding birds, and, perhaps surprisingly, in birds feeding on earthworms. These last were slightly lighter than the shore-feeding birds. In contrast with the adults, first, second and third year immature Oystercatchers followed the pattern of weight changes in other waders with an increase until mid-winter followed by a decline in weight. There are two possible explanations for this; either the immature birds failed to increase in weight because they would not be undertaking a migration to the breeding grounds in the spring, or they were less able to cope with increasingly difficult feeding conditions during the winter. In view of the fact that adult males have a winter weight gain of some 75 g and females of 95 g, averaging about 0.4 g per day (27) in Morecambe Bay, the former explanation perhaps seems the more likely. Dare speculates that the winter increase in weight in Oystercatchers is related to their early breeding. They return to Scotland as early as February, and to Iceland and Norway in March and early April, before any possible spring increases in food supply, and certainly this lends support to the suggestion. If indeed this winter increase is attributable to the success with which the species obtains its main normal food supply (bivalve molluscs) it is perhaps surprising that it is equally successful when it turns to an alternative supply in the form of earthworms. The implication is surely that the adults of the species are able to obtain their food requirements easily, whichever food supply is chosen.

There is evidence, at least in some species, that the experience adults possess enable them to cope better than younger birds with difficult winter conditions. In periods of cold weather juvenile Bar-tailed Godwits fare less well than adults, in that they lose significantly more body fat (47). The fat reserves carried in mid-December totalling some 30–40 g are estimated as providing maintenance energy for about three days, provided no food is taken in. Were this to happen, there would be some loss of insulation, and there would be no further reserves to support either a longer cold period or a flight to a more suitable feeding area. Such situations must arise very infrequently and even in very bad winter conditions in the north of the wintering range it seems likely that waders take in some food. In some cases they are also prepared to seek new feeding areas, and hard weather movements occur in many waders. The estuaries freeze over less frequently than inland feeding sites so that in hard weather Lapwings will move onto estuaries as will Snipe and Golden Plovers, though Snipes will often move to river banks first.

The study of bird movements by radar has shown that winter movements occur frequently and some migration occurs in every month of the year (125). In winter, wind direction is of primary importance in the movement of birds and temperature is of relatively little importance. Winds from the north or east bring about hard weather movements and under these circumstances many birds cross the North Sea, from the continent, into the British Isles. The density of movements is not so great as in autumn or spring and generally speaking involves inland soil feeding species such as Lapwing. On the continent winds from the north and east generally bring hard weather, frost and snow cover, under which circumstances Lapwings in particular would have difficulty in feeding. They then move west or south-west, with a following wind and in many cases cross the English coastline and move inland. A reversal of the wind direction will cause the birds to retrace their path across the North Sea.

In December arrivals from the east are common but only occur with east winds, no matter how cold it is. There is clearly benefit in their crossing the North Sea under these conditions, but it is not so easy to see why they return so quickly when westerly winds prevail. Lack (125) suggests that with a thaw on the continent, more food becomes available than there would be in the crowded conditions in Britain, and so during winter there is a continuous shuttle service across the North Sea. The flight of 120 miles or more seems to present no difficulties even to small passerines, so that the energy requirements for these movements must be readily available. It is clearly of advantage for the birds to move before hard weather is upon them, but the extent to which such movements occur was very much under-estimated before radar studies. Apart from arrivals from the continent departures also occur from the British Isles, again with following winds. Northerly winds may cause Lapwings to leave the British Isles in a southerly direction, and many ringing recoveries of British Lapwing occur in the Iberian peninsula in winter. There is probably also some movement into Ireland, and it may well have been Lapwings which overshot Ireland which arrived in numbers in Canada in December 1927 and January 1966. Amongst the Lapwings driven across the Atlantic in December 1927 was one British ringed bird. There can be little doubt that these birds had no intention of crossing the Atlantic, but their survival on these two occasions in relatively large numbers demonstrates their capability of such journeys under suitable weather conditions.

Many wading birds winter year after year on the same small piece of coastline but it is clear that considerable movement takes place during the winter season from the data which have been acquired through the BTO/RSPB Birds of Estuaries Enquiry. These counts have shown that each year there is a mid-winter peak in those waders which tend to feed away from the shoreline. Lapwings, Golden Plovers, Common Snipes and Jack Snipes all tend to move into the British Isles in winter, probably due to the poor weather conditions on the continent, though some of the estuarine increases may result from birds moving to coastal feeding areas from inland. Whilst this is to be expected, it is perhaps more surprising that there are mid-winter peaks in the numbers of several species of estuarine waders. Oystercatchers, Grey Plovers, Bar-tailed Godwits, Knots, Dunlins and Purple Sandpipers all have midwinter peaks, and only the Redshank appears to decrease in number as the winter proceeds. This increase in numbers in the British Isles is reflected in a decrease in numbers on the shoreline of the European continent, and probably the movement westward is again a weather movement.

Curlew counts in mid-winter tend to be lower than at other times because of the absence of this species at this time of the year from the estuarine roosts.

Not all estuarine waders remain in the area where they have moulted for the winter. Many moulting in western Europe move on to Africa, but others make much shorter journeys to a suitable wintering area. Knots, Dunlins, Bar-tailed Godwits and Curlews move from the Waddenzee to the British Isles (14) and ringing recoveries have shown that Knots and Dunlins moulting on the Wash may winter on the west coast of the British Isles.

During the winter season the majority of wading birds is found on a relatively small number of estuaries. Only 30 estuaries in Europe and North Africa each regularly support over 20,000 waders in mid-winter and a further 17 support over 20,000 at times (199). North Africa supports only 25% of the numbers in the area, with 75% in Europe. Knowledge of the rest of the African continent is sparse but Summers, Pringle and Cooper (234) have provided data for South Africa, from the South Western Cape. These are incorporated in Table 18 which is based largely on data compiled by Prater (199). Whilst the overall numbers from the South Western Cape, with its 45 wetlands and 680 miles of coastline, harbours only the equivalent of the numbers to be found on the Cheshire Dee, very significant wintering populations of Turnstones, Sanderlings, Little Stints, Curlew-Sandpipers, Greenshanks and Whimbrels occur. Elsewhere in Africa little is known of the size of wintering populations of waders but it is likely to be smaller than those wintering in Europe.

The British Isles act as a wintering area for more than half the waders in Europe. Three estuary complexes are of supreme importance, the Wash, the Solway and the Morecambe Bay/Ribble/Dee mudflats. Together they harbour more waders in January than the Waddenzee, though there are times of the year when they accommodate many more than in January.

It is of particular interest that more than three-fifths of the wintering waders in North Africa and Europe are found north of latitude 48°N in January, that is north of Cape Finisterre. The implication is certainly that most waders find the north European wintering grounds well suited to their needs at this time of the year. However, there are several probable disadvantages in remaining there for the winter. Apart from the cold, and consequent energy dissipated in heat loss, there is the possibility of the feeding grounds freezing over; the days are shorter and the time available for daylight feeding often reduced even further by the feeding grounds being covered by the tide. It is generally assumed that food might be short, possibly due to competition, or that it might be difficult to obtain even if it is there, and that conditions generally are far from ideal. Since such large numbers of waders use the northern wintering grounds it is likely that such assumptions may be difficult to justify and they will be further examined in Chapter 9. The balance between whether a population is migratory or relatively sedentary almost certainly depends on the strategy selected producing the highest survival rate for that population. Different strategies were obviously adopted as the wader populations increased after the last inter-glacial minimum. It is probable that migration as a strategy was adopted because a movement away

TABLE 18. Numbers of the principal wader species wintering on the estuaries of the Atlantic coast of Europe, north-west Africa and the south-west Cape. (After Prater 1975 and Summers, Pringle and Cooper 1976.)

The figures are in 1000s; + indicates that less than 50 were counted

	Ireland	Britain	Wadden-zee	Delta	France	Spain	Portugal	W. Europe	Morocco	Banc d'Arguin	N. Africa	S.W. Cape
Oystercatcher	25.0	200.0	210.0	81.0	40.0	1.9	0.5	558.4	1.5	3.0	4.5	—
Ringed Plover	2.5	8.0	+	—	2.0	3.3	4.0	19.8	10.0	13.0	23.0	1.5
Kentish Plover	—	—	—	—	+	—	+	—	1.5	3.0	4.5	—
Grey Plover	1.0	7.0	1.3	1.3	13.0	0.6	5.0	29.2	10.0	3.5	13.5	4.6
Turnstone	1.0	8.0	1.7	1.7	0.5	—	—	12.9	0.4	10.0	10.4	9.1
Little Stint	—	—	—	—	0.1	—	—	0.1	5.0	5.0	10.0	6.0
Dunlin	100.0	550.0	85.0	65.0	300.0	10.0	70.0	1180.0	50.0	180.0	230.0	—
Curlew-Sandpiper	—	—	—	—	—	—	—	—	+	38.0	38.0	54.7
Knot	55.0	350.0	65.0	14.3	110.0	10.0	5.0	609.3	5.0	130.0	135.0	3.8
Sanderling	2.0	6.0	1.3	0.1	0.3	—	0.2	10.0	3.0	13.0	16.0	14.8
Ruff	+	1.1	0.1	+	—	—	0.3	1.6	+	—	+	4.2
Spotted Redshank	+	0.1	+	+	0.1	—	0.1	0.4	0.1	—	0.1	—
Redshank	17.0	80.0	4.7	1.9	5.0	0.3	15.0	123.9	10.0	100.0	110.0	—
Greenshank	0.5	0.2	—	—	—	+	0.1	0.8	0.4	0.8	1.2	1.3
Black-tailed Godwit	10.0	4.0	—	—	15.0	0.1	11.0	40.1	30.0	0.1	30.1	—
Bar-tailed Godwit	17.0	43.0	21.0	2.1	5.0	0.1	1.0	89.2	5.0	210.0	215.0	0.1
Curlew	15.0	60.0	35.0	17.2	15.0	2.2	1.5	145.9	3.0	2.5	5.5	0.4
Whimbrel	—	—	—	—	—	+	—	—	—	3.5	3.5	1.2
Avocet	—	0.1	—	0.2	7.0	+	11.0	18.3	4.0	—	4.0	2.2
Total:	246.0	1317.5	425.1	184.8	513.0	28.5	124.7	2839.9	138.9	715.4	854.3	103.9

from a relatively dense winter feeding population resulted in the mobile population obtaining food more easily. Generally speaking birds will feed in areas of greater relative abundance of their food supplies; food does not necessarily have to be in short supply for there to be movement to a better supply.

It is likely that population sizes are limited by the availability of either suitable breeding or wintering areas. There can be little doubt that during the last inter-glacial period populations of arctic waders were limited by the availability of arctic breeding conditions. For such small populations the potential wintering areas must have been immense, and largely unoccupied during winter. As populations increased so more of the potential wintering area was occupied. At present, probably, the arctic breeding area is near its maximum, as any southward expansion of the ice would be likely to cover suitable breeding areas almost as fast as more southerly ones were created. If this is the case then arctic wader populations must be near the maximum ever if breeding conditions control numbers. In winter the number of wading birds results directly from the success of the previous breeding season, which in the British Isles may provide a wintering population varying between one and one and a half million birds. There is no evidence to suggest that our estuaries are less able to cope with the latter figure than the former, though feeding studies will no doubt eventually provide data on which estimates of carrying capacities may be made. This will be discussed further in the consideration of feeding in waders. However it is possible that at the maximum of the last glaciation, higher populations of waders occurred than exist now.

In the light of our present knowledge, it is reasonable to take the view that the wader population expansion resulting from the southward spread of the ice after the last inter-glacial has been limited by the availability of suitable breeding areas rather than by the extent of the wintering areas. If this is the case then the wintering grounds may well be able to support greater populations than they do at present. Feeding studies should go some way towards providing evidence for or against this view but probably the most important and relatively neglected area of research is the breeding biology and breeding season feeding ecology of wading birds. Not until we have further knowledge of wading birds during the breeding season will we be able to appreciate fully the biology of waders in winter.

CHAPTER 7

COMMUNAL ROOSTING

AT the end of the breeding season most European species of wading birds form flocks which persist throughout the autumn and winter. Many of these flocks spend the winter around the coasts of Europe and Africa, but some species, particularly Lapwing and Golden Plover, may remain inland. The form and size of the flocks may vary from the loosely-knit groups of Redshanks to the very large flocks of Knots or Dunlins which, closely packed, often look like smoke on the horizon. Most of these flocks remain on the coastline for the winter, feeding on mudflats and areas exposed at low tides and because of this their feeding activities are limited by the tide cycles. On high spring tides they may be entirely excluded from the areas on which they normally find food. When this occurs tight flocks are often found high on the salt marsh or on exposed islands, spending the period of high tide roosting.

Whilst the time spent roosting varies between species, the pattern is generally determined by the state of the tide. Between August and March the wintering flocks are driven off their feeding grounds on approximately two-fifths of the tides and, since the high tides occur twice a day, a considerable time is spent at the roosts, and in moving between them and the feeding grounds. The geographical location of the flocks is also of importance in the timing of roosting. For example, spring tides in Morecambe Bay and the Ribble and Dee estuaries tend to occur during the two hours before and after midnight and mid-day, forcing the flocks to roost during a large part of the daylight period. On the Wash high tides are seven hours later, giving the highest tides in the early morning and evening and enabling winter roosting to take place almost entirely during the hours of darkness. Consequently, on the Wash, more daylight hours are available for feeding than on the Ribble. The significance of this will be discussed in Chapter 9.

Most wader roosts, and certainly the larger ones, are not transitory phenomena but are established by long tradition. For example, the Crossens roost on the Ribble marshes, probably the largest known single roost, has been in use for over a hundred years. As the tide comes in the waders do not seek refuge on the nearest point of dry land, but fly to these traditional roosts. In many cases this involves a journey of 15 kilometres or more and, during the course of the two daily tide cycles, this may necessitate flying up to 60 kilometres or more. Clearly there must be advantage in expending the energy required for such flights, particularly in the winter when difficulty might be experienced in obtaining it in the first place. This problem will be considered later in this chapter.

The estuarine complex of the Ribble/Morecambe Bay/Dee accommodates between 750,000 and 1,000,000 birds annually and these use some 30 roosts. The location and size of these roosts is shown in Fig. 39. Many of these roosts contain all the species of waders feeding on the mudflats, but some species such as Redshanks, Curlews and to some extent Oystercatchers and Black-tailed Godwits, tend to roost in single species groups.

Movement towards the high tide roosts begins with the turn of the tide. Whilst some birds, such as Godwits, follow the tide right out, others – Knots, Dunlins, Sanderlings, Oystercatchers and Grey Plovers – tend to have favoured feeding areas and remain on these until displaced by the flow. As the tide turns, the Godwits move on before it, walking a short distance and then running up the shore, all the time continuing to feed.

Up to as much as three hours before high tide, Oystercatchers will form sub-roosts on the mudflats. On the neap tides these may constitute the roost itself but on the spring tides they serve only as a temporary refuge. Oystercatchers are always the first birds to roost and often many are sleeping when the flooding tide overtakes them. Frequently these birds will hop along before it on one leg, not bothering to remove their bills from the scapulars until some small wave disturbs their equilibrium causing them to run before the tide, eventually to take flight and find a dry refuge on the salt marsh.

Oystercatchers may form a compact roost or sub-roost an hour before other species appear and it is usually the larger species of waders which follow them into the roost. Bar-tailed Godwits and Curlews straggle in untidy 'V' formations and ragged lines across the flats, while the last of the Oystercatchers, call noisily to each other. In early autumn they often tumble into the roost in very erratic flight but later in the year, and in winter, they tend to glide down onto the roosting areas.

As with the Oystercatchers, Knots often form sub-roosts and pack densely together about 1–2 kilometres out on the mudflats before moving into the final roost. The sub-roosts build up as parties of birds, numbering anything between 10 and 1000, move in and jostle for space in what always appears to be an unnecessarily compact assemblage. Different estuaries have peak numbers of Knots at different times of the year, but late August and early

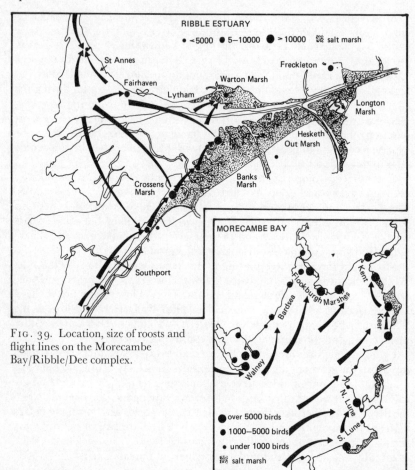

FIG. 39. Location, size of roosts and flight lines on the Morecambe Bay/Ribble/Dee complex.

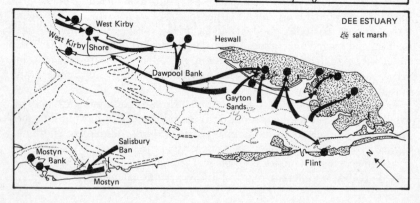

September is the time for Knots on the Ribble. At this time many are still in summer plumage, providing a splash of colour on the grey carpet which in autumn might comprise 100,000 individuals in the largest of the roosts on the Ribble estuary.

Grey Plovers return to the roost in small groups of 5 to 15 birds at the same time as the Knots and Dunlins, except on the Wash where they are amongst the first arrivals. Whilst these small groups may initially remain in separate sub-groups, single individuals often arrive with other species and become scattered amongst the Oystercatchers and some of the more loosely dispersed Knots. An hour before high tide the smaller waders, Dunlins, Sanderlings and Ringed Plovers are moving before the tide, alighting, feeding for a short time and flying on again until they arrive at the traditional roosting area.

On the lower tides the smaller waders remain dispersed above the tideline but on the higher tides form more compact roosts with the larger species. On the highest tides of all the roosts tend to break up, large single species groups dispersing to find refuge on those parts of the salt marsh which are still above water. As the tide flows in and the roost becomes more compact each species moves to its traditional place within the larger roost or, in the case of those species which tend to form single species roosts, to the selected part of the flats or salt marsh.

One species is always to be found on the seaward side of the roost. Here the Bar-tailed Godwits spend most of the period of the high tide asleep, often with water up to their bellies. Farther up the shore stand Knots in a compact flock, seldom with any other species amongst them at this stage of the tide. At the same level of the shore the Oystercatchers roost, usually separately although sometimes accompanied by Grey Plovers. At the highest part of the shore Dunlins and Sanderlings occur, but they remain active, feeding wherever possible throughout the period of the high tide and so can hardly be said to roost.

On the highest tides the orderly arrangement of the different species tends to break up and the waders are forced onto the salt marsh. In these circumstances different species roost where they can by finding a convenient islet and then small groups of Knots can be found in the middle of flocks of Godwits. The Knots stand out as they are always more tightly packed and such a situation does not normally occur on the mudflats. Even on the salt marsh Dunlins often attempt to feed during the period of high tide and because of their activity they do not normally become surrounded by other species. Oystercatchers too tend to remain separate, but like Grey Plovers, Curlews and Redshanks are occasionally found in the middle of a flock of another species.

Once the waders have taken up their stations on the high tide roost there is little aerial activity and the volume of sound, such a feature of the establishment of the roost, diminishes, at times to total silence, as many of the birds fall asleep.

It is often possible to approach within 300 metres of a roost on mudflats and salt marsh without disturbing the birds. The use of a hide placed on or near the site of a roost enables closer observation of the establishment of the roost to be made. On areas of mudflats the siting of hides is more difficult to judge than on more steeply sloping shorelines. On mudflats a change of tide height through varying meteorological conditions might cause a roost to form half a mile from the expected site and leave the observer with nothing to observe. In contrast Hilbre Island, off the coast of the Wirral, slopes steeply into the Dee estuary and so the birds cannot form their usual roosting patterns. The result is a pattern similar to that caused by very high tides on a salt marsh and provides such suitable conditions for the photographing of roosting waders that Hilbre Island is now famous.

Observations of roosts from light aircraft were originally initiated to obtain photographic confirmation of the numbers counted on the ground. This original aim was successful but other uses of aerial spotting were also found. For example, new roosts could be easily located, the distribution of the species within the roosts could be observed, and birds even followed from their feeding grounds to the roosts. Surprisingly, whilst Oystercatchers on salt marsh were easily located from an aeroplane, it was initially very difficult to locate them on the mudflats. In contrast, flocks of Knot could be seen from a distance of 7–8 kilometres when they showed up in the sun as a cream coloured carpet on the flats.

Some species, such as Redshanks and Curlews cannot be seen from the air because they roost mainly on the salt marsh or at its edge. Whilst Redshanks often roost on the open cropped grassland of the salt marsh, they may roost on the edge of the *Spartina*, and Curlews frequently spend the high tide period roosting in high *Spartina* where they are difficult to observe and count. Fig. 40 shows a plan of the large Crossens roost, on the Ribble Estuary. This is typical of open, mudflat/saltmarsh roosts.

Except in absolutely still conditions, with no wind, all the roosting birds face into the wind. In moving from sub-roosts to the main roost, or occasionally in flights around the main roost, flocks of waders may perform the most complex aerial manoeuvres. These take place mainly in autumn and Knots are the premier performers, although Godwits, Dunlins and sometimes Curlews take part less expertly. Almost invariably such flights are carried out by single species flocks. When performed by large flocks in sunlit conditions they can be very spectacular as on occasions flocks will rise up to 300–400 m in the air and literally tumble back into the roosts showing remarkable coordination as they turn, twist and tower up into the air. More commonly the birds fly directly into the roosting area and plane down in a long glide before turning into the wind to alight in a clamour of sound.

On alighting there is initially much movement on the ground, but the larger species, such as Godwits, Curlews and Oystercatchers quickly settle down to sleep. Redshanks and Grey Plovers also spend the high tide period

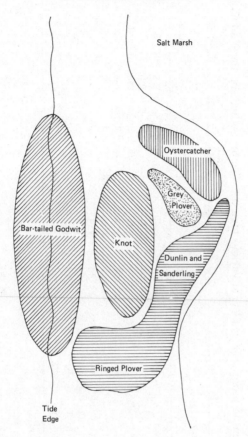

FIG. 40. Plan of the Crossens roost and location of species in relation to the tideline. Medium-high tide, autumn and winter.

resting, but Dunlins, Sanderlings and Ringed Plovers continue to feed whenever possible. All species spend some time preening at the roost, and after the birds have returned to the feeding grounds the roosting area can be found to be covered with feathers, particularly in the autumn. During the resting period waders frequently regurgitate pellets. Although pellet regurgitation is not limited to the roosting period, the roosts are the best places to collect pellets. Here they are usually cast in relatively dry places and disintegration of the pellet is less likely than out on the wet feeding grounds.

As the tide ebbs, the Dunlins, Sanderlings and Ringed Plovers follow it out onto the near mudflats, feeding continuously. The Knots are next to leave, often moving out as a flock onto the inner mudflats and again forming a subroost. These are followed by the Bar-tailed Godwits which behave similarly,

TABLE 19. Mean time (in minutes) spent in roosting by waders at various high tide heights (actual) on the Ribble Estuary (after Greenhalgh 1975).

	Height of tide (in metres)										Mean
	7.3	7.6	7.9	8.2	8.5	8.8	9.1	9.4	9.7	10.0	
Oystercatcher	102	83	115	166	197	184	248	244	316	318	184
Turnstone	—	—	27	91	73	101	195	182	176	209	136
Curlew	—	—	—	—	143	176	234	221	236	270	178
Black-tailed Godwit	—	109	—	148	—	188	261	276	288	307	191
Bar-tailed Godwit	—	89	*	92	—	156	167	178	226	251	162
Redshank	0	0	*	67	100	145	139	200	191	214	141
Knot	†	†	43	69	148	167	180	185	230	245	155
Dunlin	†	†	†	61	119	118	114	130	188	220	112
Sanderling	†	†	†	12	35	52	88	121	157	142	87

* less than 15% roosted between 18 and 28 minutes
† no real roosting, just loose associations at the tide edge

remaining in the sub-roost for up to 30 minutes and then making for the tide's edge. Curlews tend to move right out onto the flats and Redshanks disperse into the empty gullies and onto the edge of the mudflats close to the saltmarsh. Oystercatchers, first to arrive at the roost, are last to leave, remaining up to an hour after the dispersal of other species. Table 19 shows the average times spent by wading birds on the roost during different months of the year.

During the summer months non-breeding birds continue to use the traditional roosts, but numbers are relatively small. Even at this time of the year Dunlins will feed on the mudflats during the period of high tide but when roosting on the saltings show no such inclination to feed in the gullies of the saltmarsh.

During particularly high tides, or when disturbed, waders will often move onto agricultural land, but a peculiar habit has developed on the Cheshire Dee during the past ten years. Because of excessive disturbance on Hilbre Island, and the adjacent shore roosts, thousands of waders of all species occasionally spend the high tide period (up to 3 hours) on the wing, circling up to a height of 1000 m and gliding down to below 300 m and then again rising, and falling, until the tide ebbs. This 'aerial roosting' has now been recorded on other estuaries where disturbance occurs.

The quality of roosting sites available to wading birds can influence the size of populations and be an over-riding factor of more importance than the availability of food. In a study of the waders of the south shore of the Forth Estuary (52), it was shown that the construction of lagoons for the dumping of ash from a power station resulted in a dramatic change in roosting behaviour. From a constant winter level of some 800 birds there was a gradual increase to a winter average of more than 7000. The largest increase was shown in Golden Plovers which formerly roosted inland, and in Bar-tailed Godwits, Knots, Curlews and Dunlins which previously performed a 30 kilometres round trip to roost. Other species, previously roosting locally, also increased, but not to the same extent. There were no increases elsewhere in the Forth Estuary so that it was reasonable to conclude that it was the quality of the roosts that determined the numbers of waders inhabiting the area.

The quality of a roost is determined by the degree of disturbance to which it is subjected by human and other factors. Furness (53), in assessing the susceptibility of species to disturbance found that consistent rankings were obtained using any of three measures of the intensity of the disturbance. These were; the average height to which the birds rise, the average time spent in flight and the average proportion of the flock disturbed. As a measure of susceptibility, Furness used the percentage number of each species present put to flight. These figures were summed hourly for each disturbance factor and these data are shown in Table 20.

Perhaps the most interesting aspect of this work was that, although Bar-tailed Godwits were most susceptible to disturbance in this particular instance they were the last species to desert the roost entirely. This was because this

TABLE 20. Susceptibility of wader species to disturbance (after Furness 1973b).

	Susceptibility to				Total
	Human	Crow	Aircraft	Kestrel	Susceptibility
Bar-tailed Godwit	110	50	35	—	195
Dunlin	30	90	—	30	150
Golden Plover	100	—	—	—	100
Knot	15	35	—	—	50
Curlew	30	—	15	—	45
Oystercatcher	20	—	—	—	20
Redshank	5	—	—	—	5
Turnstone	—	—	—	—	0

species had the largest distance to fly (15 kilometres) in order to find an alternative roost, whereas other species had alternative roosts nearby. These findings are of particular value in planning conservation strategies on estuaries which are threatened by industrial development.

So far consideration has been given only to the communal roosting of estuarine waders, the behaviour of which is largely determined by tidal cycles. Waders which feed mainly inland, such as Lapwings and Golden Plovers, also roost communally outside the breeding season, and in many ways behave similarly to the estuarine species. Both these inland species tend to be relatively inactive as dusk approaches and are often widely spread over the daytime feeding areas. At this time small parties move off and gather in what are equivalent to the sub-roosts of the estuarine waders. As birds approach the sub-roosts, calling increases in frequency and both species may indulge in 'crazy-flying' and a variety of aerial evolutions reminiscent of their estuarine relatives. When they eventually alight the birds do not pack together as they would in the roost, but scatter, and begin to feed actively in the increasing gloom. This activity continues for some 20 to 30 minutes and has been carefully observed and documented in the Lapwing (229). In some instances feeding continues until it is almost dark and it seems impossible that under these circumstances the birds can be finding food items by sight. That they are finding food is certain; observations made using image intensifiers and a technique of lying down flat to view Lapwings and Golden Plovers outlined against the western sky showed on several occasions that the birds were taking earthworms. Possibly they were using a combination of hearing and touch in searching for their prey, but they are undoubtedly successful in finding prey at this time of the evening.

Having fed in this way for some time, the birds usually then fly directly to the roost – termed a 'night station' by Spencer – where several small flocks come together. The birds remain much closer to each other than at the sub-roost and are inactive, although a little calling may take place and some aggressive behaviour may occur. In Golden Plovers there is usually a single roost, but in Lapwings several such roosts may be used in the summer and early autumn, and a single large roost later in the year.

Lapwing and Golden Plover roosts do not appear to have the long tradition of usage that the estuary roosts do. It may be that inland roosts are more subject to disturbance, and the fact that undisturbed roosts on airfields have been known to exist for many years goes some way to support this suggestion. However, as Spencer comments, Lapwings may move their roosts for no apparent reason. Neither of these inland roosting species tends to fly as far as do the estuary waders from feeding ground to roost, and in many cases the movement may only be a matter of a few hundred yards. However, dusk movements are almost always made to roosts away from feeding areas.

A most important aspect of wader roosting behaviour was observed by Spencer (229) who described a lunar periodicity in Lapwing activity. For the two or three nights before and after a full moon Lapwings remain feeding over the areas which normally form their sub-roosts, instead of congregating, and sleeping, at the final roost. At this time of the month the birds are active throughout the night and never form the final roost. Perhaps the most remarkable aspect of this behaviour is that it takes place even if the moon is not visible.

Whether the moon is full or new, Lapwings are active more than fifty minutes before dawn. This also applies to other waders which winter inland, such as Golden Plovers, Snipes, Curlews and Redshanks. During this time Lapwings probably feed, but some twenty minutes before dawn they pack together and rest quietly (229). Around dawn, and up to eight minutes after, they gradually awake and disperse over the nearby fields. The subsequent behaviour is determined by the state of the moon. During the period of the full moon most Lapwings will sleep and preen in the daylight hours as they have fed during the night. By contrast, away from the full moon period they sleep at night and feed during the day.

The term 'roost' implies that the birds sleep there, so that the term 'night station' as coined by Spencer, is perhaps more appropriate for the area where birds spend the night. During the full moon periods birds congregate at a daytime roost, with birds arriving from many night stations. Areas of standing water are particularly attractive to Lapwings, and lakesides, reservoirs, flashes and flooded fields are favoured for the daylight roosts. Numbers build up on these roosts around the time of the full moon, and A. W. Boyd made a series of counts (which appear as an appendix in Spencer (229)) of roosting birds at Witton Flashes, Cheshire, from 1948 to 1952. The results of these counts are shown diagramatically in Fig. 41. Whilst ideally regular daily counts would have provided the best possible illustration of the build up of birds on the day roost during the full moon period, these data do support the findings of Spencer concerning the changes in roosting behaviour with the lunar cycle. There can be little doubt that other inland feeding waders behave

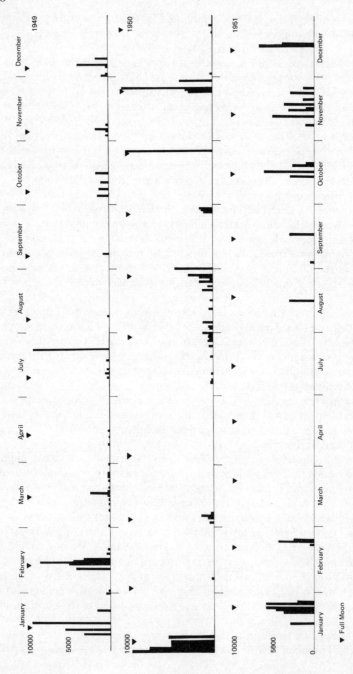

FIG. 41. Numbers of Lapwing at Witton Flashes, Cheshire roosting during daylight hours from 1949–51 (data from Spencer 1953).

similarly, although in most cases the evidence is poorer than that provided by the Lapwings. Some good evidence however, is provided by data that I have collected in relation to the communal roosting of Curlews in the early breeding season.

The bulk of my observations of the early spring roosts was made on a small area of moorland between Blackburn and Clitheroe, in east Lancashire, and this roost normally contained about thirty birds. Observations of the roost were made from a permanent hide in a dry stone wall which permitted views from within twenty-five metres without being seen on either approach or departure.

Curlews return to their breeding ground in the north of England by the end of the third week of March, and in recent years have tended to arrive earlier. Prior to breeding they spend the daytime feeding, spread over the fields and moorland, but at night the majority roost communally. At large roosts the birds may arrive from several kilometres away but on the smaller more typical roosts of between 25 and 50 birds the distance travelled is seldom more than 3 kilometres. Between 45 and 60 minutes after sunset the birds arrive at the roosting site and sing as they alight when birds on the ground frequently join in. The time of arrival at the roost is determined by the available light and the

TABLE 21. Numbers of paired and unpaired Curlew roosting communally at an east Lancashire roost in 1957.

Date	No. of pairs	No. of single birds
23.3	5	3
24.3	8	3
27.3	7	6
28.3	6	8
29.3	4	3
30.3	4	1
31.3	5	6
1.4	12	5
2.4	10	8
3.4	9	7
4.4	11	4
5.4	9	8
6.4	9	8
7.4	11	2
8.4	11	1
9.4	10	3
10.4	1	2
11.4	4	3
12.4 – 20.4	Total of 2	None
21.4	2	2

overall light intensity of the dome of the sky correlates well with the mean arrival time. Immediately after alighting at the east Lancashire roost the birds preened for some time and fighting between members of different pairs frequently took place. Both birds of a pair participated in fighting and frequently the adversaries would flutter up to 3 m in the air with bills locked together.

Most birds seemed to arrive on the breeding area already paired although unpaired birds were always present at the roost. In 1957 a series of nightly observations were carried out over a period of one month and Table 21 shows the numbers of paired and unpaired birds using the roost. Clearly, birds did not always use the roost and this was established by walking over the breeding fields after dark when pairs were occasionally disturbed. Single birds were never disturbed in this way and probably they either used the communal roost or moved out of the area. However, even after roosting on the breeding fields birds retired to the communal roost on occasions. In this year (1957) full moon occurred on 14th April and until the 9th April birds remained on the roost until dawn. On the 10th April only two birds were present, though others were active on the shore of a nearby reservoir and on 11th April birds arrived at the roost but left after a few minutes. Fig. 42 shows the number of birds seen at the roost, together with the number of pellets and gizzard linings collected on the following day. As in the Lapwing, there appears to be a desertion of the night roost during the period of the full moon, although a clear return to full usage after the full moon period does not take place because of the onset of breeding.

Communal day roosts do not occur in the Curlew during full moon periods.

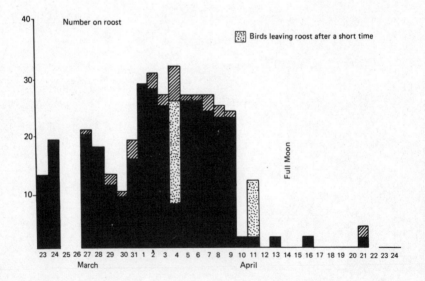

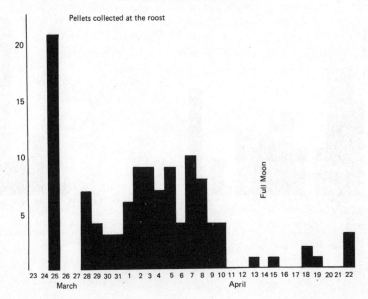

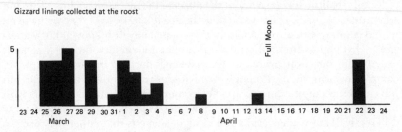

FIG. 42. Numbers of Curlew recorded on an inland roost in early spring, together with numbers of pellets and gizzard linings collected.

At this time of the year the birds remain on the breeding areas, sleeping in pairs. A measure of the inactivity at this time is shown by counts of songs during a two-hour morning period (Fig. 43). Whilst weather affects this activity to some extent, it is clear that the behaviour is different during the full moon period than at other times. Again, as in Lapwings, the visibility of the moon has no effect. An additional piece of evidence comes from the finding on the roost, after the full moon period, of pieces of the shells of *Scrobicularia* in pellets. These must have come from the coast, and whilst the possibility that these were regurgitated from newly arrived birds cannot entirely be discounted, their number strongly suggests that Curlews had made a night journey to the coast during the full moon period to feed.

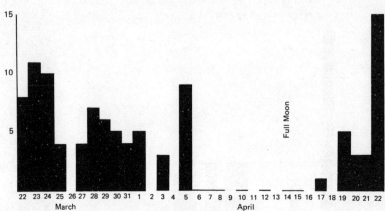

F IG . 43. Diurnal activity of the Curlew shown by the number of songs recorded in a two-hour period (10.00–12.00hrs).

Relatively little is known about the effect of the moon on wading birds and a great deal of work needs to be done before it can be said that we have an understanding of their behaviour in this connection. It is known that waders can feed at night without the aid of moonlight and, in fact, their behaviour is exactly the same on overcast nights during the full moon period as on completely clear nights. Probably behaviour is related to the tidal cycles but this can be no simple relationship since, although the full moon coincides with the highest tides, so too does the new moon when waders behave quite differently. That waders feed at all at night suggests that either they are not obtaining their food requirement during the day or that they are able to feed more efficiently at night. In the case of Curlews returning 30 kilometres to the shore during full moon periods, it appears that they are able to feed not only better, but better by a difference of at least the energy equivalent of a 60-kilometre flight. If this is the case, then why is the behaviour limited to the full moon period? Possibly the answer is that under these conditions the birds can navigate more easily, but this would not explain the behaviour of Lapwings and Golden Plovers. Probably, in all cases, the solution is that there is a greater efficiency in feeding at night in that the food organisms are more active then and possibly themselves have a lunar periodicity in activity. This is known for many littoral and marine invertebrates.

Communal roosting, and the flocking behaviour associated with it, are clearly of adaptive significance to wading birds. Several suggestions have been put forward in explanation of these phenomena. Three of these are worthy of consideration:

PLATE 9.
Ruffs on the 'hill';
the opening attitude
of the courtship
display.

Ruff and Reeves;
two satellite males
displaying to two
females.

Ruff copulating
with Reeve.

PLATE 10. *Above*, Reeve incubating in typically deep vegetation. *Below*, Woodcock brooding on woodland floor.

PLATE 11. *Above*, Greenshank at nest in typical Scottish habitat. *Below*, Oystercatcher nesting on top of a dry stone wall.

PLATE 12. *Above*, Black-winged Stilt at built up nest. *Below left*, Oyster-catcher mobbing predators; *right*, Lapwing wing-lifting, a common habit in most waders.

PLATE 13. *Above*, Avocet and chicks feeding in shallow water. *Below left*, Redshank chicks just out of nest; *right*, newly hatched Ruff chicks.

PLATE 14. *Above*, migrant Common Sandpiper. *Below*, migrant Dotterel resting in a hayfield.

PLATE 15. *Above left*, Bar-tailed Godwits at nest. The male (left) has a significantly shorter bill than the female. *Above right*, Curlew preening. *Below*, Purple Sandpipers at high tide in winter.

PLATE 16. *Above*, Common Snipe probing deeply in gaps between snow cover. *Below*, Knot during autumn passage. Oystercatchers in winter plumage in background.

1. As a means of bringing members of a population unit together so that regulation of numbers might take place through epideictic ('meant for display') behaviour (254)
2. As a means of protection from predators (127).
3. As a means for the efficient exploitation of unevenly distributed food resources by serving as 'information centres' (249).

There can be no doubt that the existence of wader roosts is actively advertised by the birds. It is not solely that wader roosts are so large and conspicuous that their presence cannot be hidden. The approach of waders to the roost in clouds of changing shape, their 'flashing' in the sunlight and, in the case of the Knot, their very clear contrast in colour with the substrate are all factors which could have been selected against. Instead, the reverse has occurred and selection has taken place to emphasise these features. Clearly, then, they must be of some adaptive significance; it must be to the advantage of the waders to attract attention to their roosting areas.

There are different interpretations put upon this. Wynne-Edwards views the situation as one in which the birds themselves are capable of assessing their overall numbers through 'epideictic' display, resulting in emigration if the overall population was too large. Whilst this may be a possibility in some species of birds, in waders it would be necessary for each roost to have a knowledge of the size of other roosts using the same feeding areas in order to assess the overall population size. This is clearly not practicable. Lack (127) considers that there is no evidence to support the Wynne-Edwards thesis for birds in general, and the above argument shows that it is certainly inapplicable in the case of waders. Lack further suggests that communal roosting has evolved through considerations of safety. The aerobatics of waders at roosts are very similar to flocks' behaviour when harassed by predators, either from the ground, or from the air. Tinbergen (242) suggested that this behaviour evolved to confuse birds of prey. Clearly, such highly perfected communal activities are likely to fulfil an important function, and since they are carried out very much more frequently in the absence of predators than in their presence, whilst the element of confusion of predators almost certainly occurs the behaviour probably has more far-reaching effects. One of these might be, as Lack (127) suggests, that undisturbed birds returning to the same roost indicate that the area is safe from predators. As a result large numbers rapidly build up which, because of the sheer size of the flock, might additionally confuse and confound potential predators.

Ward and Zahaví (249) go further; they suggest that communal roosts (and other assemblages of birds) have primarily evolved for the exploitation of unevenly distributed food supplies by acting as 'information centres'. The way in which this might operate is that birds joining a roost may follow experienced birds to known, good feeding areas after the roosting period is over. Viewed in this context the roost takes on an importance far greater than that of a sanctuary at high tide; it is probable that, as an 'information centre' and, through its quality, as a means of influencing the overall size of a population, the communal roost plays a critical part in the population ecology of wading birds.

CHAPTER 8

MOULT

FEATHERS are relatively fragile structures subject to wear and abrasion, and the individual birds must maintain their plumage in good condition. Efficient flight, temperature regulation and protection of the body surface depend upon the condition of the plumage so it is important that from time to time feathers are renewed. This is done by the process of moult. In waders all feathers are renewed at least once a year and in the case of the body feathers twice, since the complete moult in the autumn gives the winter plumage, while in spring the body feathers are moulted to produce the breeding plumage. When wader chicks hatch they are initially covered in down which gives way to the juvenile plumage during the fledging period. The juvenile body feathers are then quickly moulted within a few weeks, to give the first winter plumage.

Two groups of terminology are used to describe moult sequences; the older one, in common usage in Europe, follows Dwight (38) while the newer one, followed in the North American Handbook, is based on Humphrey & Parkes (104). Table 22 shows the general moult sequence and the equivalent terminology for each stage.

About a week after hatching, the down which covers all wader chicks begins to give way to contour feathers on the back and scapulars, soon followed by others on the breast and wing coverts. During the second week of life the first flight feathers appear and some down is then lost. The tail feathers do not appear until relatively late in the production of juvenile plumage but

TABLE 22. Moult sequence and equivalents of terminology.

Dwight (1900)	Time of occurrence (months)*	Humphrey and Parkes (1959)
Down	5 - 7	Down
Post natal moult	5 - 7	Post-natal moult
Juvenile plumage	5 - 9	Juvenile plumage
Post juvenile moult	8 - 11	Pre-basic I moult
1st winter plumage	10 - 4	Basic I plumage
1st pre-nuptial moult	2 - 5	Pre-alternate I moult
1st nuptial plumage	2 - 9	Alternate I plumage
1st post-nuptial moult	7 - 11	Pre-basic II moult
2nd (adult) winter plumage	10 - 4	Basic II plumage
2nd pre-nuptial moult	2 - 5	Pre-alternate II moult
2nd (adult) nuptial plumage	2 - 9	Alternate II plumage

* Jan. = 1, Dec. = 12.

in some species, e.g. Snipe, the young are capable of a fluttering flight before the tail feathers appear. Traces of down remain amongst the juvenile plumage for some weeks after fledging. The primary feathers do not reach their maximum length until some time after fledging, and in the case of many arctic waders this may be late in July, although earlier in more temperate regions. These primaries are retained until the moult in the second autumn of life in most species and so are in use for 13–18 months. In such circumstances they are clearly more subject to wear than are the primaries of adults, which are normally present for only twelve months, so when comparing wing lengths of first year birds, with those of adults it is important to bear this factor in mind.

As long ago as 1918 Jackson (107) gave a detailed account of the moults of different species of wading birds, and whilst there are small differences between some of the major groups, there is a general pattern. Most species have a characteristic juvenile plumage which is similar throughout the range of the species, even where considerable geographical variation occurs in the adult plumage. For example, Sandpipers have the feathers of the upperparts notched and margined with light buff while in the smaller Plovers, the feathers of the upperparts are also margined with pale buff; Grey Plovers have a characteristic juvenile plumage but in Golden Plovers it is less distinct, and the golden markings are paler on the upperparts and wing coverts.

The post-juvenile moult gives rise to the first winter plumage. Only in Coursers and Pratincoles are the flight feathers renewed at this moult which in other waders is confined to the body feathers, some or all of the tail feathers, some innermost secondaries and some wing coverts. The retention of some juvenile feathers, on the wing coverts, the tertiaries or on the tail in birds otherwise resembling adults means that these first winter birds can be positively aged. However, there is a good deal of individual variation within a species; for example, some juvenile Redshank lose the central, pointed tail feathers, but others retain them into the following breeding season. Jackson (107) found that the tail does not appear to be renewed in Golden Plover; Lesser Golden Plover; Lapwing; Upland Sandpiper; Dunlin; Baird's, Solitary, Purple and White-rumped Sandpipers and Grey Phalarope. Purple Sandpiper and Grey Phalarope also retain the innermost secondaries and most wing coverts.

The moult from first winter to first summer plumage is usually similar to the pre-nuptial moult of the adult although in some cases winter feathers persist. This retention of winter feathers is not characteristic of first summer birds as has been suggested by Jackson but is now thought to be an indication of secondary hybridisation. Stilts are exceptions in that first winter birds moult their tail feathers in spring whereas this does not occur in the adult; Stilts are also anomalous in their first post-nuptial moult in that adult winter plumage is not attained until the third year.

After the first summer there is a full post-nuptial moult which in most waders is complete by December. In some species which moult in the winter range, e.g. Common Sandpiper and Stints, the primary moult may continue into the spring. In the past this has given rise to the assertion that these species moulted primaries twice a year, which is not the case in the Common Sandpiper and occurs in few Stints.

The second pre-nuptial moult gives rise to the adult breeding plumage by a limited moult. This might be confined to some body feathers and a few innermost secondaries and wing coverts, e.g. in Lapwing, Stilt and Woodcock, but in most waders it extends to all the body feathers and most of the innermost secondaries and coverts. The pre-nuptial moult, as its name implies, gives rise to the breeding plumage. In waders this is almost always produced by the growth of new feathers and general overall colour changes which occur once a plumage is assumed are due either to abrasion or bleaching. Dunlin nesting in the British Isles seem particularly prone to abrasion of their breeding plumage, and wear of the chestnut-red edges, typical of April birds, results in a much darker bird in July; this wear does not appear to be so great in other Dunlin populations. At the end of the breeding season many waders can be seen with paler feathers, due to bleaching. This is particularly the case in the Ringed Plover and individuals of this species often have pale mantles in July.

There is, however, a third method by which colour change occurs in the fully grown feather, and this is known as aptosochromatosis. Staples and Harrison (232) drew attention to this in the Snow Bunting (*Plectrophenax nivalis*), but the phenomenon also occurs in waders where it consists mainly of a darkening of feathers in the region of the rachis and a spreading of the coloration into the barbs of the feather. It is particularly obvious in the

Greenshank, where, as in the Dunlin, July birds are much darker in colour than April birds due, not to abrasion, but to darkening of individual feathers from a light grey-brown to a dark chocolate. It also occurs, but not to the same extent, in the Redshank where retained winter feathers develop a dark coloured rachis during the breeding season. Occasionally this also happens in winter. The mechanism of this phenomenon is unknown but possibly it is a result of some oxidisation of materials present in the feathers.

In the majority of waders the pre-nuptial moult produces brood patches in those birds which do the incubation. The area of the incubation patches is defeathered prior to increasing the vascularity, and this is initiated by the hormone prolactin. In addition, secondary sexual characters are often accentuated at this moult; for example, the facial warts on the Ruff. Generally speaking, in species which are sexually dimorphic, the brighter colours of the breeding plumage are accentuated in the male, but in Phalaropes and the Dotterel, it is the females which are the brighter. In many species there is no sexual dimorphism, and both sexes can either assume a distinct breeding plumage or, as in the case of the Oystercatcher, acquire a breeding plumage little different from the winter plumage.

In some species of wader the first pre-nuptial moult may only be partial, e.g. Turnstone, and in others it may not occur at all, e.g. Grey Plover and Knot. Very often these birds remain in small flocks, south of the normal breeding area, and spend the summer in the estuarine environment which is normally their winter haunt. These flocks are not always composed entirely of first year birds and amongst them can often be seen adults which, due to some slight physiological disorder, have failed to move north. These birds may either remain in winter plumage, or, as is often the case in Grey Plover, take on the full breeding plumage. Relatively little is known of these summering non-breeding flocks, and a careful study of their ecology would, no doubt, provide much useful information.

Breeding waders usually arrive back at the breeding area in the full nuptial plumage which has been taken on during the period of migration and in the last few weeks in their winter range. Whilst the energy requirements for the partial spring moult are significantly less than those required for the autumn moult, nevertheless it will be considerably greater than that required to maintain the normal metabolism of the bird. This additional energy requirement, which occurs at the time when many waders are putting on weight for the spring migration, is clearly not too difficult to acquire, since it is only in exceptional circumstances that the spring moult does not take place. This provides yet further circumstantial evidence that the winter food supply has not been depleted to an extent where it cannot easily support the requirements of the wader population. The spring moult does not appear to put any great stress on those individuals which undergo it but the situation may be different in autumn.

It may well be that the autumn moult places a much greater burden than the spring moult both on the food supply and on the birds themselves. From a purely theoretical point of view it would be of advantage to birds migrating south to have a new, and presumably more efficient, plumage in which to carry out the journey. Certainly the young of the year have such a plumage, where the flight feathers are, at the most, only a few weeks old. Adult birds, with the feathers abraded through the exertion of the breeding season, and the flight feathers having been present for nearly twelve months, would surely benefit from a new plumage before migrating. Whilst some species do moult on the breeding ground, the majority move south either to moult at staging posts on migration, or to moult in the wintering area. The adoption of these strategies strongly suggests that the breeding areas cannot support these birds at this time in terms of their food requirements, and it seems most likely that they move to areas where they can feed easily and efficiently during the period of the moult, despite the fact that in many cases their flying efficiency and body insulation is reduced by the presence of old feathers and, in some cases, by a suspended moult.

In autumn the moult of the primary feathers usually spans the moult of the rest of the plumage and, largely because primary moult is relatively easy to quantify and quick to estimate in trapped birds, it is used in most studies as an overall estimate of moult. There are normally eleven primaries in waders, the first ten of which are large and counted in the primary 'score'; the small eleventh primary, carried on the bastard wing, is usually ignored. The primaries are numbered from the juxtaposition with the secondaries, from 1 in the proximal position to 11 in the distal position on the bastard wing (Fig. 44). In 'scoring' the moult each primary is given a rating, ranging from 0 (=old feather) to 5 (=new feather, fully grown) and partially grown feathers are given a rating in relation to their proportionate growth. The ratings are then summed so that a completely new wing would have a 'score' of 50. This method follows Ashmole (4) and is the one normally employed in

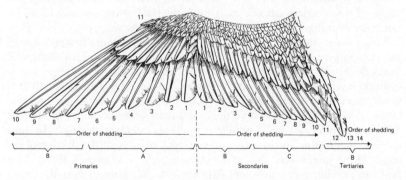

FIG. 44. Generalised wing-feather arrangement of a wader showing sequence of shedding of main flight feathers. A first, C last.

scoring primary moult though other methods have been used in the past, for example in Holmes' (93) study of the Dunlin. Here, flight feathers were scored in relation to their size, but in this case the whole moult was studied with scoring based largely on feather dry-weight, where body feathers accounted for 80% of this, primaries 11%, secondaries 6% and rectrices 3%. In the Dunlin moult of the body feathers begins on the head and spreads posteriorly along the spinal tract. Body feathers are shed quickly and almost simul-taneously and the last area to moult is usually the ventral side, so that in the Dunlin the black belly patch is the last remaining trace of the breeding plumage.

The sequence of primary moult begins with primary 1 and proceeds outwards with the longest feather, primary 10 being the last to be shed. Different populations, even of the same species, behave differently as far as the moult is concerned. Normally, in the British Isles, moulting waders drop the first five or six primaries nearly simultaneously over a period of a few days and no new feathers appear during the shedding. Once these are shed there is a very noticeable gap in the wing which can easily be seen in birds in flight, but this does not obviously impair the individual's ability to fly, although Lack (128), records that Curlews in such condition increase their wing beats by 40 strokes per minute. The new primaries grow rapidly and are almost fully grown within a period of 3–4 weeks; further primaries are then shed, two or three at a time and as new feathers grow more of the outermost primaries are dropped. The moult of the outer primaries tends to be slower than that of the inner feathers, but Minton (159) suggests that this might be because new feather material is created steadily throughout the moult and these feathers take longer because they are larger. Secondary feathers are not shed until the inner primaries are grown, and then the outermost secondary (1) is shed first and moult proceeds proximally to secondary (10), though the tertiaries (the proximal four feathers) are shed soon after the first secondary as are the central tail feathers. Moult of the tail proceeds from the centre outwards. The moult of the wing coverts occurs at the same time as the secondaries and is normally complete before the last primary is fully grown.

Moult takes different times in different species and generally larger species take longer over the moult. By catching birds from the same populations at intervals during the moult period and plotting moult scores against date of capture, it is possible to estimate the times of start and finish of the moult, and so get a measure of its duration. This method was first developed for passerine birds (225, 44, 167, 168) where the moult score increases linearly with the date, and in many waders a similar assumption can be made (193). In some species, such as the Turnstone, problems arise because of the slowing of the moult in the later stages, but, as Pienkowski rightly points out, this is not a problem providing that sufficient data are available from early in the moult period. A further problem arises in estimating moult duration where suspen-ded moult occurs, as this clearly interferes with a linear increase in moult score. In suspended moult those feathers which are moulted first, complete their new growth before others can be shed, and this may not occur for some time after the completion of growth of all of the first moulted feathers. This produces a wing which is made up partly of old feathers and partly of new feathers, but there is usually little difficulty in recognising this. The delay in continuing the moult may last for some time but even when moult is recommenced the fact that it has been suspended can often be seen because of the distinct difference in growth of the newest fully grown primary (the outermost) and the immediately adjacent growing feathers; where such a difference cannot be seen it is not possible to recognise that there has been suspended moult, though this might be suggested in some cases by the date, but as time progresses there is obviously a stage at which the pattern in birds with suspended moult merges with the normal pattern. The term 'arrested moult' is often used to mean the same as suspended moult; however, it is best retained for periods of a year or more without a moult as, for example, described by Prater *et al* (201) in the Oystercatcher.

The timing of the autumn moult is clearly related to several factors including the effectiveness of the old plumage during the migratory journey and the availability of sufficient food to provide the additional energy required in the moult. Even if sufficient food is available for normal metabolism and moult whether or not this could also provide the additional resources for migration might be a problem. Depending on the food supply at the breeding

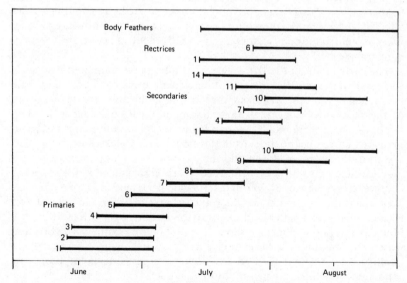

FIG. 45. Post-nuptial moult of the Dunlin at Barrow, Alaska (after Holmes 1966).

ground, and the exigencies of the journey, it is not surprising that different strategies have been adopted in relation to the timing of the moult.

The Dunlin provides an excellent example of different populations catering for the moult in different ways, and in this species can be found populations moulting on the breeding grounds, on the wintering grounds and on staging posts between the two. The North American population of the Dunlin (Red-backed Sandpiper) nesting around Point Barrow, Alaska, begins its moult into winter plumage soon after its arrival on the breeding ground (93) and the innermost primaries are lost during the period when the males are actively territorial. This can be seen in the moulting schedule of this species shown in Fig. 45. A point of interest here is that the northerly migration is carried out with very old flight feathers, so that the advantage of a southerly flight with new plumage is to this extent cancelled out. Also the onset of moult coincides with egg-laying in the female and together these must cause a significant increase in the birds' energy requirement during this period.

Usually the moult of the Dunlin's flight feathers is complete before the departure from the breeding grounds, but some leave without completing the moult during an early migratory phase, a slow, southerly movement not requiring the high fat reserves of long distance migration and which Holmes (93) terms 'migratory drift'. However, by the time the birds arrive in California almost all Dunlins have a fully renewed set of flight feathers. Apparently a shortage of food during the breeding season may affect the moult, and Holmes records that in 1963 adverse weather conditions did, in fact, cause a food shortage which apparently affected the body moult but not the moult of flight feathers. Clearly there is adaptive significance in the body moult being first affected, as the flight feathers must be replaced before the southward journey. Only about half the body feathers are normally moulted before the beginning of migratory drift.

The early moult in the Point Barrow Dunlin population, and its overlap with breeding, is clearly an adaptation to high arctic conditions where the season is short and the weather severe and unpredictable. 10° further south, on the Yukon–Kuskokwim delta, a slightly different situation occurs where the birds again begin moult before moving south in autumn, but the young here are hatched before the start of the moult. This is clearly associated with the extended breeding season and there is not the overlap of breeding and moult which occurs further north. A comparison is made in Fig. 46 of events on the two breeding areas. In this delta region birds tend to move to the coast to complete the moult after breeding, and before migration, and this may well be associated with a better food supply in this location (97). It is clear that the Point Barrow population has responded evolutionarily to the shorter breeding season by moulting at a faster rate; this results in the flight feathers being moulted and renewed in a period of some 60 days at Point Barrow as compared with about 90 days in the delta regions (Fig. 47). Pimm (194) has drawn attention to the fact that where figures referring to populations, rather

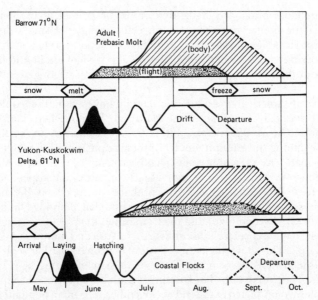

FIG. 46. Comparison of breeding season schedules of two Alaskan Dunlin populations (after Holmes 1971).

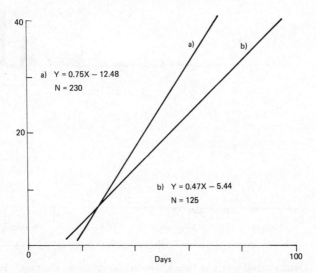

FIG. 47. Regression of moult scores of flight feathers on time for Alaskan Dunlin populations at a) Barrow and b) the Yukon-Kuskokwim delta. Time axis is given in days from when the first individual was recorded in moult (after Holmes 1971).

than individual birds, are used, 'time' must be plotted as the dependent variable if the moult duration is to be correctly estimated. Using 'score' as the dependent variable tends to result in an under-estimate of the moult period, whereas using 'time' correctly estimates the duration of moult and the variance about the time is a measure of the variability of starting and finishing dates.

The North American populations of Dunlin have a moult schedule which contrasts markedly with that of the European Dunlin where many of the typical form *Calidris alpina alpina* and of *C. a. schinzii* arrive in North Africa before beginning the autumn moult. In these populations the moult has not begun in many cases at a time when it has been completed in North American birds. However, there are some individuals which exhibit suspended moult and in these individuals moult was probably initiated on the breeding ground, as suspended moult has been demonstrated in moulting Dunlins from Finland (134), Sweden (230) and the Camargue (51).

Primary moult scores for autumn Northern African Dunlins are shown in Fig. 48 (191). This shows the typical pattern of primary feather replacement in waders in general, based on the European system of scoring (4). From this figure it can be seen that the last Dunlin to moult began to do so in September and moult was completed at the end of November. The main population takes a period of some 150 days to complete the moult, much longer than on the

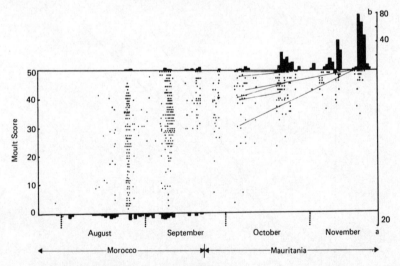

FIG. 48. Primary moult scores of Dunlin plotted against date of capture. Each dot represents one bird. Lines join scores for birds recaptured in the same year. **a** = number of birds caught at moult score 0. **b** = number of birds caught at moult score 50 (after Pienkowski and Dick 1975).

North American breeding grounds, though each individual's moult duration is about 70 days. The frequency of retrapping marked Dunlin in Morocco compared with retrapping results in later months in Mauretania suggests that the Moroccan birds may well have migrated further south, and were thus in full moult whilst actually on migration (191). Whilst this in itself is interesting there can be little doubt that many birds began moult only when they reached their wintering areas in September (Fig. 48).

Intermediate between those populations of Dunlin moulting on the breeding grounds and those moulting on the wintering grounds can be said to be those moulting at a southerly migration staging post. As far as Dunlins are concerned the Wash and the Waddenzee are staging posts for many southerly migrating birds which are mainly of the typical form *C. a. alpina* and originate from northern Scandinavia, Russia and western Siberia. After moulting on the Wash these birds move on to the western and southern coasts of Britain, into France and Iberia and possibly into north-west Africa. On the Wash they are replaced by birds which have moulted on the Waddenzee and Dunlin moulting there also move on into southern Europe and north-west Africa. Primary moult scores for Dunlin moulting on the Waddenzee are shown in Fig. 49 and it has been calculated that there is a mean moult duration of

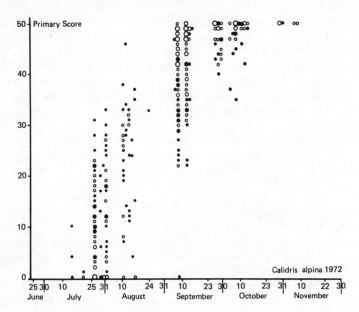

FIG. 49. Primary moult scores of Dunlins in 1972 plotted against dates of capture. Number of observations:
· = 1, o = 2–3, ● = 4–5, o = >6 individuals (after Boere 1977).

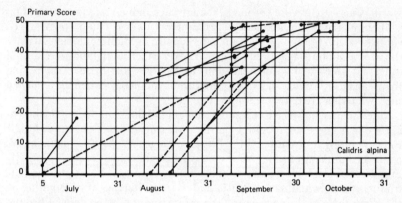

FIG. 50. Increase of primary moult scores of Dunlins retrapped during the same moult season. Broken lines indicate dates of beginning or termination of moult unknown (after Boere 1977).

87 days from Dunlin retrapped during the same moult season (Fig. 50) (14). This period is greater than that for either the southern or northern wintering populations.

The North American population of Dunlin at Point Barrow, Alaska, is usually referred to the sub-species *C. a. sakhalina*, which extends into eastern Siberia, and there can be little doubt that all this population moults on the breeding ground. Somewhere between the Verkoyhansk Mountains and the Yamal Peninsula the general moulting strategy changes, but some of the more eastern birds apparently find their way to western Europe as some 20% of the birds examined were in suspended moult when passing south-west through Finland (134).

Boere (14) further raises the interesting point that birds found in suspended moult in western Europe may well be males, which have remained on the breeding area longer than the females, using food resources present there after the departure of the females. Data for primary moult score in sexed Dunlin were shown by him to indicate a difference in timing of the moult with females completing the renewal of the flight feathers as much as 3 weeks in advance of the males (Fig. 51).

The majority of each of the different populations of Dunlins behave similarly in regard to the timing of the moult, but all workers have found a percentage of individuals which does not conform to the norm. It is therefore easy to see how, by very slight changes in selection pressure, moulting strategies can be changed, and thus it is not surprising to find several moulting strategies within a single species.

It is, perhaps, a little surprising that moulting on the breeding area is confined to a relatively few species. Icelandic Oystercatchers and Golden

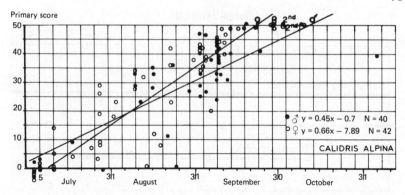

FIG. 51. Primary moult scores in male and female Dunlins plotted against dates of capture, with regression line (after Boere 1977).

Plovers both begin the moult before the breeding activities are finished and remain in Iceland until the beginning of October when the moult is completed, giving a moulting period of about $4\frac{1}{2}$ months. A short migration then takes place to the principal wintering grounds in the western parts of the British Isles. Snipe and Woodcock also moult before migrating with the first primaries shed in mid-June. The moult may last well into October and, whilst the main arrivals in the British Isles are in this month, northerly populations from the arctic move south earlier. Fig. 52 shows the moult schedule of the American Woodcock based on a large number (2500+) of specimens. As in other waders the primaries are shed in sequence outwards, but the secondary moult begins proximally in Woodcock, shortly followed by the fall of the distal feathers so that feathers are replaced in sequence from both ends of the feather tract (180). Jack Snipe also moult on the breeding ground (118) but Great Snipe moult during migration.

Some species begin their moult on the breeding ground but complete it during the subsequent migration. This occurs in some juvenile birds which have just produced new primaries in their first plumage e.g. Jack Snipe and in the Lapwing. In populations of this species in Great Britain moult begins in June and continues until the end of September. It may well be that during the moult these birds are not carrying out extensive journeys, or possibly that some may be in suspended moult, but there is insufficient information to come to a conclusion on this point. Goodyer (56) estimates the duration of the moult period in the Lapwing as 105 days, but Snow & Snow (226) estimate about 60 days for an individual though this is now recognised as too short a period. In the latter work a technique was developed for the collection of moulted feathers on a roost site, and because of the characteristic markings of individual primaries it was possible to allocate scores to individual birds on the

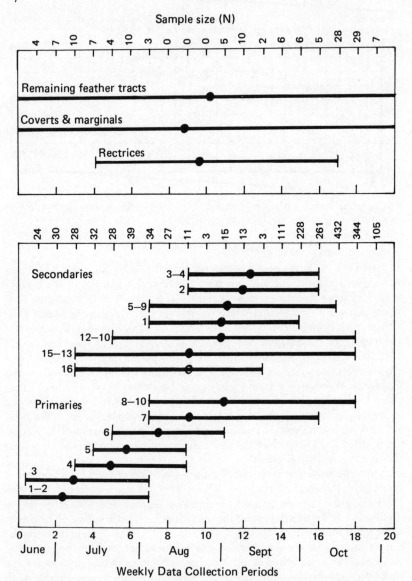

FIG. 52. Chronology of moult of adult American Woodcock 1969–1970. Each dot represents the time of highest intensity of moult (after Owen and Krohn 1973).

basis of the moulting of a particular feather. This, of course, necessitated knowing scores at which particular primaries were moulted but it was possible to obtain this information from BTO moult cards, so that P1 = 1, P2 = 4, P7 = 29 and P10 = 41. The fit of the results of this technique to the normal scores from trapped (dated) birds is shown in Fig. 53. This technique could profitably be used on other species if the results are shown to be accurate, and has the obvious advantage of not having to trap the birds.

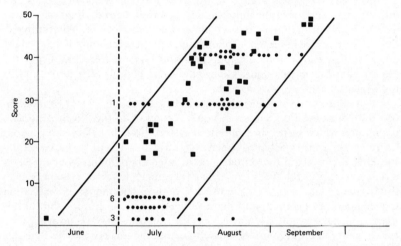

FIG. 53. Primary moult score plotted against data for Lapwings. ■ Data from BTO moult cards and specimens in the British Museum. ● Calculated moult scores from flocks assessed by date of dropping primaries (after Snow and Snow 1976).

Most wader species which moult on the breeding grounds are not high arctic breeders, with the exception of some populations of the Dunlin which, as has already been described, carried out a rapid moult before migrating. Another species which apparently behaves similarly is the Purple Sandpiper which, in Iceland, carries out the autumn moult in a period of 40–50 days, but unlike the Dunlin the moult is not started until breeding activities are ended (162). Apparently females arrive at the shore and commence moulting some 8 days before the males as the latter are still tending the chicks during the later part of their fledging period. Not all Purple Sandpipers migrate; many remain in Iceland, and this species is the most northerly wintering wader, recorded by Salomonsen (210) as remaining in Greenland during this season; however, it seems likely that the short moult has been evolved in relation to the autumn migration. Bengtson (10) also found a short moult period in the Purple Sandpiper in Spitzbergen. In many cases birds of this population will move only a short distance to the north coast of Norway, so that there can be no great selection pressure to complete the moult in the breeding area. The fact that this species does so may well be associated with a plentiful food supply in the rocky shoreline habitat in which this species feeds.

The staging posts at which many waders pause during their southerly autumn migration serve not only as a refuelling area but also as a resting place in which the moult, or part of it, can take place. The Waddenzee is perhaps the best known of these moulting areas (14) but in the British Isles the Wash and the Morecambe Bay/Ribble/Dee complex are of great importance in this context. Such areas are utilised in different ways by different species and different populations of the same species. Knots and Sanderlings may carry out the whole of the moult in such areas and then move on. Alternatively, Grey Plovers arrive in suspended moult and complete their moult here, whilst other species, e.g. Common Sandpipers and Greenshanks may begin the moult on the European estuaries and complete it, possibly after suspension, in the wintering area.

On the European moulting grounds Knots seem to complete their moult in one particular locality. This is in marked contrast to the North American population which suspends its moult in eastern Canada before carrying out the rest of the journey to South America by an over-sea route (153). Generally speaking Knots begin the primary moult later than Dunlins, but the body moult is begun at a relatively earlier stage of primary moult in a similar way to the Bar-tailed Godwit (14). As in the case of the Knot, there is no indication that Sanderlings begin moult from a suspended state in Europe, but in this species once the moult has started several primaries may be growing concurrently and there are signs of difficulty in maintaining continuous flight for long distances.

Grey Plovers often arrive from their Siberian breeding areas in suspended wing moult. Branson and Minton (17) suggest that this may possibly be associated with lack of breeding success so that time is available for a partial moult before the southerly migration starts. Such suspended moult occurs in up to 40% of arrivals in Britain and in the majority of these 50% occurred with two new primaries, in 20% with one new primary and in 30% with three. It is likely that suspension takes place before departure from the breeding ground and it apparently occurs only in birds older than one year. On the Wash, Grey Plovers complete their moult by the middle of November except for a small proportion (16%) which remain in suspended moult until March, when moulting is restarted before the northward movement.

In contrast to the situation in Grey Plovers, Green Sandpipers passing through the British Isles arrive without having started to moult and in many moult progresses as far as the seventh primary before the birds move south (116). However, there is evidence of suspended moult occurring at or before this stage and subsequent southerly migration takes place with moult having been suspended in many individuals.

Examples have already been given of waders which moult on their wintering grounds, but these have been in northern Europe, on estuaries where others of the same species have used these areas only as staging posts. Some waders move to the extreme south of the Palaearctic/African migration system before moulting. Common Sandpipers and Little Stints arrive at the rift valley lakes in Southern Kenya before starting to moult (184) and other species, such as Greenshanks, Marsh, Wood, Green and Curlew-Sandpipers and Ruffs complete the moult which has already begun further north on arrival. In Common Sandpiper the moult normally begins after arrival, in October, and may finish in some individuals as late as March. In the Little Stint, moult begins by mid-September and may be completed by December, though some individuals experience suspended moult and may not recommence moulting until February or March. Alternatively, birds which have completed the primary moult by the beginning of December sometimes renew the outer primaries again in the intervening period of five months before the spring migration. Pearson (184) estimates that some 20% of adult Little Stints may moult some of their outer primaries twice, and in this Stints are relatively unusual.

Moult in tropical wintering areas is a much more leisurely process than in more temperate regions. It is probable that the extended lack of a full complement of flight feathers is associated with the lighter weight of the fat-free birds in these areas, and the fact that they are not likely to be called upon to make movements in response to the weather. In other words, waders wintering in the tropics have a relatively easy time and do not require a high quality plumage. An additional factor in retaining an old plumage might be the excessive wear to which a new plumage would be subjected both by sunlight and abrasion. It is clearly of advantage to produce a new plumage as near to the time of the northerly flight as possible.

It is frequently suggested that suspended moult may be a result of a relatively low food supply and is an adaptation to conserve energy. Suspended moult occurs frequently in the tropical winter range where the food supply is almost certainly not limiting in any way. It also occurs on the breeding ground, late in the season, and if food were limiting at this time it is difficult to see why the birds remain. It is much more likely that suspended moult is an adaptation to take advantage of an over-abundance of food, particularly before the onset of migration, and on the northerly wintering grounds it may well be a device to allow a more rapid increase in weight as it occurs at a time when weight is building up to the winter maximum.

So far, for the autumn moult, only that of the adults has been considered and in juvenile birds there are considerable differences. Thus, the primaries and secondaries are not normally moulted in temperate wintering areas but in some species, e.g. Woodcock, the proximal secondaries are replaced in the first autumn of life. Moult of tail feathers occur in some species occasionally, but generally the autumn moult is limited to body feathers. However, this does not apply to species wintering in the southern hemisphere, as here juvenile birds often moult their flight feathers. Some Ruffs and Greenshanks return north at the end of their first winter still wearing their juvenile flight feathers but, according to Pearson (184) many birds in this worn plumage summer in Africa and have low weights in spring compared with migratory birds. Curlew-Sandpipers and Wood Sandpipers renew four to six outer primaries in their first winter, whereas in Greenshanks, Marsh Sandpipers and Ruffs only odd outer primaries are replaced. The Common Sandpiper has a complete moult of both primaries and outer secondaries in the first winter in Africa, and the Little Stint and Ringed Plover have a complete moult like the adults. A similar situation occurs in South America, where the Least Sandpiper has a complete moult in Surinam but when wintering in California does not moult the primaries. It appears that first year waders moult some or all of their primary feathers in winter where extensive northerly journeys are expected in the following spring. If such a moult did not take place first year Curlew Sandpipers might retain their first flight feathers for a period of up to eighteen months. However, it should be remembered that Dunlins wintering in temperate regions have to make three migratory journeys, perhaps totalling in excess of 12,000 km, on their first set of primaries.

Birds which do not breed in their first year and remain to summer south of their normal breeding area, begin post-nuptial moult earlier than adults. This is the case in Turnstones and Knots on the Wash and primary moult may begin here in late May. In these circumstances, the moult period is more drawn out than in adult birds beginning moult two months later and may take up to a month longer. Oystercatchers do not normally reach maturity until their third year so that non-breeding first- and second-year birds are present on the estuaries in summer. First-year birds moult from May to the middle of September ($4\frac{1}{2}$ months), second-year birds from mid-June to mid-October (4 months) and adults from the end of July to mid-November (3 months).

Differences in moult duration are not limited to age classes, as has already been pointed out in the case of Dunlin. Populations wintering in different habitats moult over different periods of time, though different species tend to have characteristic moulting periods (see Table 23). Dunlin on the moulting area furthest north take only 60 days for the primary moult, whereas on the breeding grounds and staging posts further south the period increases to 90–97 days and reaches 100 days in the southerly wintering areas. The increase in moulting rate can be brought about by increasing the number of feathers in growth at one time, and Morrison (162) has drawn attention to this. Fig. 54 illustrates this in relation to the moult duration of several species of birds. The alternative strategy is to grow feathers more rapidly, and Pienkowski (190) records that in comparisons of the moults of Little Stint and Curlew-Sandpiper in Morocco and in the southern hemisphere (156, 241) this was shown to occur, as it was in Dunlins in Alaska (97). In either case, the daily energy requirements involved in the simultaneous growth of several feathers will clearly be greater than if they were grown in sequence, so that it is

TABLE 23. Duration of moult in wading birds.

		Country	Source	Duration of Moult (days)
Oystercatcher	1st yr.	UK	Minton (1977)	140
	2nd yr.	UK	Minton (1977)	120
		Holland	Boere (1977)	130–140
	Adult	UK	Minton (1977)	110
		Holland	Boere (1977)	100–110
Grey Plover		UK	Branson & Minton 1976	90
Ringed Plover		UK	Minton & Waterson in Pienkowski 1972	90
		Morocco	Pienkowski 1972	80–90
Lapwing		UK	Goodyer 1976	105
		UK	Snow & Snow 1976	60–70
Curlew		Holland	Boere 1977	100
Black-tailed Godwit		Morocco	Pienkowski 1972	c. 90
Bar-tailed Godwit		Holland	Boere 1977	104
Redshank { Continental population Icelandic population		Holland	Boere 1977	{ 125 135
Turnstone		Iceland	Morrison 1976	c. 70
		Holland	Boere 1977	70–75
Woodcock		USA	Owen & Krohn 1973	c. 120
Knot		Holland	Boere 1977	90–100
Sanderling		Holland	Boere (1977)	c. 50
Western Sandpiper		Alaska	Holmes 1972	c. 70
Red-necked Stint		Australia	Thomas & Dartnall 1971	110–115
Little Stint		Morocco	Pienkowski 1972	c. 56
Purple Sandpiper		Iceland	Morrison 1976	40–50
Dunlin		UK	Boyd & Ogilvie 1966	60
		Holland	Boere 1977	90–94
		Alaska (N) Alaska (W)	Holmes 1971	70
		Morocco	Pienkowski 1972	100
Curlew Sandpiper		Morocco	Pienkowski 1976	40
		Australia	Thomas & Dartnall 1971	125–130

likely that food is readily available at the time where such growth is a regular occurrence. The greatest recorded discrepancy in moulting time occurs in the Curlew Sandpiper, which takes only about 40 days on its Moroccan staging post but may take 125–130 days in Tasmania, during the northern winter. Presumably, the rapid northern moult is associated both with the need to move further south and with an excess food supply. In Tasmania the extended moult period is surely not because this is the only sufficiently long period free

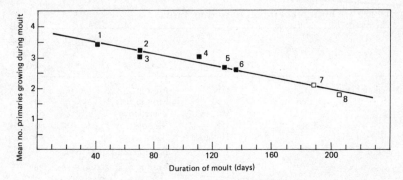

FIG. 54. Relation of duration of moult to the mean overall number of primaries growing during moult for a number of species of waders and gulls. (■1) Purple Sandpiper, (■2) Dunlin, (■3) Turnstone, (■4) Red-neck Stint, (■5) Curlew Sandpiper, (■6) Oystercatcher, (□7) Greater Black-backed Gull, (□8) Glaucous Gull (after Morrison 1976).

from physiological strain (241) but because the surplus of food per unit time is greatest and the spread of the moult minimises the demand at any one time (190).

There can be little doubt that the production of new feathers during the moult requires energy, which might be derived either from an increased intake of food, or from the utilisation of energy reserves in the form of fat deposits or muscle proteins (47). If the latter source of energy was utilised a reduction in weight of individual birds would be expected during the moult, and this has been recorded in some species, e.g. American Woodcock (180) and Snipe (243). Minton (158) states that moulting adults have a relatively constant weight, and are largely fat free, during the moulting period July–October. Boere (14) studied in detail the weight changes during the course of moult in seven species of common shore waders and demonstrated constant mean weights throughout, with a tendency to increase towards the termination of moult. Fig. 55 shows weight changes in relation to moult score in the Curlew, which is typical of the seven species studied.

In Morocco, Mauretania and countries further south, moulting waders are lighter in weight than are individuals of the same species moulting in Europe. This suggests that the European moulting birds are maintaining some reserves, as those moulting further south do not normally increase their post-moult weight until the time of the next northward migration.

It does seem, then, that moulting is normally carried out in areas of good food supply. In the case of those species remaining in the breeding area the Purple Sandpiper lacks competition of any sort (unless Turnstones can be regarded as competitors) while in the North American Dunlin its congeners in

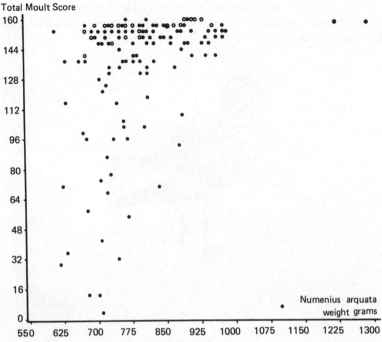

FIG. 55. Relationship between total moult scores and bodyweight in Curlews. (Birds with score zero are omitted). Number of observations. · = 1, o = 2–3, ● = 4–5, O = >6   (after Boere 1977).

the breeding area (Pectoral, Baird's and Semi-palmated Sandpipers) have moved south to moult in the winter range. In both cases the species are capitalising on an abundant food supply in the absence of competitors. Moult fits into the annual cycle in a variety of ways, and only rarely overlaps with breeding. Moult and rapid migration are normally mutually exclusive, and here mechanisms (e.g. suspended moult, use of staging posts) are evolved to ensure the production of efficient flight mechanisms for migration. The events of the annual cycle are the evolutionary results of selecting for optimum use of energy availability within a population. Moult almost certainly occurs when other stresses are minimal, so that it might be argued that during the moulting period there is a super-abundance of food on the moulting areas. Within any population of wading birds it is likely that environmental factors may have effect upon the hormonal control of the moult cycle to produce a degree of variability in the timing of onset of moult. There is probably also a large inherited variability, so that selection for change in moulting strategy with changing environmental conditions may be rapid and the fact that different strategies occur in populations of the same species is a reflection of the great adaptability of the birds to the timing of the moult.

CHAPTER 9

FEEDING ECOLOGY

In many wading birds the habitats occupied during the summer and winter are very different, and their food and feeding techniques may differ because of this. For the most part waders feed inland during the breeding season, although there are obvious exceptions, while in winter many species feed on the coasts and estuaries; thus a study of feeding in any particular species has two aspects. It is not surprising that most studies have been carried out during the non-breeding season, on an estuarine environment. It is here that the birds are found for most of the year, and the threat to these wetland environments by reclamation schemes, and possibly barrage construction, has resulted in money being made available to study the effects of such schemes on the environment and its occupants. There are several reasons why feeding during the breeding season has been a neglected area of study, not least of which is the difficulty of getting to the breeding areas of many waders. However, where such studies have been carried out, interesting results have been obtained and this is a very promising area for future research. For the purpose of this discussion, winter feeding ecology will be examined, first in the estuarine environment and then inland, and feeding in the breeding area will be considered last.

Except during the periods which are spent at high tide roosts (Chapter 7), most shorebirds live and feed in winter between low and high water mark, in a mud-flat environment otherwise occupied almost exclusively by marine invertebrate animals. The food supply of waders feeding here consists of animals of three main phyla-molluscs, crustaceans and marine worms. Typical den-

TABLE 24. Mean monthly density ($/m^2$) of estuarine invertebrates preyed upon by waders.

	Ribble Estuary (Greenhalgh 1975)	Morecambe Bay (Anderson 1972)
Annelida		
Nereis diversicolor	596	750
Nephthys sp.	294	*c*. 100
Scoloplos armiger	190	—
Pygospio elegans	3620	—
Arenicola marina	128	222
Crustacae		
Corophium volutator	22,000	8700
Corophium arenarium	3220	—
Bathyporeia pelagica	4200	—
Haustorius arenarius	480	—
Eurydice pulchra	1420	—
Carcinus maenas	10–12	—
Mollusca		
Hydrobia ulvae	47,000	8525
Macoma balthica	2440	4000
Tellina tenuis	365	875
Scrobicularia plana	132	—
Cardium edule	40+	100

sities of the more important species are shown in Table 24. Of the Annelid worms, two are of particular importance, *Nereis* in the case of the smaller waders and *Arenicola* in the case of the Godwits. *Corophium* is the most important Crustacean but small crabs (*Carcinus*) are also taken in large quantities. Of the molluscs, cockles (*Cardium*) are taken mainly by Oystercatchers (and small specimens by Knot) but *Macoma* and *Hydrobia* are of particular importance to the smaller waders. However, large individuals of these species may be taken by Oystercatchers, Bar-tailed Godwits and Curlew, and the fact that different species of waders take different sizes of prey must be recognised when estimating the abundance of prey species. In western Europe, *Nereis*, *Corophium*, *Hydrobia*, *Cardium* and *Macoma* are the most important food organisms for waders living on mud-flats, but in rocky environments other invertebrates become important, e.g. mussels (*Mytilus*) for Oystercatchers.

Many factors affect the distribution of the invertebrates in estuarine conditions, and their distribution is very patchy. Like soil animals they tend to be aggregated in certain areas, and they occur in low densities on the higher banks, and in high densities in the gullies. All species, even the deep-burrowing molluscs, are to some extent subject to movement, largely by the effect of wave action, though *Corophium* and *Hydrobia* are frequently moved during the incoming tide. Because of such movements causing aggregation and patchiness in the distribution, it is difficult to sample accurately, and there are wide margins of error on most population estimates. Even in still water cockles will move quite large distances (up to 1 metre in 24 hours) so that, even in supposedly relatively sedentary organisms such as this, monthly sampling suffers from the same inaccuracies. Nevertheless, different food invertebrates are generally found at different levels on the shore and Fig. 56 shows the distribution of the more abundant species in relation to shore level on Morecambe Bay.

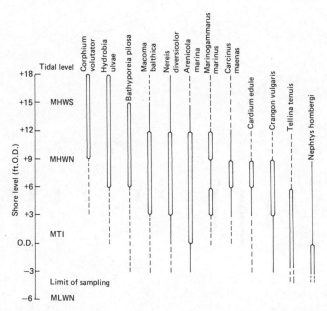

FIG. 56. Distribution of the twelve most abundant invertebrate species surveyed in Morecambe Bay in relation to shore level. Open bars indicate densities greater than the mean; ———, densities greater than half the mean; ------, present (after Anderson 1972).

The annual cycle of the invertebrates is of importance in terms of food supply for waders. At the end of the winter in western Europe the invertebrate populations are at their lowest numerically, and the total biomass is also at its lowest. However, the mean weight per individual is at its highest and theoretically a wader needs to work less hard to obtain a given weight of food. In Fig. 57 mean density and biomass are shown in each month of the year for

Hydrobia and *Corophium* on the Ribble mud-flats; in addition the mean dry weight of an average individual is shown in each month. Similarly shaped curves occur in other prey species. In spring, migrant waders are able to put

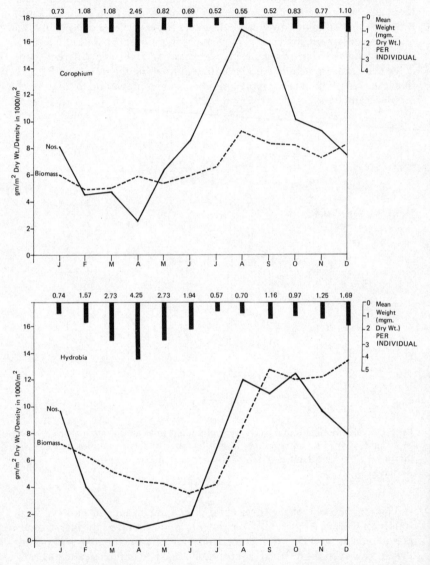

FIG. 57. Density and biomass of *Corophium* (top) and *Hydrobia* (bottom) on the Ribble mudflats (after Greenhalgh 1975).

on weight (Chapter 5) by feeding upon individual prey which then have greater weight per individual than occurs at any other time of the year, whereas in autumn, those birds using our estuaries as staging posts take advantage of the highest biomass which occurs throughout the year. It also happens that in autumn population densities are at their highest so that the likelihood of a bird encountering prey is greater than when densities are low. However, although the likelihood of encountering food items is greater, it does not follow that the rate of eating increases accordingly. There is a density of prey at which the predation rate levels off, and this is very much lower than might be expected. Fig. 58 shows that in Redshanks preying on *Corophium*, this is at the level of 1000/m^2, and in Oystercatchers preying on cockles, it is at the level of 250/m^2 (61, 62). It is interesting, however, that whilst the predation rate levels off, the intake, in terms of biomass, continues to increase, as in areas of high density birds tend to take larger individual prey.

The relationship between predators and their prey is one that has interested ecologists for many years, and the wader/invertebrate prey interaction provides a situation that has many aspects which can be studied relatively easily. The wading birds crop the invertebrates so that it is clearly of importance to know the annual production of the prey – the biomass of potential food produced by the prey populations over a year. This will enable a comparison between different areas where the percentage of the total annual production taken by waders is known, and on this basis it may be possible to forecast whether a given estuary could support waders displaced from another. Clearly in a situation such as this, much more information would be needed, for example the presence of other predators on each site, the effects of predation on the productivity of the prey, and whether or not total numbers were limited by other factors. Nevertheless, production in the prey species is an important parameter in any study of feeding in wading birds, and several methods of measurement are available. Crude estimates can be obtained by summing the positive biomass increases over a year; in Fig. 57 this gives a production estimate of 6.3 g dry wt/m^2 in *Corophium* and 10.8 g dry wt/m^2 in *Hydrobia*. Usually estimates of production using positive biomass increases are under-estimates because no account is taken of mortality, and figures derived from life tables, which are often very difficult to construct, are more reliable. Greenhalgh (66) gives corrected estimates of production on the Ribble, allowing for mortality, of 9.8 g dry wt/m^2 for *Corophium* and 11.9 g dry wt/m^2 for *Hydrobia*.

Many factors affect production estimates but the predation itself is one of the most important. Estimates from positive biomass increases and from life tables are almost invariably based on sampling of populations which are predated, and to obtain a figure for *total* production, the biomass removed by the predators must be added to the estimate obtained by sampling. In the estuarine environment the wading birds are not the only predators on the invertebrates, and the effects of fish and invertebrate predators, e.g. *Carcinus*

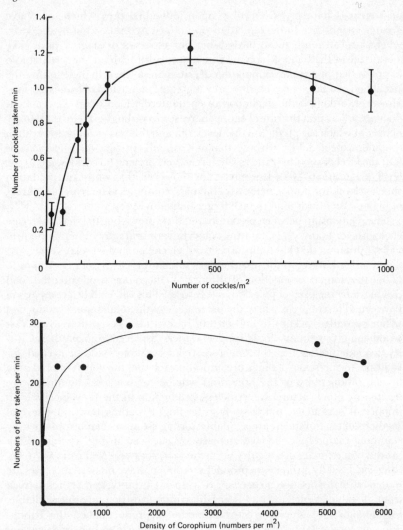

FIG. 58. *Above*, feeding rate in relation to density of prey. The feeding rate of Oystercatchers in relation to the numerical density of *Cardium* 16–42mm long. Curve fitted by eye; Vertical bar = 1 S.E. (after Goss-Custard 1977a). *Below*, The number of small prey taken per minute by individual Redshank in relation to the density of *Corophium* (after Goss-Custard 1977b).

must be taken into account. Estimates of predation by fish are particularly difficult to obtain since the predation occurs only during tidal cover when the predators move onto the mud-flats, and they retreat with the tide, so that their density and level of predation are very difficult to estimate.

Attempts have been made to exclude waders and other predators from areas in which the invertebrate populations are regularly sampled, and theoretically a comparison of the densities of the prey inside and outside such exclusion areas should give a measure of the predation. In practice little useful information has been obtained using such techniques in estuarine situations (except perhaps where sedentary polychaetes such as *Lanice* and *Arenicola* are concerned), as marine invertebrates are notoriously mobile and the manufacture of pens in which they can be artificially retained affects the movement of the substrates, causes siltation and traps debris, all of which affect the experiment.

In an inland habitat, Bengtson, Nilson, Nordstrom and Rundgren (11) record the results of an interesting exclusion experiment in Iceland where Golden Plovers were kept out of areas in a hayfield using nets, so that the earthworm population beneath the nets was protected from them. Over a period of 22 days the earthworm population outside the exclusion areas was reduced from $238/m^2$ to $107 \ m^2$, whilst other observation showed that the Plovers were taking about 4.5 lumbricid worms per m^2 per day. The density of earthworms was thus more than halved during this period, but attempts to set up similar experiments on tidal mud-flats have proved inconclusive and there is the additional problem here of predation by fish during tidal cover.

There is clearly a lot of potential food present in the estuarine habitat; that it is there is one thing, but its availability to the waders is another. Throughout the tidal cycles, different areas of mud-flat are uncovered and available to the waders. During spring tides, much greater areas are uncovered than during neap tides, but on spring tides waders may be driven right off the estuaries so that even Dunlin are unable to feed. There is no doubt that the distribution of the invertebrate prey with depth is an important factor in their being taken by waders, and on areas remaining uncovered by neap tides the invertebrates are often largely unobtainable by the birds. This is also the case when low temperatures reduce the activity of the invertebrates (58) when the frequency with which they are taken is reduced, or the birds change to different prey species. On the Ythan (58) Redshanks took mainly *Corophium* at temperatures above 6°C, but during one winter, in one area, *Macoma* was taken more frequently at lower temperatures as was *Nereis* in another area. Similar results were obtained on the Ribble (66). There may also be a reduced efficiency of feeding during the hours of darkness and under these circumstances cloud cover, and the states of the moon, may be important. The geographical location may also be of importance in this respect, as in north-west England the highest tides are around midnight and midday, whereas in the south-east they occur in the evening and early morning, leaving areas available to birds throughout the daylight hours only in the south-east. Blowing sand also affects feeding efficiency, and during high winds and neap tides, when relatively dry areas occur on the flats, this can be a real problem, not only to the birds but to those trying to observe them.

From a knowledge of the topography of the estuarine habitat, and the records of tide heights, it is possible to obtain a figure for the area of substrate exposed in terms of hectare-hours suitable for feeding. Theoretically, it is also possible to make allowance for other variable factors affecting feeding.

To determine the intake of food in terms of either biomass or energy, it is necessary to know the feeding rates at different times of the day and different times of the year, and the size or energy content of the food items. This information can only be obtained by direct observation of the number of food items and their size taken over a given period of time. Two major parameters need to be measured, firstly the time spent feeding and secondly the food intake during that time.

Different species of waders spend different amounts of time feeding during the daily cycle, and within a given species the proportion of the time spent feeding also differs throughout the year. Dunlins spend more time feeding than most other species and Curlews spend the least time; this amounts in mid-winter to some 75% of the tide cycle (9 hrs) in the former species and about 47% in the latter. Such estimates can only be obtained by direct observation of the birds throughout several tide cycles at different times of the year and whilst this is relatively easy during the hours of daylight, at night it is more difficult. During periods of the full moon, when the sky is not overcast, it is even possible to use binoculars to observe feeding birds, but under most circumstances an image intensifier is necessary. In areas where there is strong street-lighting e.g. Morecambe, waders can often be seen feeding at night, but here the lighting itself may create an artificial situation. There can be no doubt, however, that waders do feed at night even in overcast conditions, but the results that have been obtained so far are in some ways contradictory. Goss-Custard et al (64) found that most Oystercatchers stopped feeding at night in January and February, whereas Greenhalgh (66) found that they continued to feed at about 50% of the daylight rate on Mytilus and 19% of the daylight rate on Macoma. (This may possibly be associated with mid-day high tides in the north-west of England.) On the other hand, Hulscher (103) found that the feeding rate in captive Oystercatchers in darkness was generally only slightly below the average daylight figure (86%) and above the feeding rate observed during the midday period. In other common species of waders, Greenhalgh (66) found that food intake during the hours of darkness was roughly half that of the mean rate during daylight hours, and that in some species there appeared to be a change of diet. Redshanks and Dunlins take more Hydrobia at night than they do during the day, possibly because of the relative difficulty of locating Corophium in their burrows at night. Even so, night feeding clearly provides the necessary quality of food and, the fact that waders do appear to increase their ingestion rate to compensate for the shorter daylength of winter, even during the shortest days, is of significance although the percentage of time spent feeding may increase. A great deal more work is needed on night feeding at different times of the year before meaningful estimates of the relative importance of daylight and night-time feeding can be made; there can be little doubt, however, that an important part of the food intake of waders occurs in the hours of darkness.

Hulscher (103) has provided information on night feeding in the Oyster-catcher and the method of locating cockles. In daylight captive birds made pecking movements apparently at surface marks made by the cockles, where-as in darkness it walked forwards with the bill at an angle of 70° and the tip below the surface; in this position 'sewing' (up and down) movements were made until a cockle was contacted. When this happened the Oystercatcher attempted to insert its bill between the valves of the cockle. The 'sewing' movement was also used by Oystercatchers in low density cockle beds (less than $40/m^2$) in daylight and it was found that this was, in fact, random searching. At higher densities, in the dark, too few cockles were found to fit the random searching hypothesis. Even so, Hulscher found no significant difference in the daylight and darkness intakes of food, from a biomass point of view. This is interesting with regard to other waders, such as Dunlins, which feed in much the same way.

Food intake can be observed easily in waders taking large food items, for example Bar-tailed Godwits feeding on *Arenicola*. In watching Godwits feed-ing it is unlikely that the observer will miss seeing such a large item but difficulties can arise when, for example, a worm is broken when removing it from the substrate. Again there is little difficulty in assessing how many cockles or mussels an Oystercatcher ingests, but observation on small *Hydrobia* or *Corophium* can be difficult. The peck rate, which can be relatively easily counted, is a crude measure of feeding rate, and using a stop-watch and tally counter, estimates of pecks per minute can be made. It is also necessary to measure the feeding success, that is the percentage of pecks which provide a food item which is ingested. Usually it is possible to detect the swallowing movement, and Goss-Custard (60) showed by reliability tests that this was a good measure of the ingestion of a food item in Redshanks. However, during cold weather, when the feathers are fluffed out, it is sometimes difficult to see swallowing movements, particularly in Knots feeding on *Hydrobia*.

In Dunlin and other small waders the rapidity of feeding movements often causes problems and in some circumstances prey items cannot be seen to be swallowed with certainty. The use of cine photography, with the possibilities of slow-motion replays, is a useful technique in such cases.

Generally speaking, problems concerning the ingestion rate in terms of numbers of items can be resolved, though often different techniques are necessary for different species of prey organisms. Techniques associated with this aspect of feeding ecology have been devised and described in a long series of publications by Goss-Custard (58–65). Estimation of the biomass, and thus the energy content, of the individual food items is more difficult. Waders do not select food items at random but in many cases tend to select larger prey, particularly as the density of the prey species increases (58, 59, 62). It is not, therefore, valid to assume that the mean size of each prey item is the mean size occurring in the substrate (Table 25). In the case of waders feeding on larger molluscs, the shells can be measured after the bird has discarded them. In other cases, food items can be allocated to size classes in relation to the bill size

TABLE 25. Seasonal changes during 1964/65 in the sizes of *Corophium* in the substrate and in the sizes taken by Redshank (after Goss-Custard 1970).

Zone	Date when prey size measured	Mean dry weight of Corophium above 4 mm in length in the substrate (mg)	Mean dry weight of Corophium taken by Redshank (mg)	% change in size taken from autumn to winter
A1	Oct. 15	0.313	0.395	
	Dec. 10	0.291	0.378	−4.3
	Feb. 19	0.250	0.347	−12.2
	Apr. 30	0.359	0.429	
A2	Oct. 15	0.214	0.317	
	Dec. 10	0.250	0.347	+9.5
	Feb. 19	0.230	0.330	+4.1
	Apr. 30	0.319	0.400	
A3	Oct. 15	0.329	0.410	
	Dec. 10	0.344	0.418	+2.0
	Feb. 19	0.284	0.373	−9.0
	Apr. 30	0.493	0.518	
A4	Oct. 15	0.395	0.453	
	Dec. 10	0.321	0.400	−11.7
	Feb. 19	0.330	0.408	−9.9
	Apr. 30	0.468	0.502	
B1	Oct. 30	0.261	0.356	
	Jan. 7	0.240	0.339	−4.8
	Mar. 9	0.228	0.330	
	May 14	0.449	0.489	
B2	Oct. 30	0.245	0.345	
	Jan. 7	0.223	0.325	−5.8
	Mar. 9	0.252	0.339	
	May 14	0.455	0.493	
			Mean:	−4.2

of the bird, and this can be checked either by subsequently shooting a sample of birds (under licence) or by trapping and using emetics to cause the bird to regurgitate the last meal. In either case the food items can be measured and weighed directly.

Shooting and the use of emetics provide information on the qualitative nature of the food intake. Quantitative estimates from these sources are impossible for various reasons. It is not possible to determine over what period of time the gut contents have been taken in and in all cases some digestion has taken place, particularly in the case of soft prey such as small Annelid worms. Emetics do not work as well on wading birds as on Passerines, due to the different structure of the digestive tract, and as a result, only a small part of the gut contents is regurgitated. Even so, these methods have provided important results and can be used to support and substantiate observational data. A study of the use of emetics on captive birds which have been provided with a known food supply would produce interesting results, as may the subsequent gut analysis of similarly fed birds. However, this approach has yet to be tried and whilst the former approach is probably justifiable, a very carefully designed experiment, using marker dyes or tracers, would be necessary to justify the latter.

It is a little surprising that the production of pellets by waders has not been exploited more in the study of their feeding. Most waders produce pellets, though they are more discrete structures in some species, e.g. Curlew, Redshank, than in others, e.g. Knot. They contain the undigested hard parts of their prey and they are egested regularly, particularly on roosting sites. They are readily identifiable in such species as Redshank, Curlew, Knot and Oystercatcher, but in other species it is often necessary to observe the regurgitations to be sure of the species of wader producing them. For these to have quantitative value in feeding studies it is necessary to know the frequency of production and just how much food intake each pellet represents. This can be done satisfactorily with captive birds, where all the pellets produced can be collected. However, field collections of pellets can provide information on diet changes and on food items which possess hard parts. Swennen (236) studied the diet of the Greenshank from pellet collections and found that the most important prey species were the goby (*Potamoschistus*), the shrimp (*Crangon*), the shore crab (*Carcinus*) and the polychaete worm (*Nereis*). In Table 26 a comparison is made between pellet contents of Greenshanks from Holland and Redshanks from the Ribble, and although this may to some extent reflect differences in habitat, it can be seen that the diets of the two species of wader are markedly different, Redshank taking *Hydrobia* and *Corophium* in the main. Swennen estimated that Greenshanks each produce about 5 pellets a day, and captive Redshanks produce about 6.

Goss-Custard and Jones (65) made a study of the diet of the Redshank and Curlew based on the examination of pellets, and the relative abundance of the hard parts of prey in them. Useful information on annual changes in diet can

TABLE 26. Comparison of contents of pellets from Greenshank and Redshank (mean numbers of individual prey in each pellet).

	Potomoschistus microps	Crangon crangon	Carcinus maenas	Nereis diversicolor	Hydrobia ulvae	Littorina sp.	Lamellibranchia	Corophium	Gammarus/Orchestia	Balanus	Diptera	Coleoptera
Greenshank (Swennen 1971)	22.57	19.50	4.00	3.43	1.00	0.03	+	0.30	0.23	+	0.07	0.07
Mean of 30 pellets %	44.02	38.03	7.80	6.69	1.95	0.06	+	0.59	0.45	+	0.14	0.14
Redshank	—	—	0.23	0.60	7.30	—	—	0.79	0.04	—	1.0	+
Mean of 186 pellets %	—	—	2.30	6.00	73.79	—	—	7.90	0.40	—	10.6	+

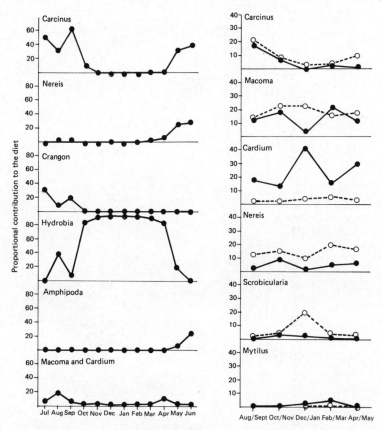

FIG. 59. Seasonal changes in the proportional contribution of the main prey species of Redshanks (left) and Curlews (right) to the total number of prey items represented in a sample of pellets.●———● east shore; o———o south shore. The data were combined into two-monthly periods because of the small number of pellets that could be examined on some occasions (after Goss-Custard and Jones 1976).

be derived from such studies and in Fig 59 the proportion of the diet of Redshanks and Curlews made up by the different prey species is shown. Redshank pellets give a better impression of the birds' diet than do Curlew pellets, as the latter species often ingests only the soft parts of the prey, particularly molluscs. Again, pellet studies in isolation are likely to produce biased results as remains of soft-bodied animals, such as Annelids and Nematodes, are more likely to be ejected in the faeces than in pellet form, and like Curlews, other waders feeding on larger molluscs ingest only the flesh, leaving the shell. The same problems found in pellet studies are to be found in studies

TABLE 27. Peck rate per minute (P.R.) and percentage of successful pecks (P.S.) of Redshanks feeding on *Corophium volutator* (after Greenhalgh 1975).

	No. observations	P.R.	P.S.	Biomass of Corophium in substrate/m²	Intake per hour expressed as		
					No.	g dry weight	kcal	kJ
August	186	64.7 ± 7.6	87.5	9.4	3400	1.20	5.1	21.4
September	114	66.3 ± 9.6	90.6	8.3	3620	1.27	5.4	22.7
October	68	59.8 ± 8.2	84.2	8.4	3030	1.24	5.3	22.3
November	49	61.3 ± 9.8	81.3	7.2	3000	1.23	5.3	22.3
December	135	62.1 ± 9.0	79.2	8.2	2920	1.19	5.1	21.4
January	102	62.3 ± 11.1	65.7	5.8	2420	0.92	3.9	16.4
February	50	65.5 ± 10.5	69.3	4.8	2730	1.04	4.4	18.5
March	91	71.5 ± 8.3	74.0	5.1	3180	1.21	5.2	21.8

Note: calorific value of *Corophium* measured in this study 4.26 kcal per g dry weight ash-included (17.9 kJ).

of the faeces and techniques for their study need to be developed and standardised. It may well be possible, particularly with larger waders, to develop techniques similar to those used in studying geese (179), where frequencies of defaecation and faecal analysis were the major parameters measured because of the difficulty in assessing grazing behaviour quantitatively.

The methods used in feeding studies of wading birds will depend largely on the objectives of the research. To show differences in feeding ecology between species does not require the same type of information as a survey of the effects of predation on the prey species, or the likely carrying capacity of an estuary. Where quantitative data are necessary on the amount of food taken in by a bird, or a population, it can usually be obtained only by watching the birds and recording the intake, though checks may be necessary using other techniques. Intake may vary from month to month so that observations need to be frequently repeated to allow for this. Using the peck rate, an estimate of the number of successful pecks, and the mean dry weight (cf. Table 25), it is possible to estimate the intake per hour in terms of biomass or energy (Table 27). Then, knowing the time spent feeding during a daytime tide cycle (e.g. 67.5% or 486 mins in Redshanks on average) it is possible to estimate the intake per cycle. Taking into account the additional variables resulting from variations in temperature, daylength and tidal cycles, it is possible to estimate the intake of individual birds and the whole population over the winter period. In general birds are most numerous in areas of high prey density because their feeding profitability is greatest here, and there is evidence that some waders may reach ceiling densities on the most preferred parts of their winter feeding grounds.

Studies on wader feeding are complicated by a species feeding on more than one prey species, and preferences apparently change in different parts of a single estuary and with time. Knots take *Hydrobia* very commonly, but where *Macoma* occurs they take this in preference (195); in the period March–May the species also takes *Mytilus* following the spat fall, when these are small. With one or two obvious exceptions the wader species which feed on mud-flats are exploiting dense populations of a relatively few prey species (Table 21) but many must take different less common prey items as they are encountered. All these aspects of the problem must be considered in estimating the daily intake of a wader on the mud-flats.

Away from the coast the feeding of wading birds during the non-breeding season presents even more problems. Plovers feed mainly on low-lying agricultural land where Annelids and insect larvae are their main food supply. Different agricultural practices cause prey population densities to vary, often even more than they do on the estuaries, and direct observation is made more difficult by the vegetation, short though it may be. Snipe, feeding in boggy situations, often take in food with their bill still below ground so that identification is impossible, but J. Swift (pers. comm.) has gone some way towards quantifying the intake of this difficult species in an inland habitat. Tentative estimates based on an intake of 20.8 g of Annelid material per day in the Snipe are particularly on the low side as even in December, Redshanks take in, during daylight, about 1.2 g dry wt of *Corophium* per hour (58,66) which compares with 0.57 g dry wt/hr of Annelids in the Snipe. The mean live weight of the Redshank concerned was about 180 g (Icelandic birds) and of the Snipe 120 g. There is little difference in the calorific (energy) values of *Corophium* (4.26 kcal/g dry wt) and Annelids (4.13 kcal/g dry wt) so that for Snipe, assuming similar activity in the two species of wader, 0.8 g dry wt/hr of earthworms would perhaps be a more realistic figure, equivalent to 29 g of live earthworms. Even this figure is low, as Goss-Custard (58) estimated that less than half the food supply necessary to a Redshank comes from the estuary during the hours of daylight; the rest must come from agricultural land at high water and from night feeding, an equivalent in excess of 32 g of live *Corophium*.

Experiments on captive waders suggest a much higher daily intake of food. In Oystercatchers, Hulscher (102) recorded mean daily intakes of between 117 and 187 g fresh weight of *Mytilus* and *Cardium* in birds weighing from 442–473 g (i.e. from 25% to 42% of the body weight daily) and Sheldon (219) records the American Woodcock, *Philohela*, as consuming the equivalent of their own summer body weight (150 g) in 24 hours. This observation, considered together with that of Liscinsky (136) that *Philohela* fed on only half their body weight daily lost 30% of their weight after 12 days, further suggests that the food requirements of Woodcocks may be greater than those of Sandpipers.

To people not involved in work on the feeding ecology of waders, perhaps the most meaningful way of expressing the food intake is in terms of live weight of food materials. In the Oystercatcher the daily intake is of the order of 40% of its own weight, and in the Redshank 30% of its weight. In a year an Oystercatcher may consume 150 × its own weight of cockles (excluding the shell), some 82.5 kg, or 182 lbs! (equivalent to 13 cwt of cockles in their shells); a Redshank may consume 110 × its own weight of *Corophium* (if it feeds exclusively on this species), some 19.7 kg or 43 lbs. The Oystercatcher may well feed on the same prey species throughout the year, but most wading birds have different diets in the breeding and wintering seasons. The examination of pellets clearly shows that the Redshank's selection of food items changes in April, when a distinct preference for insect foods is shown, even in the saltmarsh habitat. Remains of beetles and dipterous insects, completely absent during the winter months, are commonly found in pellets throughout the summer. The energy content per unit weight is greater in insect material than in marine invertebrates and this is shown in Table 28. In feeding on insects waders are, then, able to obtain their daily energy requirement through the intake of a smaller amount of food, and the time taken to do this may well be smaller than for birds feeding on marine invertebrates. In

TABLE 28. Energy equivalents of different invertebrate prey species (kcals per gm dry wt).

Annelida		
Earthworms	4.1256	C. & W.
Tubificidae	5.137	Teal 1957
Nereis	4.910	
Mollusca		
Hydrobia	1.860	
Cardium	4.590	
Mytilus	4.950	Dare 1973
Macoma	5.030	
Scrobicularia	4.475	Hughes 1970
Arthropoda		
Corophium	4.26	
Insecta		
Coleoptera	5.926	Kendeigh 1967 (in C. & W.)
Tipulid larvae	5.44	G. R. J. Smith
		and J. C. Coulson (per. com.)
Diptera	5.796	C. & W.

C. & W. = Cummins and Wuycheck 1971.

saltmarsh breeding species, Tubificid worms are of importance, particularly to chicks and these too have a relatively high calorific value.

On the northward journey, in spring, waders often take advantage of staging posts to pause, feed and increase their weight for onward migration. These areas are often those occupied by other, wintering wader populations and they are clearly not so depleted of their invertebrates as to fail to provide for their new arrivals. In fact, there is no direct evidence that waders have difficulty in obtaining their food supply during the winter except when the feeding grounds are frozen over, a relatively rare event. In most cases the return to the breeding ground results in a diet different from that of the winter, but initially problems may be found by potential breeding birds in finding an adequate supply of food, particularly in the high arctic where snow is still on the ground.

Most waders turn to insect food during the breeding season. In the high arctic the insect fauna is dominated by Diptera, and Holmes (94) has shown that more than 80% of the insect biomass available to birds is in the form of crane flies (Tipulidae) and non-biting midges (Chironomidae), and their larvae. When birds first return to the breeding grounds they feed very largely on Tipulid larvae, but in mid-season Dunlins turn to Chironomids; in late summer their preference is again for Tipulids and whilst to some extent this reflects the abundance of the various foods Holmes (94) has demonstrated that preference is shown by the adult Dunlin for Tipulid larvae in early and late summer. In mid-season they prefer Chironomid larvae, and newly hatched birds feed entirely on small-sized, adult Chironomids. There appears to be no food overlap between adult and young Dunlins and the available food supply appears to be very efficiently exploited. In the first part of the breeding season in Barrow, Alaska, the Dunlins remain on the high ground and the lower ground, consisting mainly of very wet marshy areas, is unoccupied. At this time the Dunlin is still territorial (Chapter 4), but territorial boundaries break down by the end of July when the food supply and diet are most varied. On the breakdown of the territorial boundaries the birds move on to the drying, lowland areas and exploit the food resources which had previously remained untouched.

Holmes (95) contrasts the high-arctic situation with a sub-arctic habitat. He concluded that the density of Dunlins in the sub-arctic, which was five times that in Barrow, was determined by the larger food resources and by the fact that the reliability of this food source was much greater than in the high-arctic where adverse weather conditions sometimes result in food shortage.

Waders turn to insect food during the breeding season in temperate areas also. The Dotterel feeds mainly on insects and analysis of stomach contents has revealed that adult cranefly and Coleoptera are taken in profusion by chicks (164). Dementiev and Gladkov (31) also record insects as the most important food in summer, in Russia, where they are also known to feed on the seeds and berries of crowberry (*Empetrum*).

Of particular interest in the high-arctic studies was the fact that three other closely related species lived in the same tundra habitat as the Dunlin, exploiting the same food resources, but Holmes and Pitelka (99) considered that the presence or absence of congeneric species does not account for the density difference of the Dunlin between high- and sub-arctic areas. There was clearly a high degree of food overlap between four Barrow species of sandpiper – Pectoral, Baird's and Semi-Palmated Sandpipers, and Dunlins (Fig. 60), particularly in June where *melanotos* and *alpina* take Tipulids in the main and *bairdii* and *pusillus* take Chironomids. In mid-June, *bairdii* switch to Tipulids, like the larger species of Sandpiper. In July, when the Diptera hatch, all four Sandpipers turn to adult Tipulids and to some extent adult Chironomids. The change to Chironomid larvae in mid-July coincides with a fall in numbers of adult Diptera, but *bairdii* does not move down to the marshy areas with the other three species but remains on the high ground feeding on beetles and spiders. By early August the impact of feeding waders on the insect population is reduced by the departure of 1) all the adult *pusillus*, 2) all adult male *melanotos*, 3) most adult *bairdii* and adult female *melanotos*. The only adults to remain in numbers are *alpina* and they return to the upland tundra to feed on Tipulids. The highest degree of overlap is shown by the two large sandpipers, *alpina* and *melanotos* (Fig. 61). It is interesting to see that the degree of overlap between male and female *alpina* is reduced after the departure of other species,

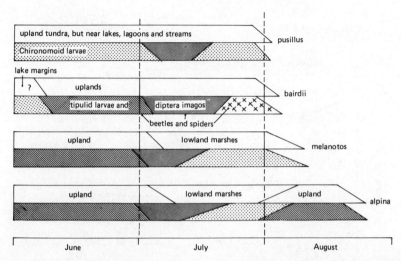

FIG. 60. Generalised scheme of time trends in breeding habitat and diet of four sympatric sandpipers, genus *Calidris*, common near Barrow, Alaska. For each species, the upper part of the double bar indicates chief habitats used, the lower part indicates the chief foods. Refer to upper half of figure for key to diet symbols. For *bairdii*, the late summer food class (beetles and spiders) overlaps with the prior two as indicated (after Holmes and Pitelka 1968).

and this, together with the early departure of other species, suggests that the reduction in food supply has some effect on the numbers of birds on the tundra at this time.

Studies of this type require the collection of samples of birds to examine stomach contents and there is an obvious and understandable reluctance to do this to any large extent, particularly during the breeding season. However, there is one important piece of work which sheds some light on the feeding ecology of sub-arctic waders nesting on peat bogs in Estonia (120). In this study, 206 waders were collected and their stomach contents analysed. Lapwing (6), Golden Plover (144), Wood Sandpiper (30), Curlew (6) and Whimbrel (20) were collected and with the exception of the Wood Sandpiper all were found to feed extensively on Coleoptera and cranberries (*Vaccinium oxycoccos*). The beetle *Plateumaris* was the commonest food organism and apart from this, Lapwings took other beetles and Dipterous larvae. Similarly, Golden Plovers took *Plateumaris* and other larvae in June but turned to berries increasingly in July, and in August berries constituted the most common food item. Wood Sandpipers took mainly soft-bodied invertebrates, including large numbers of insect eggs and some beetles, whereas Curlews took beetles and cranberries, but fed to a large extent away from the bog area. Whimbrels took berries more frequently than the other species and whilst insect food constituted a signi-

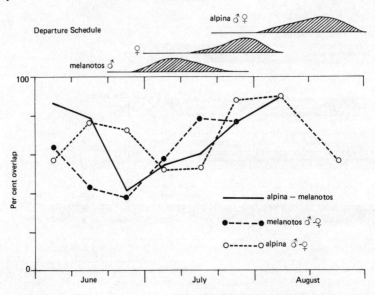

FIG. 61. Indices of diet similarity (per cent overlap) between the sexes of Dunlin and Pectoral Sandpiper respectively, compared with the index of overlap between those two species. Departure schedule at top (after Holmes and Pitelka 1968).

ficant proportion of the diet, wireworms (*Elateridae*) were virtually absent, as they were in Curlews. The most significant aspect of this work was the frequency with which berries were found in the gut contents and clearly, in areas where they occur commonly, they form a significant contribution to the wader food supply during the breeding season. This is also apparently the case in the European Woodcock which Gordon (57) records as consuming great quantities of blackberries (*Rubus fruticosus*) during the autumn.

It is clear from the study made by Kumari that just as there is a large food overlap between species during winter, a similar situation occurs during the summer on the breeding ground, though here different food organisms are concerned. During both periods of the year a relatively small number of prey species, which have a large biomass, are fed upon by several species of wading birds. In arctic Alaska the four species of sandpiper previously discussed in relation to the work of Holmes and Pitelka (99) formed the basis for a study of the ecological determinants of species diversity by MacLean (141). In this latter study it became clear that other sandpiper species which bred regularly, but in small numbers, on the tundra, had their populations restricted in numbers by the presence of the other four species. Several ecological factors might account for this, but food limitation is certainly one of the most probable. Schoener's study of bill size differences in sympatric congeneric species of birds (216) showed large ratios (length of larger species bill: length of smaller species) to occur when congeners feed on low food supplies, and this was the case in arctic Alaska (94), certainly in part of the season. MacLean found that overlap in feeding style was complementary to overlap in feeding habitat, being greatest in late July when the overlap in feeding habitat is least. He concluded that habitat overlap is related to food abundance, and the available evidence indicates that food is a limiting factor on the arctic tundra in this case. Food is most abundant in mid-July and the impact on the food resources is greatest in July and early August during the period when young are actively growing. It seems likely that the departure of adults from the breeding grounds is associated with the decreasing food supply, or has at least evolved to ensure a sufficient food supply for the young; this in itself is indicative that the food supply is being exploited close to its limit, particularly in view of the fact that whilst the food supply is seasonally abundant it is not dependably so. In this it is markedly different from the estuarine and coastal food supplies of the non-breeding season.

Little comparative information exists on the feeding ecology of waders on the breeding ground and on the wintering areas. However, Baker and Baker (7) compared the foraging behaviour and habitat utilisation of six wader species under winter conditions in Florida and on the breeding grounds in eastern arctic Canada. They assumed that under the influence of food limitation, birds of a given species will withdraw into the ecological niche for which they have been selected; in other words they will feed in a specific habitat and in such a way as to provide an optimum return. The authors argue that where there is a super-abundance of food there is probably little direct competition (contrary to recent foraging theory) and food items are taken as they are encountered; when food becomes relatively scarce competition between species occurs, so that it is clearly of benefit to seek prey items in the manner to which they are best suited. Baker and Baker outlined eight foraging methods primarily based on how the bill was used, the method of locomotion and the rate of feeding. By quantifying these aspects of behaviour and relating them to particular microhabitats, statistically different resources were defined. The data thus obtained tended to show a small niche breadth in winter where the waders showed a low behavioural and microhabitat diversity and a low resource overlap between species; in summer a higher behavioural and microhabitat diversity was exhibited and a higher overlap between species. Using the techniques involved, these results might well have been expected. In winter, waders tend to feed in flocks and birds of a species tend to keep together, thus excluding flocks of other species from their immediate vicinity. In summer, most waders feed solitarily, and are not influenced by the presence of other birds near to them, once breeding has started. It is possible that the data obtained by Baker and Baker (7) were affected by the different dispersion of the birds at different seasons, but even if this was not the case their interpretation of the results go beyond that justified by the data. If we accept that, generally, during the breeding season waders occupy a broader niche than in winter, and that there is greater competition for food in winter, this does not necessarily imply that waders are limited through competitive processes occurring on their wintering grounds. It would be interesting to carry out a similar study but to compare results on a monthly or fortnightly basis throughout the year. Comparing seasons does not allow for food being limited only at a specific time of the year. Nor would either study take account of bird movement taking place before a potential shortage of food, which is apparently exactly what happens in the studies of Holmes and Pitelka (99) and MacLean (141) where in some species adults of one sex leave the breeding ground immediately after the hatch; under these circumstances the remaining adults and young would presumably show a higher resource overlap between species than if the other adults had remained. Clearly it is of advantage to the birds to leave an area *before* food becomes short and this is exactly what happens towards the end of the breeding season.

From what we know of wader feeding it is likely that at least some species, e.g. the Golden Plover, are dispersed in the breeding area in densities determined by territories. Whereas territoriality is apparently not associated with an initial food supply, it ensures a dispersion which guarantees sufficient food later in the season, so reducing competition. Thus any examination of food overlap, either inter- or intra-specific, is largely superfluous from the point of view of population limitation if this has already been determined. The results obtained by Baker and Baker (7) are exactly those to be expected if some mechanism, such as territoriality, has determined the breeding season density. Such matters of evolutionary significance will be further considered in Chapter 11.

Lack (142) suggested that if food is the main factor limiting numbers it will be most critical either in late summer when birds are most numerous or in late winter when food is scarcest. A great deal of attention has now been paid to waders in winter, with as yet relatively inconclusive results; work on feeding during the breeding season, to date a neglected area of study, may well prove to be a rewarding area for future research, which might intially be directed to the comparative feeding ecology of a single species throughout the year.

CHAPTER 10

ENERGY BALANCE

OUTSIDE the breeding season most waders obtain their food from the intertidal zone and are dependent upon invertebrates which in turn feed upon suspended matter, in the form of detritus, in the water columns of the ebbing and flowing tides. Other waders feed, to some extent, on invertebrates grazing algae from rock surfaces, some take small fish and yet others rely on earthworms and insect larvae living in soils above the high water mark. During the breeding season most species of waders rely on insect food, earthworms and to some extent berries, and intertidal foods are of little importance.

Between the tides the organisms upon which the waders feed depend almost entirely on detritus suspended in the water but some detritus and algae may be taken from the surface of the mud flats. In general the detritus is derived from material brought down by the river, brought in from the sea by currents and washed off the salt marsh. In a very simplified form the food web of the estuary, which consists of many food chains, is shown in Fig. 62. It is very difficult to quantify such a system, since there are so many inputs to it, the detritus, on which the majority of the invertebrates depends, being contributed to by the zooplankton, the salt marsh vegetation, the algae and the decaying remains of animals and plants which have died.

Probably the best means of illustrating quantitatively what is happening in the estuarine ecosystem is to express the relationships between the component parts in terms of energy exchange. As in all other ecosystems the initial energy comes from the sun and is fixed by photosynthesis. The amount of radiant

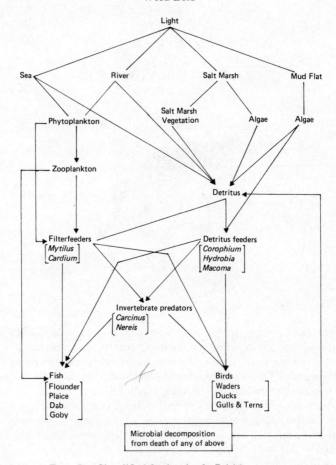

Fig. 62. Simplified food web of a British estuary.

energy transformed into the chemical energy of plant tissues varies between 1% and 5% of the total, depending upon the plant populations fixing it. In some ecosystems, such as the oceans, the plants are then grazed by animals, and this grazing food chain is the most important in terms of energy flow; however, in the estuarine ecosystem the detritus chain is of greater importance than the grazing chain and it is through this chain that the majority of the energy flows through the different trophic levels, first into the main invertebrate detritus feeders, and then into their predators, such as fish and birds. At each level in the food chain energy is required for respiration and for growth and it is only the latter portion of the energy flow which is potentially

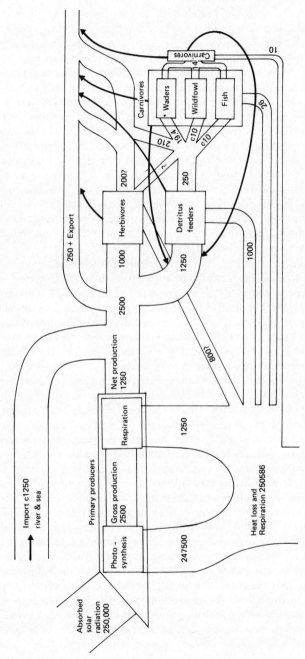

FIG. 63. Hypothetical energy flow diagram for the Ribble Estuary, Lancashire. Figs in kcal/m²/year.

available to the next level in the chain. Energy fixing plant communities are virtually absent from many parts of the estuary and therefore every thousand units of solar energy which are put into the estuarine ecosystem, approximately only 10 are utilised by the photosynthetic plants (primary producers), about 5 for respiration and about 5 for building new plant material. Of these latter 5 units perhaps 2 will be utilised by grazing animals, but the other 3 may well find their way to the decomposers (mainly Bacteria and Fungi) to become potentially available to the detritus feeders. It is therefore probable that significantly less than $\frac{1}{4}$% of the energy from the initial solar radiation is used, in respiration and in forming body material, by the detritus and filter feeders upon which the wading birds themselves feed, while approximately an equal amount comes from material washed in by the river and the sea. Assuming that the quantity of solar radiation falling on an estuarine ecosystem in the British Isles is of the order of 250,000 kcal/m^2/year, less than 1250 kcal/m^2/year would be a reasonable estimate of the energy flow through estuarine detritus and filter feeders, assuming that half of this was imported from the river and sea (Fig. 63).

To obtain an estimate of the energy content of the food supply of the prey species of wading birds would be immensely difficult. However, some indication of the energy flow through those populations of invertebrates on which waders feed is possible through sampling at intervals throughout a full calendar year. A series of between ten and thirty sample units of known area and depth taken from the mud flat substrates and carefully sorted for the animals, which are then counted, gives a mean number of each species per unit area on which may be placed an estimate of error in terms of the standard deviation or standard error of the mean. Such a sampling programme will normally give population estimates within an error of 10–15% of the mean. From the point of view of the effort involved it is fortunate that the number of prey species is small, or can be considered to be from the point of view of the exercise. In an average estuarine situation the main detritus feeders are *Corophium*, *Arenicola*, *Hydrobia* and *Macoma*; the main filter feeders are *Mytilus* and *Cardium* and the only invertebrate predators of significance are *Nereis* and *Carcinus*. In some circumstances other amphipods may replace *Corophium* in terms of their significance as a food supply, and molluscs such as *Scrobicularia* may be of local importance; in other areas one or two important food species may be entirely absent, but on the whole a consideration of the ecological energetics of these eight wader food species will give a reasonably accurate picture of the state of affairs on a generalised British Estuary. Table 24 gives mean monthly densities of estuarine invertebrates on the Ribble and Morecambe Bay, but these data are for the various species where they occur. For example, on the Ribble the impression is given that *Nephthys* sp. occurs in densities only half that of *Nereis*, but this is only in very small areas where it replaces *Nereis* so that for the purpose of these estimates it can be ignored. On most estuaries *Mytilus* and *Cardium* occur in isolated beds of high density, and to some extent this also applies to the lugworm *Arenicola*, so that for the most part the mud flats are mainly inhabited over most of their area by mixed populations of *Nereis*, *Corophium*, *Hydrobia* and *Macoma* with some *Carcinus*. Together (Table 29) these have a net production of 202.1 kcal/m² yr. Molluscs make up the greater part of this estimate. It has been shown that

TABLE 29. Estimated mean standing crop and net production of common invertebrate prey species in a temperate estuarine ecosystem.

	Standing crop (g dry wt/m²)	Estimated production biomass (g dry wt/m²)	Energy content kcal/m²
Annelida			
Nereis	5.2	7.8	38.30
Arenicola	100	150	736.5
Crustacea			
Corophium	6.5	9.8	
Carcinus	2.5	3.8	41.7
			16.0
Mollusca			
Hydrobia	7.9	11.9	
Macoma	11.1	16.7	22.1
Mytilus	142.3	213.5	84.0
Cardium			1053.0

Estimates based on hand sorted samples only, without correction for predation.

respiration accounts for 79% of the energy flow through a population of *Scrobicularia* (101) and 86% of the flow through salt marsh *Littorina* (177) so that, accepting a figure of 80% respiration, the total energy flow through the mixed *Nereis*, *Corophium*, *Hydrobia*, *Macoma* and *Carcinus* population would be of the order of 1010 kcal/m²/yr approximating to the 1250 kcal/m²/yr estimated by taking 0.5% of the incident solar energy as passing through the detritus chain. However, the former estimate takes into account only the density of animals which have been derived from the sampling programme. In other words, no account has been taken of animals removed from the flats by predation. Thus, in order to obtain a figure of true net production over the period of a year, the biomass taken by birds and fish must be added. The estimate of annual production thereby becomes considerably more complex as the amount (biomass) of various prey taken needs to be estimated.

Where almost single species populations of invertebrates occur, there appears to be a greater productivity and in all three species *Arenicola*, *Mytilus* and *Cardium*, the energy flow is considerably more than the estimate based on

incident solar energy and, with the addition of the fraction taken by predators, this will be even greater. This can probably be accounted for, however, by the relatively small areas occupied by such populations in terms of the
whole estuarine complex, and the fact that other mud flat areas are significantly less productive so that, on average, the energy entering the detritus
feeders might still be of the order of 1250 kcal/m². Even so, there can be little
doubt that this figure is exceeded in some estuaries, but in terms of net
production of potential wader food some 200–250 kcal/m², plus the fraction
taken by predators, is produced annually in temperate estuarine conditions.
This does not mean that this sum is even potentially available to waders, and
this problem needs examination. From direct observation it can be seen that a
large part of the fraction taken by predators is taken by wading birds and it is
equally clear that this is available to them. It is possible, though improbable,
that all the net production estimated by sampling is unavailable to waders
(and other predators) but the fact that a large part of it is present throughout
the year, at or close to the surface of the mud, suggests that it is available
should it be required. Availability of food has already been discussed in
Chapter 9, but it is worth stressing that invertebrate prey within bill depth of
the various species of waders are almost certainly available when uncovered
by water and when their activity is sufficient (the temperature high enough)
to attract the attention of feeding birds.

In order to estimate the fraction of the invertebrate productivity which is
taken in by the wading birds, it is necessary to know the numbers of wading
birds of each species feeding on the area in question, the amount of food each
species takes in a given time, the duration of feeding each day and the number
of days each year that each species feeds. To date there has been only one
comprehensive study which has attempted to provide this information and
that is the work carried out by Greenhalgh (66) on the feeding ecology of
wading birds on the Ribble Estuary. In this study regular counts of all the
waders were made from the ground and checked by aerial surveys of the type
described in Chapter 7. A figure for annual 'bird-days' for each species was
calculated and food intake was measured by direct observation and by
collection of specimens under licence. The basic data obtained in this way are
shown in Table 30. Only the main species of waders and the main prey species
of invertebrates are shown together with a figure of standard metabolic rate.
The standard metabolic rate (SMR) is the minimum rate of metabolism in a
resting bird in an environment with a temperature the same as its own body
heat, whilst not digesting or absorbing food. During normal activity waders
probably utilise between two and five times the energy requirement of the
SMR, though the data obtained by Greenhalgh (66), from actual feeding
rates, suggests that the variation may be from $1.77 \times$ SMR (Redshank) to
$6.30 \times$ SMR (Oystercatcher). Clearly, in estimating the daily food intake of
waders there are several sources of error, but it seems likely that the daily
energy intake, on average, is likely to be around $4 \times$ SMR. In captivity
Oystercatchers took in a maximum of 231 kcal/day (calculated from Hulscher

TABLE 30. Energy utilisation of wading birds on the Ribble Estuary.

	Bird days × 1000	Standard metabolic rate kcal/day	Daily food intake in kcal/day	kcal × 10⁶/year				Total for general feeding area	Mytilus bed
				Nereis	Corophium	Hydrobia	Macoma		
Oystercatcher	637	47.6	300*	—			95.60	95.60	95.50
Grey Plover	161	25.0	[75]	Feeds mainly outside estuary					
Ringed Plover	5.6	11.0	[33]	0.06	0.06	0.06	—	0.18	
Curlew	132	44.0	130*	5.54	—	—	11.62	17.16	
Black-tailed Godwit	58	39.0	86*	4.99	—	—	—	4.99	
Bar-tailed Godwit	1186	34.3	97 (Nereis)* 148 (Macoma)	57.50	—	—	87.76	145.26	
Redshank	785	22.6	40*	3.14	26.16	1.96	—	31.26	
Turnstone	30.4	14.0	[42]	Feeds mainly on mussel beds on other invertebrates					
Knot	9885	21.0	67*	—	—	62.56	599.73	662.30	
Sanderling	955	12.6	[37.8]	Feeds mainly on Bathyporeia					
Dunlin	9429	10.2	38.5*	—	47.15	235.70	80.10	362.95	
Total consumption of each prey species kcal × 10⁶/yr				71.23	73.37	300.28	874.81	1319.70	95.50
Total predation by waders /m²/yr				1.05	1.08	4.42	12.85	19.40	4.89
Total production not taking into account predation /m²/yr				38.30	41.70	22.10	82.50	184.60	1053.00
Total production taking into account predation by waders but not fish /m²/yr				39.35	42.78	26.52	95.35	204.00	1057.89
% of production taken by waders and calculated from Greenhalgh (1975)				2.66	2.52	16.67	13.47	9.51	0.46

[]   estimated from SMR

(102)) and American Woodcock about 78 kcal/day (calculated from Sheldon
(219)). These figures are roughly equivalent to $5 \times$ and $4 \times$ the SMR.
American Woodcock fed on 49 kcal/day ($2 \times$ SMR) lost weight as described
in Chapter 9, and whilst captive birds do not utilise the amount of energy that
wild birds need, these results suggest a necessary intake of energy of approximately $3-4 \times$ the SMR. In the estimates in Table 30 only the Redshank and
Black-tailed Godwit fall below this level; it is possible that the Redshank takes
a proportion of its food supply, not allowed for in Table 30, from the salt
marsh and inland fields. Pellets show *Carcinus* to be an important constituent
of the diet and almost certainly this prey is obtained from channels on the salt
marsh. Black-tailed Godwits may take some small prey which go unnoticed
during observations, but it is unlikely that this species takes much more than
the estimated food supply and so the energy intake possibly is below
$3 \times$ SMR.

In the estimates shown in Table 30 it has not been possible to allow for the
fractions of the net production of the invertebrate populations which are
taken by wildfowl and by fish. Shelduck undoubtedly take a significant
proportion of *Hydrobia* as do flat fish and it may well be that failure to allow for
this has caused the relatively large figure for the percentage of total production taken by waders. Overall, it appears that less than 10% of the total
invertebrate net production is cropped by the waders. *Hydrobia* and *Macoma*
have a higher percentage of their production cropped (17.0% and 14.0%
respectively) than other invertebrates and this is not surprising since both
form the food of the Knot which accounts for more 'bird-days' on the Ribble
than any other species of wader. The levels of production of other prey
cropped by waders are much lower (Table 30), 2.66% in *Nereis*, 2.52% in
Corophium and 0.46% in *Mytilus*. These are much lower figures than might be
expected, particularly in the case of *Mytilus* which is cropped by Oystercatchers. Oystercatchers cropping *Mytilus* and *Cardium* in other estuaries take
a much higher proportion of the prey, which suggests that the relatively small
mussel bed on the Ribble could support a higher population of Oystercatchers. On the Ythan, Milne and Dunnet (157) estimate that Oystercatchers
take 7.2% of the production of mussels, whilst Eider Duck, which are absent
on the Ribble, take 2.1%.

It may be that estimates of the order of 10% of the annual productivity, as
the proportion taken by wading birds on the Ribble, is not typical of estuaries
as a whole. The tentative estimates for the Dee, Wash and Burry Inlet are
higher (Goss-Custard pers. comm.) but are not yet published and may be
subject to some modification. It is important to consider cropping in terms of
annual productivity since, firstly, much of the production of invertebrates
occurs when the birds are absent yet remains to be taken when they arrive
and, secondly, estimates of what is cropped in relation to the standing crop
(the biomass present at any one time) will give a very false picture of the
proportion of potential food.

A tentative energy flow diagram for the Ribble Estuary is shown in Fig. 63. It may well be that in this diagram the grazing food chain is shown to have a greater significance than in fact it has; what is significant, however, is to stress that the detritus food chain is of paramount importance and depends basically on dead plant material washed from the salt marsh and other organic material and detritus washed in from the sea and down the river. It may well be that in Fig. 63 both the net production of the primary producers and the energy import from outside the estuarine ecosystem are underestimated. It is this import from outside the ecosystem that gives rise to the relatively high productivity of the estuary and to the 'nutrient trap effect' described by Odum (176). This is particularly important in considering conservation strategies within estuaries and this is examined further in Chapter 13.

Before leaving the topic of energy balance in the estuarine ecosystem it is worth considering the relative contributions to it of the different wader species. On the Ribble the Knot accounts for almost half of the energy flow through the wader population and this is not surprising considering the numbers which are present. What is perhaps surprising is that the species, despite its large numbers, consumes less than 5% of the productivity of the invertebrates over the year. Next in order of importance is the Dunlin which accounts for 28% of the energy flow and compared with these two species in these terms all the others are of relatively little importance. The Bar-tailed Godwit is responsible for 11% of the energy flow and the Oystercatcher only 7%. This latter is perhaps somewhat anomalous on the Ribble as these populations are much lower than they were twenty years ago, before the crash of the cockle population in the winter of 1962–63. In most estuarine situations Oystercatchers would be responsible for a greater part of the energy flow than they are on the Ribble and this possibly accounts for the fact that less than 10% of the annual productivity is cropped by waders. This leaves the rest of the wader populations accounting for only 4% of the energy flow, so that in this context even such common species as the Redshank, Curlew and Sanderling can be considered to be of relatively little significance.

Several factors contribute towards the errors involved in estimating the energy intake of wading birds, and, at least theoretically, some check on the accuracy of the estimate should be obtainable by measuring the energy output. This, in general, involves the estimation of the parameters of the equation:

Food intake = Tissue production + Respiration + Waste material
              (growth and reproduction)   (faeces + nitrogenous
                                                  excretion + pellets)

Ideally a study of the energetics of a population should aim at solving the whole equation, but, under field conditions, this is often very difficult. Some discussion has already taken place on estimating food intake, where errors can be large; on the right-hand side of the equation equal difficulty occurs, but different groups of organisms provide different problems. For example, in geese the estimate of waste materials is much easier than in waders, since the faeces are more compact, dryer and form a mass which does not coalesce with particles in the substrate on deposition.

In estimating the parameters on the right-hand side of the equation Tissue Production, in terms of what is added to the population, can be considered to constitute the energy going into egg production and chick growth, whereas Respiration (eggs, chicks and adults) takes account of replacement tissues, heat maintenance and general metabolism; Waste Material, measurable from faeces production accounts for a significant loss of energy intake. The estimation of the energy involved in each of these parameters requires the measurement of a large number of variables which could involve large errors. Considering first Tissue Production there is little difficulty in measuring the energy equivalent of the eggs, as this can be done directly by burning the material in a bomb calorimeter. However, once hatched, it becomes necessary to estimate the mortality at different stages before fledging. This mortality is affected by weather conditions and the presence of numbers of predators which may vary from season to season. Different species may have different growth rates and different ages and sizes at fledging, and these factors must also be taken into account. In order to obtain information for a particular habitat where the production of prey organisms might be known, it is necessary to follow through the fledging period sample broods of all predator (wader) species in the area. This is an immense task and only one good example occurs in the literature where several species have been followed simultaneously; this is the work of Norton (175) where four species of Calidritine Sandpipers were studied in Alaska. In this study chicks were reared in captivity, weight increases recorded, respiration measured and faeces collected and burned to obtain their energy equivalent. At the same time increases in weight were recorded in marked birds in the field and, using a combination of laboratory and field data, Norton estimated that a single Dunlin chick utilised some 1135 kcal between hatching and fledging. Carrying out similar exercises with the other three species he calculated that the surviving fraction of chicks (those fledging) utilised some 560 kcal/hectare during their growth, and adding the energy used in the mortaility fraction (those dying before fledging, my calculation) this gives an overall estimate of 1105.1 kcal/hectare (Table 31).

From these data it follows that the daily energy intake of Dunlin chicks, in Alaska, must range from 4–6 kcal/day in the first day or two after they hatch, to about 80 kcal/day immediately before fledging, with a mean of 51.6 kcal/day. This is high compared with the estimate for wintering adult Dunlin in the UK, where the daily intake was estimated to be 38.5 kcal/day, this being a mean over the whole of the non-breeding season. Again, Heppleston (85) gives figures of 50.1 kcal/day and 81.0 kcal/day (mean 66 kcal/day) for food intake in the two halves of the fledging period of the Oystercatcher; as a

TABLE 31. Energy intake of *Calidris* chicks between hatching and fledging at Barrow, Alaska.

| | Weight gain | Chicks fledged/nest | Density nests/hectare | Energy intake | | Total kcal/ha [2] |
				Surviving fraction kcal/chick	Mortality fraction kcal/chick	
Dunlin	49.5	1.43	0.11	1135	2217	348.7
Baird's Sandpiper	35.9	0.76	0.18	822	1606	219.7
Pectoral Sandpiper	71.6	1.40	0.09	1640	3205	403.8
Semi-palmated Sandpiper	21.7	1.38	0.10	493	963	132.9
Total						1105.1

Based on data from Norton 1973 (recalculated)

proportion of the daily winter intake of adults (300 kcal/day) these figures are significantly below the arctic estimates for the Dunlin. However, considering the growth factor, and the low temperature experienced on the breeding ground, the two estimates for adult Dunlins and chicks are of the same order of magnitude. Again, estimates for adult male and female Dunlins on the breeding ground are significantly above the wintering estimates and Norton (175) gives a figure of 67 kcal/day for the male Dunlin and 73 kcal/day for the female Dunlin. These estimates are nearly twice those of wintering birds obtained by Greenhalgh (66), whose estimates were made by calculating the food intake, whereas Norton's estimates were made largely from respiratory studies.

The gross energy requirements of the Alaskan Sandpiper is shown in Table 32, together with the daily requirement, and from this latter figure it can be seen that this requirement is of the order of 6 × the standard metabolic rate; approximately twice that estimated by Greenhalgh for metabolism in a

TABLE 32. Gross energy requirements of *Calidris* sandpipers in Alaska (after Norton 1973).

| | ADULTS | | CHICKS | |
	*Maximum** metabolic rate kcal/Bd/day	*Gross energy intake kcal/Ha*	*Energy intake kcal/Ha*	*Total kcal/Ha*
Dunlin	♂ 67	835		
	♀ 73	915	348.7	2098.7
Baird's Sandpiper	♂ 52	427		
	♀ 60	315	219.7	961.7
Pectoral Sandpiper	♂ 110	422		
	♀ 86	397	403.8	1222.8
Semi-palmated Sandpiper	♂ 39	185		
	♀ 44	196	132.9	513.9
Total		3692	1105.1	4797.1

* Equivalent to daily food intake kcal/day in Table 30.

temperate winter situation (66). In estimating these figures allowance has been made for loss of energy in faeces and excretion, so that totalling the overall energy requirements of adults, chicks and egg production should give an estimate of the energy content of the food intake. This amounts to 4797.1 kcal/ha (my calculation) or to less than 0.5 kcal/m^2, less than $\frac{1}{40}$th of the level of the estuarine predation on the Ribble by waders.

The arctic tundra in Alaska provides an ecosystem which is in many ways easier to sample for its invertebrate population than are most temperate ecosystems. MacLean (142, 143) and MacLean and Pitelka (144) have provided information on the insect fauna which is the main food supply of the Sandpipers. In Chapter 9 the main food organisms of the Sandpipers were seen to be Tipulids (Craneflies) and Chironomids (non-biting midges), and whilst other organisms are taken they are of little significance in providing the energy requirements of the four main species of Sandpipers. Holmes (94) has shown that in the Dunlin (Red-backed Sandpiper) more than 95% of the food of adults is provided by the Tipulid population and 85% of the food of chicks. This amounts to 1662.5 kcal/ha for adults and 296.4 kcal/ha for chicks, a total of 1958.9 kcal/ha/annum. MacLean* (175) estimated the annual production of Tipulids as some 20,000 kcal/ha, so that Dunlins alone are responsible for cropping 10% of the annual productivity. The level of energy uptake by the wading birds as a whole (4797.1 kcal/ha) is of the order of 24% of the production of Tipulids. Norton (175) estimates that 25% of the total *Calidris* requirement comes from adult Tipulids (1200 kcal/ha) so that a maximum of 3600 kcal/ha is required of the larval population. This is only 18% of the productivity of the larval population (all Tipulid productivity is larval). However, according to MacLean (142) predation by adult *Calidris* species is limited to 4th instar larvae which over a period of two years were responsible for only 62.5% of the total productivity. It therefore follows that the waders were obtaining 2700 kcal/ha from Tipulid larvae (the other 900 kcal/ha was from adult Tipulids) which had a productivity of 12,500 kcal, so that in fact they were cropping over 20% of the available productivity. The energy content of the whole of the emergent population of Tipulids is smaller than the total *Calidris* requirement so that the larval population is essential to provide the necessary food supply for the birds which are present for approximately 45 days on the tundra. The hatch is spread over only 15 days, so again the larval population is necessary from this point of view, and it may well be the low productivity, the low growth rate and the long period of vulnerability of the prey which allows high densities of breeding waders in arctic conditions. In the case of the Alaskan *Calidris* this density was of the order of 50 nests per km^2, a density reached elsewhere in non-colonial birds only in salt marsh conditions, where the productivity of the food organisms is high.

To some extent the breeding waders are probably responsible for the short period of the adult Tipulid presence on the tundra. MacLean considers that the first emerging Tipulids are taken immediately by birds, and only the emergence of very large numbers at one time ensures that some lay before they are taken as food. It seems likely, therefore, that early and late emergence in tundra Tipulids is selected against because of the likelihood that they will be eaten before they lay. Norton (175) regards it as likely that considerably more than this original estimate of 25% of adult Tipulids are taken by waders at Point Barrow, as at the height of the emergence parts of undigested Tipulids

* In Norton.

occur in the waders' faeces, which suggests that the birds are eating more than their normal requirements.

There can be little doubt that the abundance of insect life in arctic conditions is responsible for the relatively high numbers of breeding waders. But is this food source as easily obtainable by the waders as their winter food supply on the estuaries? From what evidence is available, it seems likely that on the breeding ground waders crop a much higher proportion of the total productivity of the invertebrates on which they feed. Even if the estimates made on the Ribble by Greenhalgh (66) are too low, and wading birds in winter have a daily energy requirement nearer 6 × the standard metabolic rate, their intake is still below the percentage of the invertebrate productivity taken from the tundra. It is often argued that under the conditions of almost continuous daylight in the arctic summer, birds are able to feed for longer periods. This may be the case in Passerines, but there is little evidence to suggest that wading birds feed less efficiently at night in winter, and there is certainly some evidence (102) which suggests little or no such reduction in nocturnal feeding efficiency. It is also likely that in the arctic summer waders do not encounter their prey as easily as they do in winter. Adult Tipulids emerge at a density of only up to 10 individuals per m², when they occur at all, and it is likely that it is immobile individuals that are taken most easily. It is probable that they are encountered less easily than most estuarine invertebrates which occur in densities of several hundreds or thousands per m², but their energy content is undoubtedly greater per individual. Again, Tipulid larvae are much more sparsely distributed than estuarine invertebrates, and almost certainly have to be sought for more carefully, as signs of their activity in the tundra soil will be to a large extent obscured by the vegetation.

As in the winter habitat, there are few signs that the food supply on the breeding ground is exploited close to its limit. In the arctic the only real evidence available is the departure in some species of one parent bird when the clutch has hatched, and from what has already been shown, were these birds to remain, they would take a significant part of the invertebrate productivity. The very fact that they do go strongly suggests better feeding elsewhere. The fact is that there is relatively little information about feeding on the breeding grounds, and Norton's (175) study of the Arctic Sandpipers is certainly the best available at the present time. It does seem likely that the energy flow from the primary consumers on the breeding ground, insects, to the secondary consumers, the wading birds, is greater in terms of the productivity of the primary consumers than the energy flow from detritus feeding invertebrates to waders on the shore. This fact, in itself, does not necessarily suggest that waders are nearer to the limit of their food supply on the breeding ground than they are on the shore, as little is known about the real availability to the waders of the invertebrates. However, it could be said that there appears to be no greater difficulty obtaining food in winter than there is in summer, though Baker and Baker (7) argue differently (see page 205).

It can be argued that an X% consumption of a large super-abundance of food may be much less damaging to the food supply than the same percentage consumption of a poorer intial supply. Certainly, on the arctic breeding grounds it is only the extended life cycles of the prey species which makes them available at all, and a relatively high percentage of the preferred size classes are taken; once these have been removed they are not replaced until the next season. On the estuaries a much greater density of food organisms occurs, but during winter a proportion of this is unavailable because of the depth at which it occurs. For example, whereas half the *Macoma* of the size range taken by the Knot are near enough to the surface to be caught in autumn and spring, only 7–9% are accessible in mid-winter (205). Similar changes in depth distribution undoubtedly occur in other invertebrate food supplies, which, with the onset of spring, move nearer the surface. Thus the food supply of the wintering area may be replenished in a way that does not occur on the breeding ground and is an additional factor which suggests that waders are nearer to the food limit on the breeding area.

Whether or not waders are nearer their food limit on the breeding ground than on the wintering area does not, in itself, indicate that food is acting as a limiting factor. However, it may be that taking a higher percentage of the available food supply increases the difficulties of feeding and increases competition to the extent that food does become limiting and, whilst this has yet to be demonstrated, the likelihood of its occurrence appears to be greater on the breeding grounds. It may well be that waders possess a mechanism (territoriality?) which prevents them coming up against the limits of their food supply, but the fact that different mechanisms and feeding strategies (Chapter 9) have been evolved suggests that it has at least been worthwhile evolving some degree of feeding partition; the fact that this partition still exists strongly indicates continuing selection pressures. An examination of these pressures and the likely areas in which they have been selected may well provide some evidence to point to the season of the year when this might have occurred, and this is done in the following chapter.

To a large extent the comparison of energy flow through wader populations in winter and during the breeding season depends on estimates of the standard metabolic rate (SMR defined p. 212) and by what factor this must be multiplied at different times of the year. This will be the case until such time as more accurate estimates of food intake and energy output are available. Variation of this actual metabolic rate from the SMR is clearly affected not only by the degree of activity of the birds but by the temperature of the environment. It may well be that breeding birds in the high arctic have a similar metabolic rate to wintering birds in a temperate climate, but it will probably be considerably lower in temperate breeding birds. It is unlikely that the energy intake in temperate regions in winter reaches $6 \times$ the SMR and Goss-Custard (62) uses a factor of $4.9 \times$ SMR for estimation of energy intake of wading birds on the Wash. This figure is derived from a union of two of his own estimates of $4.2 \times$ SMR for Redshanks on the Ythan and $5.8 \times$ SMR for Oystercatchers on the Wash, together with two estimates of $5.2 \times$ SMR and $4.5 \times$ SMR for Bar-tailed Godwits at Lindisfarne (221). Using a factor of $6 \times$ SMR waders take 15.5% of the invertebrate productivity on the Ribble; using $4.9 \times$ SMR, 13%. It is likely that on average waders use considerably less energy than $6 \times$ SMR as this is the increase recorded by Pearson (186) in continuously flying humming birds as compared with birds at rest. It is likely that energy intake in wading birds wintering in the British Isles is of the order of 10–13% of the productivity of the invertebrates; in other words somewhere between the estimate made by Greenhalgh (66), Goss-Custard (62) and that calculated from estimates of the proportion of the standing crop removed. Different species of waders may not necessarily have the SMR increased by the same factor, even under similar conditions as some species may use energy-expensive methods, so that the factor of $6.3 \times$ SMR, which results from the measured intake of food in the Oystercatcher on the Ribble (compared with $5.8 \times$ SMR on the Wash (62)) and the factor of $3.77 \times$ SMR for Ribble Dunlins could both be accurate estimates. On the other hand Norton's estimates of energy intake on the breeding ground (175) are of the order of $6 \times$ SMR, but even allowing for this, the percentage of invertebrate productivity taken by the Alaskan waders on the breeding ground is higher than the percentage taken from estuarine conditions.

It may be that the food requirements of some populations of breeding waders are greater than their requirements in winter, particularly as some arctic breeding waders may well experience lower temperatures during the breeding season than in winter e.g. Curlew Sandpiper. In winter their food intake balances energy loss in maintenance of body temperature, flight and food gathering; in summer there are the additional drains on their energy resources of breeding, in the form of display, egg production and rearing young, though this last factor will be small in waders.

The effects of wind, tides, temperature and daylength have already been discussed in relation to feeding and Evans (46) has reviewed their possible effects in relation to the distribution and movements of waders in winter. Of particular interest is his consideration of a situation which occasionally arises where food gathering is not cost-effective. Occasionally situations occur where, due to the weather, food gathering becomes difficult and as a result the behaviour of the feeding birds changes. The extreme situation occurs where no feeding takes place at times when birds would normally be feeding, and this has been recorded in very cold weather and during gales. However, before this state is reached in the Bar-tailed Godwit, a different feeding method is adopted (221). Above 3°C the Godwits feed largely on *Arenicola* searching an area between 9 and 10 m²/min. Below 3°C, as the *Arenicola* become less active, the birds search smaller areas and take more *Scoloplos*, walking more slowly and thus reducing energy output. Theoretically there comes a point when the energy costs of foraging are no longer replenished by food intake, at which point it is more profitable to stop feeding. Clearly this is an abnormal situation and one which occurs either very infrequently (cold winters) or very temporarily (gales), but the change in feeding strategy, as this point approaches, is of more than theoretical interest. Adaptability to different situations is important in the energy balance of wading birds and has certainly contributed to the success of the group.

It may be that under some circumstances it is necessary to minimise the time taken to obtain the necessary energy intake and in this context Evans (46) draws attention to the influence of predation on some wader populations. In California, Page and Whiteacre (181) have shown that up to 21% of Dunlins, 12% of Least Sandpipers, 8% of Western Sandpipers, 13% of Sanderlings and 16% of Dowitchers are taken by raptor predation in winter so that in these circumstances food is obtained in the shortest possible time to allow flocking to take place for longer periods as an anti-predator device. In Europe the level of predation is much lower, but it is possible that feeding grounds, where the required energy can only be acquired slowly, might be made unusable by heavy levels of predation. This might also be the case in some breeding areas. In the British Isles predation is not a very common cause of mortality, and starvation in winter is generally regarded as the greatest cause of mortality. Goss-Custard *et al* (64) had shown that even though mortality is normally low, waders are, on average, ten times more likely to be found dead in winter than in autumn and spring. They are also most likely to be found dead in an emaciated condition in cold spells, which suggests that at least some birds are not able to maintain an energy balance during very adverse conditions. Heppleston (84) estimated that 33% of Ythan Oystercatchers died in one cold spell. The likelihood is that on most British estuaries, and those further south, waders have a plentiful supply of food normally available to them. In conditions where the activity of the prey species is reduced, and where freezing conditions prevent access to it, waders are unable to take in sufficient food, and under these circumstances some mortality occurs. High winds and blowing sand occasionally make feeding difficult, but it is unlikely that such conditions would persist long enough to prevent feeding; almost certainly food is present in sufficient quantities for wading birds both on the summering and wintering grounds, if they can get it. Availability is probably the over-riding factor, and it appears to be only when food becomes difficult to obtain in the available time that large numbers of deaths occur, particularly in small waders that feed near the top of the shore (198). Should adverse weather conditions affect the invertebrate food supply of the waders, as was the case in the crash of the cockle populations of Morecambe Bay and the Ribble in the winter of 1962–63, then the waders move elsewhere. If waders are present for any length of time, there is almost certainly more than sufficient food for them to maintain their energy intake without too much difficulty, provided it remains available to them. If the food was insufficient, or difficult to obtain for any length of time, there would be few or no waders; their presence implies an adequate food supply and energy source to meet their needs.

PLATE 17. *Above*, Oystercatchers showing the white collar of their winter plumage wait for low tide. *Below*, Redshanks and Curlews roosting at high tide in winter.

PLATE 18. Godwits alight at their high tide roosts.   *Above*, Bar-tailed God-wits; *below*, Black-tailed Godwits.

PLATE 19.
Inland communal
roost of Curlews
during breeding
season; mid-Wales.

Grey Plovers in
flight, showing the
gaps left by the
moult of the inner
primaries.

Adult Grey Plover
moulting in
autumn.

PLATE 20. *Above*, Spotted Redshank in full moult. *Below*, wader pellets. Top row, summer (left) and winter (right) pellets of Redshank; bottom row, Curlew pellets containing cast gizzard linings.

PLATE 21.
Feeding waders.

Avocets 'sweeping'
in deep water.

Red-necked
Phalarope
'spinning'.

Black-tailed Godwit
shading water
surface in the
fashion of a Sun-
Bittern, whilst
attempting to take
small fish.

PLATE 22. *Above*, high tide roost on salt marsh; Bar-tailed Godwit, Oystercatcher (top right), Dunlin (foreground) and a small clump of Knot (centre). *Below*, mud-flat roost on a lower tide; Knot (left), Bar-tailed Godwit (top left), Oystercatcher (right centre) and Dunlin (foreground).

PLATE 23. *Above*, tightly packed Knot on a sub-roost on the mud-flats. *Below*, an active sub-roost of Knot on the mud-flats.

PLATE 24. *Above*, Oystercatchers alighting at a roost on agricultural land before a high spring tide. *Below*, Dunlin reach high numbers even where industry encroaches onto the estuaries.

MORTALITY AND EVOLUTION

CERTAIN aspects of mortality in waders have already been examined. It is likely that the mortality rate is lower than is shown by ringing recoveries, and that the highest level of adult mortality occurs in winter as a result of cold weather and starvation or, in some populations, as a result of predation (181). In the biology of wading birds, mortality has two important aspects; firstly, in relation to population regulation and, secondly, in relation to the evolution of various characteristics, where differential mortality results in their selection.

As in most other animal groups, the population sizes of different wader species vary between upper and lower limits in such a way that the total population of each species fluctuates relatively little about the mean value. Clearly some mechanism must operate to maintain this level and density dependent factors are the most likely agents. Density dependent factors may affect either, or both, of the birth and death rates, but in most cases the latter. Most species of wading birds usually lay a clutch of four eggs, so the birth rate is not affected by variation in clutch size. The birth rate could be affected if some birds are prevented from breeding when numbers are high; this is the mechanism suggested by the results of Holmes' (95) work on the Dunlin in Alaska. From a comparison of two breeding populations of different densities he concluded that the density of breeding Dunlins is related to the abundance and availability of food, and that territorial behaviour disperses the population in relation to food. It does seem that this situation exists since the experimental removal of breeding birds resulted in recolonisation of the vacant territories by other birds, thus demonstrating the existence of a pool of non-breeding birds. However, since in each study area the territory sizes remained the same over the period of study, it seems likely that they had been arrived at by a process of natural selection, and were not subject to modification at short notice as a result of varying food supplies. Soikkeli (227) considered that territory in the Dunlin is related to pairing and other features of sexual behaviour, and that the density is regulated by factors which are themselves density dependent, and which control small variations in breeding success. The implication of Soikkeli's argument is that the breeding success, at least in the Dunlin, is controlled by the action of density dependent factors on the mortality of chicks during the fledging period rather than by any effects on the birthrate.

It is very difficult to determine the pattern of mortality throughout the year although, from an evolutionary point of view, this is not particularly important. Most mortality is likely to be density independent, but where starvation occurs in winter there is a possibility that some differential mortality might be involved. The important aspects of mortality are those which are density dependent and those where differential mortality results in the maintenance of the characteristics of different populations. Since such characteristics as breeding plumage are clearly selected for use in the breeding season and on the breeding ground, it may be possible to find other characters which have a particular use at a particular time of the year and thus pinpoint the timing and location of selective forces. Establishing when and where density dependent mortality occurs is more difficult and this whole area is one of speculation rather than the analysis of known facts leading to a reasonable conclusion. However, some speculation is justified in that this might point to fruitful areas of research.

There is a little evidence to suggest that in winter flocks there is a higher mortality among larger groups. Page and Whitacre (181) have shown that Merlins have greater success attacking flocks of over 50 waders than smaller ones although there is an even higher success rate in attacking single birds. There may be an element of density dependent mortality here and this probably merits further investigation. Whilst predation may be responsible for some density dependent mortality, it is difficult to see other factors, apart from disease and the possibility of food shortage, acting during the non-breeding season. In this connection it has not proved possible to demonstrate that food acts as a limiting factor (Chapters 9 and 10) except when it is unobtainable, and then mortality is not density dependent. The fact that it has not proved possible to demonstrate density dependent mortality does not, of course, mean that it does not occur, but certainly in winter it is difficult to see when and where it might.

Transferring attention to the breeding season, similar problems occur; predation, disease and food shortage are again the most likely causes of density dependent mortality. Soikkeli (227) found a high mortality rate of 27% for breeding Dunlins in Finland. This does appear to be very large in relation to annual mortality; however, there is no indication from this work that predation increases with density, though I have certainly got the impression that this is the case with the Redshank. Certainly nest losses are higher in dense breeding populations, and both carrion crows and ground predators (fox, mink, rat) take a higher proportion in densely nesting salt-marsh populations than they do in inland, more sparsely distributed populations. Both egg and nest losses, and chick losses, are far greater in the dense salt-marsh populations than I have recorded elsewhere. In some ways the Redshank might be considered to be a poor example to choose, as it is largely non-territorial, and groups of nests tend to be lost if a predator finds one. Redshank appear to stimulate the nesting of other Redshanks in the immediate vicinity of the nest (say within 20 m), and groupings of clutches laid within a few days of each other are to be found in dense salt-marsh situations; a predator finding one of such a grouping often finds others. Disease cannot be discounted, but there are so few records of it affecting wader breeding populations that its effect is probably insignificant, though of course, a very small density dependent effect can have considerable significance in population regulation. Food shortage, again, is as difficult to demonstrate during the breeding season as in winter. It may be that on the initial arrival at the breeding grounds (particularly in arctic breeders) there is difficulty in obtaining food, and this could well act in a density dependent way; however, it has not been shown to do so in waders, although this might be a profitable line of research to follow. If a shortage of food occurs at all it is likely to be later when the chicks hatch but in many species the establishment of a given breeding density through territoriality ensures that this does not happen. Adults are able to move considerable distances to feed, whilst chicks cannot and, as has been described earlier (Chapter 2), they are often led to suitable wet areas to feed. In certain circumstances such wet places may be few, and food shortages could then give rise to density dependent chick mortality. It is possible that in particularly dry seasons normally suitable wet feeding spots will dry up so that movement to other areas becomes necessary, leading to increased mortality of chicks because of their greater vulnerability while moving. This is much more likely to occur in temperate areas than in the arctic. Under some circumstances it is possible that competition between pairs with young may also result in mortality. Occasionally waders will attack the young of other pairs of both their own and other species; on the other hand as has already been described, wandering chicks are sometimes adopted.

With a limited number of suitable feeding areas, mortality will be more severe at high densities than at low densities, though the availability of suitable areas will depend largely on the climate. This is of some theoretical interest ecologically, since climatic vagaries usually result in density independent mortality. Here, climate is acting in conjunction with the paucity of feeding areas in a density dependent manner and might therefore play a significant part in population regulation. In the high arctic, such a situation is less likely to arise, but adverse weather conditions can have important effects on the availability of insect food (95) and this in turn results in a poorer, survival of wader chicks. Adult Dunlins respond to such a situation by leaving the breeding area and moving to the coast, presumably after the loss of young. Most of the mortality involved in such cases is density independent, in many cases resulting from failure to maintain body temperature under cold, wet conditions, but it is possible that a density dependent element may arise if some birds find pockets of adequate food supplies. In these circumstances a situation similar to that caused by drought conditions in more temperate areas could well result.

Much of this discussion is mere speculation, but on the whole it does seem likely that most, if not all, density dependent mortality in waders occurs in the breeding season and that chicks are most likely to be involved. There is a higher mortality rate amongst young birds immediately after fledging and perhaps for the first six months of life, as compared with adults (15). In birds generally, Lack (123, 127) maintains that the size of population is mainly governed by density dependent mortality of the young from leaving the nest to the onset of winter, and that the main density dependent factor is food. There are no reasons to think that waders should be considered to be different from other groups in this respect, but real evidence is wanting. The difficulties of estimating fledging success and chick mortality are very great in wading birds, but this should be regarded as a priority area for future work, as conservation strategies may depend upon information of this sort.

It has already been seen in the discussion of geographical variation (Chapter 3) that populations of the same species of wading birds possess different characteristics in different parts of the range. These characteristics are selected for by pressures in the areas where they occur, so that a study of them is likely to indicate where selection pressures exist and when competition for the various resources for which the characters are selected occurs. Variation in overall size in wading birds has probably received more attention than other characteristics, and it is probable that an examination of this may well provide information which has more far-reaching consequences than are initially evident. Two of the so-called eco-geographical rules are of interest in relation to size. Bergmann's Rule, which has already been commented on in Chapter 3, is defined by Mayr (146) as stating that individuals in populations of a species of warm-blooded animals (homoiotherms) which occur in cooler climates, tend to be larger on average than individuals of the same species living in warmer climates. Allen's Rule (1) is an extension of Bergmann's Rule which states that in homoiotherms there tend to be a reduction in size of protruberant parts of the body in cooler climates. In both cases the effect on the organisms concerned is to conserve heat. From the point of view of warm-blooded animals, cold is generally associated with the winter season, but this is not necessarily the case in wading birds. Many waders spend the winter in warm climates and breed in the arctic so that, at least in some cases, it is the breeding season during which they experience cold; probably the only time of the year when many species, e.g. Curlew-Sandpiper, Greenshank, experience freezing conditions is at the beginning of the breeding season when they first arrive on the breeding area. It has been shown in Chapter 3 that in waders there are, generally speaking, east-west clines in overall size shown during the breeding season. In Fig. 13 this is related to temperature for the Redshank, and it seems likely that in other species showing similar variations in overall size the relationship is again with temperature. This is not necessarily always the case in birds, and Snow (224) demonstrated a 'latitude' effect in titmice, where the limitation in size was apparently related to the effects of shorter day-length in northern latitudes on feeding time. In waders the reverse could be the case if larger birds were found in the northerly areas; during the breeding season, the time when waders are in the north, a longer daylength is available to them for feeding. But, with the exception of some of the Icelandic waders, e.g. Redshank, the most northerly birds are not the largest. Again, waders are quite capable of feeding at night which also militates against a 'latitude' effect.

Williamson (251) considered size in relation to migration and concluded that selection operates most powerfully during the actual period of migration. This suggests that a greater body weight, coupled with an increase in wing and tail length, would occur in birds making a sea crossing (Greenland/Iceland to Continental Europe) as compared with those moving overland, and in Redshanks, Whimbrels, Purple Sandpipers and, to some extent, Oystercatchers, this appears to hold. The Black-tailed Godwit apparently provides an unexplained exception. Here again, as in Salomonsen's interpretation of selection for size (Chapter 3), only the Western Palaearctic has been considered and the argument that long wings/large size are associated with overseas migration appears to fall when, for example in the case of the Redshank, birds of equal size and wing length are found to occur in Western USSR where no overseas migration is necessary.

In 53 species of North American birds, Salt (214) showed that larger birds occurred on the edge of the ranges and in the centre of the range birds were relatively small. He interpreted this as an increase in overall efficiency unrelated to the habitat, pending the evolution of specific adaptations to new habitat requirements. This argument does not appear to apply to the majority of waders, though it is an interesting concept. Hemmingsen's (82, 83) studies of size do have relevance to the behaviour of waders, for he found that in several Asian species of birds the timing of migration was correlated with body size. Birds arriving first at the breeding grounds were larger, those arriving last smaller. This is exactly the situation described in Chapter 3 for the Redshank, where the small brown birds from Lapland breed later, and is probably also the case in the Ringed Plover (246). It can be considered that the timing of laying is related to temperature (Chapter 3), so that smaller birds are laying in warmer conditions and larger birds in colder conditions; in the strict sense this is really an example of Bergmann's rule as is the case where size has been related to altitude (203, 160 and 108).

Geist (in press) puts forward the proposal that large forms of warm-blooded animals have been a feature of periglacial ecosystems throughout evolutionary history, whereas smaller forms occur in warmer areas. He argues that the high productivity of such evolving systems makes large amounts of food available to large, long-lived and infrequently producing organisms. Such an argument seems to have little basis in fact since, today at least, such primitive ecosystems are characterised by small, frequently reproducing and short-lived animals.

There seems little doubt that variations in size in wading birds are related to temperature, though Salomonsen (211, 212) claims that selection for size takes place in the winter range. His conclusions are based on the observation that, in the Redshank and Ringed Plover, large birds tend to winter in the north of the wintering range and small birds in the south. The argument is largely based on the various populations of these two species being allohiemic (Chapter 6), and he rightly points out that the allohiemy is seldom complete and does not need to be to affect the evolution of a species. There can be no doubt that the populations of both the Redshank and Ringed Plover are to some extent allohiemic, but whether sufficiently so to ensure selective adaptation of the type suggested by Salomonsen is open to question. Figs 33 and 37 show that birds from eastern Europe and western USSR complicate the picture provided by Salomonsen to an extent that in several areas large and small birds winter together. Under these circumstances it is difficult to see how that particular environment can have resulted in the selection not only of the size of bird appropriate to the proposed winter cline, but also of the different size of groups. A very different genetic make-up allowing selection to operate on each group is one possible explanation, and another is that recent changes in wintering areas have resulted in large and small birds wintering together; neither is a likely explanation, particularly since selection for a common size is likely to take place rapidly, as is evidenced in changing wing lengths in Scandinavia (Chapter 3).

It has already been explained (in Chapter 6) how Salomonsen obtained indirect measurements of wintering populations. The validity of his argument has now been assessed by obtaining actual winter measurements of a series of birds from the wintering range (from Museum collections). The data (wing lengths) obtained for the Ringed Plover are shown in Fig. 37 and for the Redshank in Fig. 64. In the Redshank data there is a clear trend showing that there is a tendency for smaller birds to occur in the south of the range in winter and larger ones to occur in the north, in both males and females. A similar trend can be shown in the Ringed Plover. However, in the Redshank, the correlation coefficients show that only a small percentage of the variability in

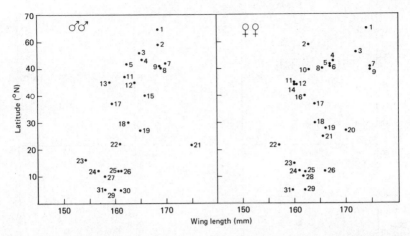

FIG. 64. Mean wing length of winter populations of Redshanks. 1, Iceland; 2, UK 1; 3, UK 2; 4, UK 3; 5, Denmark/Germany; 6, Western USSR; 7, Holland; 8, UK 4; 9, Belgium; 10, Czechoslovakia; 11, Austria/Hungary; 12, Italy; 13, Eastern USSR; 14, Rumania; 15, Tien Shan; 16, Greece; 17, Tunis; 18, North-west India; 19, Syria; 20, North-east India; 21, Arabia; 22, China; 23, Burma; 24, Philippines; 25, Siam; 26, Aden; 27, Sierra Leone; 28, South India; 29, Malaya; 30, Somalia; 31, Nigeria (after Hale 1973).

the data is accounted for by these regression lines (39.7% for males and 31.4% for females). When the data are separated and shown in groupings according to longitude (each group 50° wide), as in Fig. 65, no variation of wing length with latitude is discernible in the regions 30–80°E and 80–130°E. Similar results were obtained from an analysis of tail length.

Even if the trend suggested in Fig. 64 is accepted this does not necessarily indicate selection for size taking place in winter. Male Redshanks from Nigeria are not significantly smaller than birds from the British Isles, 50° of latitude further north, nor are the females any different; birds from the Malay Peninsula are similar in size to birds from the British Isles, again 50° of latitude further north. Many similar examples can be found in both wing length and tail length which suggests that size is not selected for in the winter range.

If size is selected for in the winter range, and the populations are al-lohiemic, it is to be expected that winter populations will have mean measurements similar to those of the breeding areas from which they originate and that the standard deviations will have similar values. Some of the data are in close agreement with Salomonsen's hypothesis; winter measurements of wing length from the Camaroons and Sierra Leone and the Gambia are identical with those from breeding Redshanks in Northern Norway and Sweden, and winter mean measurements from Tunisia are similar to the measurements of breeding Redshanks from Austria and Hungary. However, the measurements

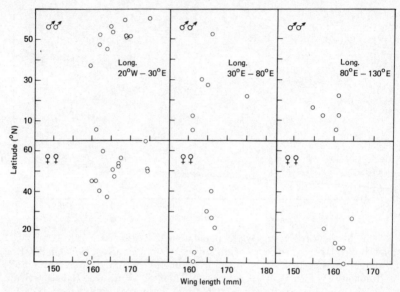

FIG. 65. Variation in wing length with latitude in different parts of the winter range of the Redshank (after Hale 1973).

of two of the Tunisian birds clearly indicate that they are of Russian origin. In Italy the measurements are greater than would be expected if the wintering population was entirely of Danish birds; again Russian birds appear to be responsible for this result. In most cases the standard deviations are greater in winter populations, indicating a greater heterogeneity of the wing measurements, but in many cases the data are few and significant comparisons are not possible.

It is quite clear that in certain parts of the range of both the Redshank and the Ringed Plover, no allohiemy exists, and this is also the case in other wader species. However, the argument will be restricted to these two species since they are those on which Salomonsen's hypothesis was based. In the Philippines and the Malay Peninsula, both the largest Redshanks (from Northern India and Tien Shan) and the smallest birds (from Eastern USSR) have their winter quarters. This was originally deduced by measurement of museum specimens, but Dr D. R. Wells was kind enough to send me a series of skins, of Redshanks in breeding plumage, recently collected by him in Malaysia, and specimens referable to all these populations figured amongst them. In the region of the Persian Gulf, small birds from Finland, and probably the Kola Peninsula, winter alongside large birds from Central Asia, and Redshanks from the USSR as large as Icelandic birds winter in the Mediterranean in

Egypt and as far west as Tunis. Whilst selection may operate in a given environment to produce quite different end results in closely related species, it seems unlikely that it would operate within a species to produce both large and small individuals, despite the fact that they may originate from geographically very different areas.

Salomonsen claims that when populations of Redshanks and Ringed Plovers are compared in their breeding areas the variation in size makes no sense. This is apparently true for the western European populations which have probably been derived from two genetically different populations (Chapter 3) and are now largely hybrid. Outside the western European hybrid zone there is an east-west cline in the wing measurements of the Redshank during the breeding season (Fig. 12), and in the Ringed Plover there is little change in measurements across Eurasia and in Iceland/Greenland but there is a suggestion of clinal changes in North America (Fig. 5). When the relationship between wing length in the Redshank and minimum recorded May temperature is examined (Fig. 13) there is a very clear pattern in the breeding season measurements and there can be little doubt that at least in this instance the overall size is selected for by spring temperature on the breeding ground.

However, it cannot be denied that there is a tendency for smaller birds to winter further south in most waders. In the Redshank, and probably the Ringed Plover, it appears that size is selected for in the summer range but that there is an advantage in smaller birds migrating further south; in other words, populations of smaller individuals of a given species winter in the south because they are small – they are not small because they winter in the south.

An apparent anomaly in the argument arises in the case of the Redshank. Across Eurasia the size of the dark cinnamon-coloured birds increases from the Amur to the Urals (73); why is it that similar selection did not result in an increase in the size of the dark-brown Redshank occupying the western European seaboard, where colder conditions prevail? A clue to this can perhaps be found in the present-day distribution of the Redshank (Fig. 8). The cinnamon birds to the east of the Central European hybrid swarm are clearly not adapted to breeding as far north as the brown form and their northerly range does not encroach beyond latitude 60°N. It is perhaps worth speculating that this may well have been because Greenshanks and Spotted Redshanks occupied the northerly latitudes in the east of the range and did not spread westwards until later. In contrast to the cinnamon Redshanks, the brown form breeds up to 71°N and has become adapted to this without increase in size. It is possible that the dark brown coloration is of adaptive significance in colonising the colder parts of its range and it is interesting in this respect that the Redshank from the high Himalayas in northern India and Tibet (up to 16,000 ft) are identical in colour with the Northern Scandinavian birds. However, it is more likely that it is the lateness of return to their breeding grounds which enables the small brown birds to breed in Northern

Scandinavia, to where they probably spread originally because of the absence of the Greenshank and the Spotted Redshank.

The majority of ringing recoveries of birds from the northern Scandinavian population of Redshanks occurs in May, so it is clear that the northerly spring movement is relatively late. Any selective pressures to which these birds are subjected on the breeding ground will not be in operation until late May or June, and this in itself may be sufficient to produce the small size, as the temperatures at this time of the year will generally be higher. June minimum temperatures from 22 stations in northern Norway, northern Sweden and Finland give a mean absolute minimum of 28°F. Following the regression line shown in Fig. 13, this temperature corresponds to a wing length of 158.6 mm, which is only slightly larger than those recorded from northern Scandinavia (73). It therefore seems probable that the wing length in the brown form of the Redshank has been selected for in the same way as in the cinnamon birds, but that the main difference between the two genotypes lies in the physiological adaptation of the cinnamon/hybrid birds to latitudes below 60°N. With the amelioration of the Scandinavian climate, discussed in Chapter 3, the hybrid birds are now spreading north and the small brown birds are at a selective disadvantage.

It seems clear that there must be a higher survival rate in the small brown Scandinavian Redshank if they migrate than if they remain in Norway and Sweden for the winter. Conversely, the survival of the larger British and Icelandic birds must be enhanced by their sedentary dispositions and it seems likely that they are able to remain in the north of the wintering range because of their larger size. The brown form probably colonised Scandinavia from the south after a cold climatic period. Whilst the cinnamon birds adapted to different climatic conditions by an increase in size in colder areas, the brown form colonised the more northerly parts of the range by selection for a later breeding season; this later breeding could account for the more northerly distribution of Redshanks in the western part of the range and for the apparent clinal winter distribution in the west.

It has been argued earlier that two populations of the same species with different genetic make-up could possibly account for the selection of different sizes in the same environment. Clearly genetic differences of the magnitude of those between the small brown and larger cinnamon birds might be sufficient for such selection, but it has been seen that to achieve the difference in the breeding season a time (temperature) differential is necessary, and similar temperatures apparently result in the selection of similar sizes. This can be considered to justify the original assertion (p. 230) that it is most unlikely that a single winter environment may produce populations of different sizes in the Redshank.

Two alternative strategies have been adopted in the past by wading birds colonising colder regions. Either a population increases the mean overall size of the individuals composing it and breeds early, or the individuals remain

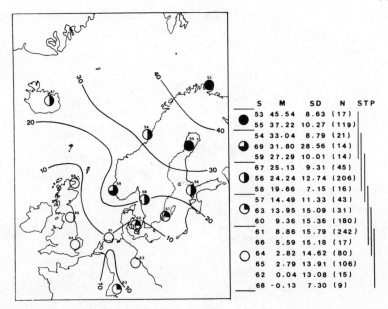

S	M	SD	N
53	45.54	8.63	(17)
55	37.22	10.27	(119)
54	33.04	8.79	(21)
69	31.80	28.56	(14)
59	27.29	10.01	(14)
67	25.13	9.31	(45)
56	24.24	12.74	(206)
58	19.66	7.15	(16)
57	14.49	11.33	(43)
63	13.95	15.09	(31)
60	9.36	15.36	(180)
61	8.86	15.79	(242)
66	5.59	15.18	(17)
64	2.82	14.62	(80)
65	2.79	13.91	(106)
62	0.04	13.08	(15)
68	-0.13	7.30	(9)

Fig. 66. Geographic variation in the date of laying in the Redshank; sample numbers 68 (Spain) and 69 (Kashmir) originate from outside the range of the map. On the right, data give sample number (**S**), mean (**M**) (here day on which the first egg of the clutch was laid, counted from 1 May), standard deviation (**SD**) and sample size (**N**). Vertical lines to the right of the columns delimit maximal non-significant (P<0.05) subsets of samples (**STP** test on ranked means). The range of means is divided by the amount of black in the circles. These, together with the isophenes, delineate the pattern of geographic variation (after Väisänen 1977).

small and the birds breed later. Dates of breeding in the Redshank and the Ringed Plover are shown in Figs. 66 and 67; considered together with Figs 5 and 9, the pattern becomes clear. Only during the breeding season is there a discernible and consistent pattern of variation in mean size in wading birds over the whole of the range; no such pattern is present in winter, and it seems reasonable to conclude that size is selected for during the breeding season. It is possible that factors other than temperature are involved in size selection in wading birds, but the evidence available at the present time suggests that this of overriding importance. If the interpretation of selection for size in wading birds is correct, then a differential mortality must occur early in the breeding season or, alternatively, low temperatures may act to prevent a higher proportion of smaller birds from breeding; either mechanism would result in selection for larger birds in cold areas.

Considerable attention has been paid in previous chapters to food and

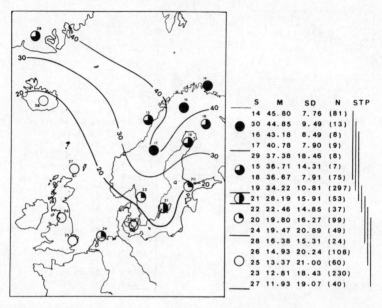

S	M	SD	N	STP
14	45.80	7.76	(81)	
30	44.85	9.49	(13)	
16	43.18	8.49	(8)	
17	40.78	7.90	(9)	
29	37.38	18.46	(8)	
15	36.71	14.31	(7)	
18	36.67	7.91	(75)	
19	34.22	10.81	(297)	
21	28.19	15.91	(53)	
22	22.46	14.85	(37)	
20	19.80	16.27	(99)	
24	19.47	20.89	(49)	
28	16.38	15.31	(24)	
26	14.93	20.24	(108)	
25	13.37	21.00	(60)	
23	12.81	18.43	(230)	
27	11.93	19.07	(40)	

FIG. 67. Geographic variation in the date of laying in Ringed Plover. For legend see Fig. 66. Sample No. 30, from Canada, lies outside the range of the map (after Väisänen 1977).

feeding in waders, and to the differences and similarities in these in the summer and winter ranges. In any comparison of waders, attention is almost invariably drawn to the variety of bills to be found in the group, usually in relation to probing for invertebrate food (usually in a winter habitat) and the depths to which different species can reach to obtain it. The point has already been made that just because an animal uses a particular structure to achieve a certain end does not necessarily mean that it has been evolved specifically for this purpose. The assumption is often made that waders' bills are for probing. Certainly many of them use them in this way, but have they really evolved for this purpose? Clearly the main use is in feeding, but some light might be shed on bill evolution by an examination of the variation similar to that carried out for overall size.

Bill size within a species is very much a reflection of overall size of the bird; large individuals tend to have large bills and small individuals, small bills. In the Redshank the bill is usually 25–27% of the wing length, but this varies in different parts of the range. In Plovers, which have bills much smaller in relation to the wing length, variation is not so great, nor is a clear pattern visible. In Redshanks, only in Sinkiang and north-west India does the bill reach 28% of the wing length, and in northern Norway and Sweden it falls as low as 25% with an Icelandic minimum of 23%. Redshank bill length measurements across Eurasia follow the pattern of the wing length and only in Iceland is there a significant difference, where the bill is considerably shorter. The winter distribution of Icelandic Redshanks largely overlaps that of birds from the British Isles and therefore it appears unlikely that the differences which occur (23% wing length as compared with 26% in British birds) could be a result of selection in the same environment. Redshanks from Sinkiang and north-west India winter alongside small birds from the extreme east of the range, as is shown by direct measurement of wintering birds and, whilst it is recognised that only a degree of allohiemy is necessary to produce different mean measurements, it is unlikely that the large differences which occur, both in actual bill length and the ratios of bill/wing length, could be accounted for by winter selection (Sinkiang 44.5 mm, 28% of wing length; north-west India 46.2 mm, 28% of wing length; eastern USSR 39.5 mm, 26% of wing length). In other waders such as the Ringed Plover, Golden Plover, Dunlin, Knot, Greenshank, Spotted Redshank, Bar-tailed and Black-tailed Godwit, similar patterns are found where mean bill lengths change gradually over the breeding area, but winter measurements show no clear pattern.

How different bill lengths are selected is obscure. In the case of the Icelandic Redshank and the Greenland Dunlin, the relatively short bill is possibly an adaptation to the low temperatures of the environment in spring (this provides examples of Allen's Rule). In the Redshank, however, it is more difficult to account for the large bills present in north-west India and in Sinkiang. A possible explanation is that whilst overall size is selected for by the low temperatures of early spring, bill length is selected later during the breeding season, possibly when there may be competition for food with young

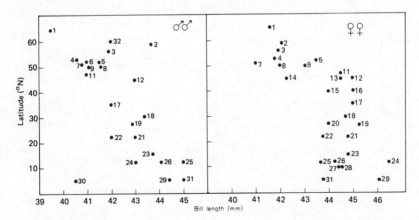

FIG. 68. Variations in bill length of the Redshank, with latitude in the winter range. For legend see Fig. 64 (after Hale 1973).

of the year. This would account for the relatively longer bills in western USSR and central Asia in comparison with Icelandic birds of similar overall size. Whilst spring temperatures are similar in Iceland and central USSR, the latter area experiences much warmer summers; this also applies in Kashmir and Sinkiang, where relatively long bills occur. Mean winter bill lengths are shown for different wintering populations of the Redshank in Fig. 68, plotted against latitude; there is little or no correlation and it is only in the data from the breeding season (73) that there is a discernible pattern over the range, indicating that selection takes place at this time of the year.

In most wading birds, variations in the tarsus length follow those in the bill length. This suggests that at least to some extent tarsus length is also related to feeding activities. Throughout the breeding range of the Redshank the tarsus length varies between 29% and 33% of the wing length, and like the bill length, varies directly with the size of the bird except in one or two specific instances. In Iceland the tarsus is at its shortest relative to the wing length, but the shortest mean tarsus measurements are from the British Isles. Here again is an example of Allen's Rule for which further instances can be found in tarsus length. The Greenland Dunlin and Iceland Black-tailed Godwit have the shortest tarsi for those species, and in all waders the pattern of tarsus length is clear only in the breeding season. The argument put forward for bill length being selected for during the later breeding season can also be applied to the selection of length in the tarsi, and Fig. 69 shows that there is no relationship between latitude and tarsus length in the Redshank in winter; a similar lack of relationship between tarsus length and latitude is found in other waders in winter and there can be little doubt that in waders generally, tarsus length is selected for on the breeding ground.

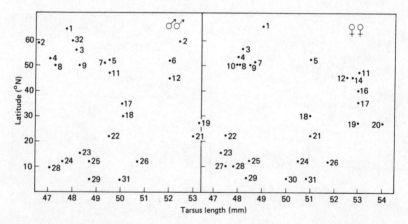

Fig. 69. Variations in tarsus length in the Redshank with latitude in the winter range. For legend see Fig. 64, p.231 (after Hale 1973).

It does appear that Allen's Rule applies to both bill and tarsus length in waders, at least in some populations. Both these structures are associated with the collection of food and are probably selected for on the breeding ground. It is possible that the selective pressures brought to bear involve competition for food, and the fact that selection takes place in the breeding season implies that greater competition occurs at this time of the year than at other times. At the end of the breeding season the wader population is at the annual peak and relatively restricted to suitable breeding areas. It may well be that at other times of the year, when selection pressures are reduced, there is a super-abundance of food except when it is unavailable due to excessive cold and ice formation. Considering all the evidence based on morphological characters, it does seem that the breeding season is the time of the year when competition for resources is greatest and selection operates to modify characters which might be of advantage to different species of wading bird.

CHAPTER 12

CARRYING CAPACITIES IN THE
NON-BREEDING SEASON

DURING recent years, threats to some of our larger estuaries involving the building of barrages and similar enclosures, have drawn attention to what might happen if such engineering programmes were initiated. Clearly, if large areas of present day mudflats were permanently inundated by fresh water, as was intended, then these would no longer be available for feeding waders. In some areas the displaced birds might move to other parts of the same estuarine complex but in other places the reclamation might well be of such a scale as to cause the birds to seek other wintering grounds. The case has already been made for the importance to waders of the system of estuaries in western Europe. From the wader counts (199) it is known that wader numbers are distributed throughout this area, but are these at or near their limits? Are our estuaries full as far as waders are concerned or could more be accommodated in all or even some of them? Does a reduction in the feeding area available to wading birds mean a reduction in overall numbers, or can present day numbers even be increased within the present complex? These are some of the questions that ecologists working on waders have been seeking to answer for some time and to date there has not yet been a completely satisfying answer to any of them.

The carrying capacity of an estuarine complex (the maximum numbers of birds it can support), from the point of view of wading birds, may depend on many factors some of which have already been discussed in previous chapters. Basically a suitable wintering area must cater for the two main needs of waders, an adequate food supply and an undisturbed roost. The particular importance of a suitable roosting site has already been discussed at length, but one factor of importance in this context has not yet been touched upon. This is the importance of an undisturbed roost at all states of the tide, in other words several undisturbed sites, on the mudflats and the highest parts of the saltmarsh for the highest tides. There is a natural advantage to the waders in the sea-ward side of the saltmarsh normally being the highest point of it, and the presence of a good spring-tide roost is one of the most important factors in those estuaries maintaining a high carrying capacity. Numbers on the Cheshire Dee have fallen significantly as a result of disturbance at roosts, and whilst waders will spend some high-tides on the wing, it is doubtful if they will continue to do this if they are continually disturbed, and their numbers will, no doubt, fall.

The lack of suitable roosting sites will not necessarily be obvious. It has already been seen that there is considerable movement between estuaries in winter and it may well be that where waders do not find a suitable roost, they move on, only for other birds to move in, which in turn might move if no suitable roost is present. Thus, an estuary may appear to be supporting numbers of birds which are, in fact, part of a transient population, and it is possible that the Cheshire Dee is such an estuary. Only the regular observation of marked birds is likely to provide evidence of this.

Apart from feeding and roosting the only other really important aspect of the estuary, as far as a wader is concerned, is as a moulting ground. If feeding and roosting facilities are adequate it is likely that it will provide a suitable moulting area, but here again lack of disturbance is of prime importance, both during feeding and in roosting, as the period of the moult is one of relatively great expenditure and replacement of energy.

Probably the single most important factor which might limit the carrying capacity of an estuary is the amount of food both present and available to the birds. Food may be regarded as a limiting factor when birds can no longer obtain sufficient for their needs. In these circumstances they will either starve to death (or a proportion will) or they will move elsewhere, usually before the effects are felt. Food may be unavailable to birds because of its absence or occurrence in small quantities, or because it is present but unobtainable. Where food is present, but unobtainable, this may be for two reasons. Firstly, it may be out of reach of the birds' bills at lower depths in the substrate, to which a large part of the prey population may move in the winter season or, secondly, it may be because of cold conditions. In these circumstances the substrate may be frozen, or sufficiently cold to reduce the prey's activity to a degree where the birds are unable to see signs of movements and discover the prey item. This second situation is usually relatively short-term in the British Isles as freezing conditions on the mudflats rarely persist for any great length of time, but the first situation is relatively long-term and a large proportion of the potential prey of waders is out of reach for a considerable time during winter.

Clearly there are several factors which may result in food being limited, but from the point of view of the birds concerned this can be viewed as a single problem to which there may be several solutions, or none.

Estuaries are amongst the most productive ecosystems (Chapter 10) so it is not unreasonable to assume intially that large amounts of food will be present. Goss-Custard and Charman (63) have commented upon the fact that waders tend to spread out over the areas available to them early in winter, when food is presumably readily available, and it may be that the waders are responding to their own density rather than to the availability of food or, possibly, in addition to it. If this is the case, then the waders may be dispersed well below the food limit, but it might also be the case that such early dispersion causes birds to be spread out over the whole of the available range and this is of value when, and if, food does come to be in short supply.

There can be no doubt that waders are well dispersed throughout the estuaries during the non-breeding season. Prater (200) has shown that estuaries tend to hold similar numbers of waders from year to year and this is shown in Table 33 which summarises the total wader counts on the principal

TABLE 33. Principal estuaries for waders in Britain and Ireland 1969–75 (after Prater, 1977).

	Average	74–75	73–74	72–73	71–72	70–71	69–70
Morecambe Bay	244.1	258.4	269.4	232.7	227.2	252.4	224.5
Wash	175.5	167.8	201.9	165.3	181.4	161.0	(65.5)
Solway	171.7	163.2	(126.4)	144.2	207.6	(79.9)	(75.8)
Ribble	168.1	219.4	219.4	158.6	123.2	119.8	(72.7)
Dee	133.5	105.1	150.9	154.1	121.8	121.4	147.9
Thames	103.1	134.7	91.0	83.7	—	—	—
Hants/Sussex Hbrs	93.6	92.7	87.7	100.3	—	—	—
Severn	93.2	82.0	121.6	75.9	(68.4)	(49.1)	(35.3)
Firth of Forth	62.6	61.1	56.6	62.5	70.2	(37.6)	(31.6)
Dundalk Bay	58.6	68.3	(48.9)	(37.0)	—	—	—
Shannon/Fergus	58.2	44.8	73.9	55.9	—	—	—
Humber	50.8	41.2	60.9	37.6	85.7	44.1	35.4
Lindisfarne	41.1	60.1	43.8	38.8	29.3	33.3	(3.7)
Strangford Lough	40.7	28.3	62.4	29.9	49.7	45.1	28.9
Burry Inlet	39.3	34.7	40.1	34.7	35.4	46.7	44.2
Mersey	32.3	49.1	44.6	29.3	18.7	19.7	—
Duddon	30.5	46.0	19.6	22.2	33.6	31.1	(17.9)
Bull	29.9	27.6	36.4	30.0	28.9	26.7	—
Clyde, inner	26.7	29.4	33.8	28.4	18.7	(17.0)	23.3
Cork Harbour	22.7	27.7	—	(7.5)	16.6	23.8	—
Blackwater	22.4	29.2	27.2	10.9	—	—	—
Hamford Water	22.1	30.0	22.7	13.2	(6.9)	—	—
Wexford Harbour	21.9	18.1	41.8	20.4	7.3	—	—
Dengie	21.4	24.8	22.1	17.3	—	—	—
Teesmouth	21.4	14.9	21.2	22.0	24.2	25.1	21.3
Exe	21.1	20.9	17.4	20.1	21.9	21.0	25.6
Conway Bay	20.2	20.8	21.8	24.4	18.4	16.9	19.0
Moray Firth	20.0	16.0	27.8	22.3	14.0	(11.3)	—
Stour/Essex/Suffolk	20.0	20.1	32.2	21.4	14.0	12.0	—
Taw/Torridge	20.0	23.5	26.9	9.6	(10.0)	(8.8)	—

* peak counts, in thousands

estuaries of the British Isles. There is a tendency for numbers to increase in years immediately after the first count, but this is almost certainly an effect of the improved counting techniques rather than an increase in numbers of birds. With few exceptions it can be seen that the larger estuaries and those with large food resources tend to hold larger numbers of birds and that these numbers tend to be similar in different years. Two explanations are possible; either the birds are dispersed as a result of their own interactions, or they have reached a ceiling level in each environment probably because they are at or near their food limit. Evans (46) has shown a high degree of similarity in the seasonal changes in total numbers of individual species of waders from year to year (Fig. 70) and of particular significance here is that the overall numbers of

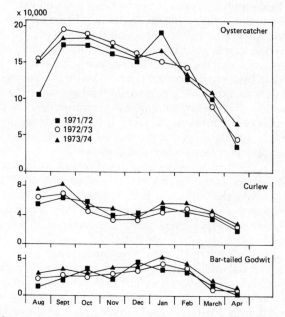

FIG. 70. Monthly counts of three species of shorebirds. Oystercatcher (top), Curlew (centre) and Bar-tailed Godwit (bottom) in the British Isles in three winters (after Evans, 1976).

birds within the British Isles follow an annual pattern. For Oystercatchers, Curlews and Bar-tailed Godwits it certainly appears as though some mechanism is maintaining an overall pattern of numbers, but there is no means of distinguishing whether this is food limitation or the even dispersal of relatively stable numbers.

In order to determine whether waders are up against a food limitation, or whether they are dispered at a level below this point, it is necessary to examine the available evidence in support of each possibility. However, it must be borne in mind that the carrying capacity of an area, if there is such a thing, might itself vary from year to year with variation in the annual production of the food organisms. If this were the case it might be possible to relate wader numbers to food supply (64); if overall wader numbers increased over a period of years where there was a clear increase in the total production of the food organisms, this would provide good evidence for the existence of a carrying capacity regulated by food supply. Even if such a situation occurred it would be virtually impossible to monitor, and where only local increases of waders and food occur, as they have done in the Cockle/Oystercatcher situation, this can still be explained on the basis of the birds distributing themselves on the basis of the food supply and not necessarily being limited by it.

It is known from ringing recoveries in Africa (161, 41) and on the Wash, and from colour-marking several species on the Tees (46), that some birds have preferred wintering areas to which they return from year to year. The implication of this is that these individuals return because they have success-fully wintered in that area before, and because there is a known and adequate food supply. It is clear that many birds are faithful to a wintering area for the whole of the non-breeding season, and though real evidence is lacking it is likely that most of the birds which move between estuaries in winter are probably young, with the exception of birds carrying out journeys initiated by hard weather. The repeated returns to the same wintering area do seem to indicate that for these birds at least, food is not necessarily limiting, and it is possible that they have some hierarchical advantage over other birds which move on. However, the indication is that these birds are not finding life difficult in winter, and this is evidence to suggest that, generally speaking, outside the breeding season waders exist in areas where food is not a limiting factor.

From the point of view of an ideal experiment, the introduction of large numbers of additional waders into an area apparently already fully occupied, would afford the sort of evidence on which conclusions might be based. Under natural circumstances this situation actually arises every few years, when there is a good breeding season and increased numbers of birds appear on the estuaries in autumn. The magnitude of such increases is illustrated in Fig. 71 for Bar-tailed Godwits, Knots and Dunlins, on the Ribble Estuary. 1973 was a particularly good breeding season and it can be seen that the autumn populations are double those of 1971; in the Dunlin, 1974 was also a good season and hence the mid-winter population was three times that of 1971. During these seasons the invertebrate populations were sampled by Green-

---

FIG. 71. Monthly totals in thousands of Bar-tailed Godwits (top), Dunlins (centre) and Knots (bottom) on the Ribble Estuary (after Smith and Greenhalgh 1977).

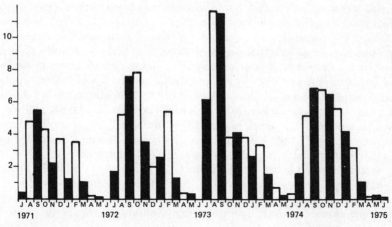

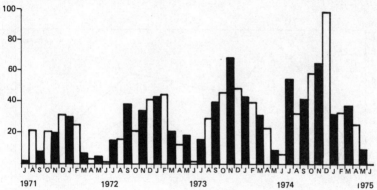

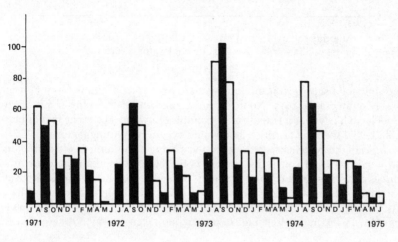

halgh (66) and there was no significant difference between the populations of
Corophium and *Hydrobia* in December 1971 and December 1973. *Nereis* and
Macoma population densities were also very similar in the two years so that it is
reasonable to conclude that Fig. 71 does not merely show an influx of birds
into an area where there is an increased food supply, but the accommodation
of larger numbers of birds in an area with a relatively stable food supply.
Assuming similar availabilities of food, it can therefore be concluded that at
least in 1971 and 1972 the main autumn wader populations of the Ribble were
well below their food limit; in 1973 other species of waders also had large
populations so that there is little possibility of these three species taking up
food which was made available by the absence of other birds.

A similar situation can be seen in the Grey Plover wintering in the British
Isles in 1971–2, 1972–3 and 1973–4. Monthly counts are shown in Fig. 72
and it can be seen that in the winter of 1973–4 significantly higher numbers
were present than in the two previous years. Nothing is known of variations in

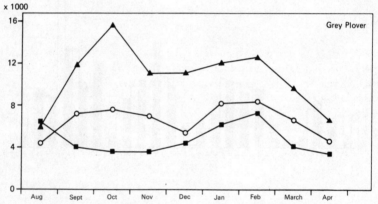

FIG. 72. Monthly counts of Grey Plover in the British Isles in three winters. Key as in
Fig. 70. Figures on the vertical axes are thousands (after Evans 1976).

possible food supply, but in October 1973 four times as many Grey Plovers
were counted as in 1971. No firm conclusions can be drawn from this but it
does seem likely that this again is an example of a wader occurring in numbers
well below the level at which food would become a limiting factor.

Most of the evidence for wader numbers being below a threshold density in
winter is far from conclusive, but several factors other than those already
discussed in this context point to waders occurring well below the theoretical
food limit. It has been seen in Chapter 10 that on the Ribble Estuary less than
10% of the annual production of invertebrates is taken by waders. Compared with the high percentage of production taken by, say, Oystercatchers

elsewhere (25, 29), this is a low figure and in itself suggests that more waders could be accommodated. Without information on the availability of the food it is difficult to come to a conclusion, but considered together with the fact that the densities of food species normally remain well above the threshold at which the predator peck rate is reduced (Chapter 9) there is a clear indication that food appears not to be limiting.

The problem of availability of food bedevils any assessment of whether food is limiting or not. It has already been noted that waders moving north in spring easily find food at their staging posts. Does this supply remain because during the winter it has been unavailable to the wintering waders, or has it been present in such super-abundance that it remains so in spring? Whilst the biomass of individual prey specimens may well be greater than in winter, overall numbers are lower in spring as a result of winter mortality. The implication is that numbers in winter were not significantly diminished through predation by wintering waders and large populations survived until spring.

Further evidence for feeding below the food limit in winter is provided by waders performing hard weather movements. In Chapter 6 it was shown that radar studies had clearly demonstrated that winter movements from the continent occurred before the onset of a cold period. Where Lapwings cross the North Sea into England they move into areas largely already occupied by other wintering Lapwings. Some may move out, as far as Iberia, but the British population is enlarged by such influxes; this again suggests that there is food available for incoming migrants in addition to that required by the normal wintering population. Although the possibility exists of an increase in mortality there is no evidence of this. These immigrants clearly have the energy capacity to make a sea crossing, which itself goes some way to show that they are not short of energy reserves. After the end of the cold period they recross the North Sea, probably not because of a shortage of food in the British Isles but because the Continental food supply is better. It appears that this food remains in the Continental areas, but the likelihood is that it is difficult to get, and the evidence for food being limiting which has so far been discussed seems to point to the probability that there is little difficulty in obtaining food except when the ground temperature is near to, or below, freezing point.

Winter weights have already been considered at some length, but here again there is an indication that at least in some species, e.g. Oystercatchers, there is little difficulty in obtaining the normal daily requirement outside the breeding season, as weight is increased throughout the winter. Other species have been seen to lose weight from January onward in temperate wintering areas, but it has also been seen that the mid-winter weights here are significantly higher than they are in tropical wintering areas. It might be argued that in these species, e.g. Dunlin, weight is put on in the autumn as an insurance against food shortage later in the winter; there can be little doubt that this is the case, but it is likely that it is an insurance against cold weather when food might be unavailable through, say, frost. Even in the latter part of winter there are times when all species of waders can be seen to be resting and preening, when, if they were really short of food, they would be actively in search of it. Many species spend long periods of inactivity and details of this have been shown in Table 19. Again, this is an indication of food in relative plenty. Conversely, there are times when waders feed continuously, and this may well indicate difficulty in getting food; however, this is likely to be a problem of availability rather than absence of food from the area in question. A final and telling piece of evidence in support of this contention comes from the high probability of selection for structures associated with feeding occurring on the breeding grounds (Chapter 11). It has been argued that, since a pattern of bill and tarsus measurements is clearly seen only in the breeding season, this is the time of greatest competition, and when selection takes place. Whilst it does not necessarily follow that because competition is likely to be greater for food during the breeding season waders must be significantly below their food limit in winter, the likelihood is that they are, and food is more difficult to come by during the breeding season.

The alternative to waders existing below a theoretical food limit is for them to be up against it. One of the most obvious probable indicators of such a state of affairs is for a species to be taking a large proportion of the available food, e.g. Oystercatchers; under these circumstances food could be limiting, and therefore additional birds might not be able to settle in a given area. There are two possible viewpoints from which to consider whether waders are restricted in numbers by their food supply; firstly, by considering the food supply, and, secondly, by observing the birds, and changes in both them and their behaviour.

Ideally, the comparison, over a year, of the fauna of areas on which waders have fed with the fauna in areas from which they have been excluded should give a measure of the level of predation. For reasons already considered, such exclusion experiments have proved of little or no value, and the results must necessarily be regarded with care. Other methods for estimating the removal of prey have provided the sort of results already discussed in previous chapters, and approximate estimates of levels of predation are available. These are relatively low for most sandpipers and plovers, in comparison with Oystercatchers feeding on *Mytilus* which, except when covered by the tide, can be considered to be readily available to the birds. The difference in levels of predation could be accounted for either by relatively lower numbers of birds or by the lower availability of the prey. However, Oystercatchers do take a high percentage of cockles which present similar problems of availability in that they may occur well below the surface of the substrate. Where prey organisms occur below the surface they may be completely unavailable to the birds because, they are too deep to reach with their bills, or they may be within bill length of the surface but not providing clues to their presence

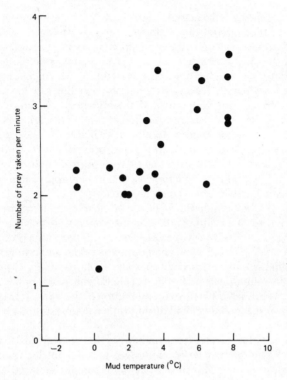

FIG. 73. Feeding rate of Knots on bivalve molluscs in relation to mud temperature. Each point is the mean of five separate observations for one minute ($r = 0.687$ $P < 0.001$) (after Goss-Custard et al 1977).

through any form of activity. The fact that some waders, e.g. Redshanks, have difficulty in feeding at low mud temperatures may well be due entirely to the reduced activity of the prey species. This seems likely in the Knot, where Goss-Custard *et al* (64) showed a decline in the number of prey taken per minute as temperature fell from 10°C to zero (Fig. 73). The same authors found no such problems confronting Curlews, Bar-tailed Godwits and Oystercatchers even at temperatures as low as 2°C, so that in these cases it is likely that the behaviour of the prey is not so important. From the point of view of depth distribution, some invertebrates, e.g. *Macoma*, tend to move deeper in response to shorter winter days so that in mid-winter fewer are close enough to the surface to be fed upon. Other species, like *Hydrobia*, are permanently in the top few millimetres of mud, so that availability is determined by both depth in the substrate and the birds' ability to detect its presence, either through its own efforts or through the activity of the prey. With the exception of *Arenicola* (221) the detailed circumstances under which invertebrates are available to waders are unknown. Since the seasonal changes in availability cannot be measured, the only alternative is to assess the feeding rate of the waders. In turn this may give an indication of the availability, which, in any case, is only of importance when it affects the feeding rate. Feeding rate has already been seen to be affected by food density and, in some species, by low temperatures. From what evidence there is, the question of availability appears to be one of importance only when food is totally unavailable due to extremely low temperature. Clearly with more prey species occurring at lower depths in the mud and reduced activity making their capture a matter of increasing difficulty, mid-winter must be a time when numbers approach most closely to the carrying capacity of the feeding grounds.

What might be considered to be a completely different aspect of food availability arises as a result of predators other than waders, e.g. wildfowl and fish, feeding on the same prey species. Clearly this must affect the food stocks, if only to a small extent, but no good estimates of the magnitude of the effect are available. So far it has not proved possible to attack the problem of possible food limitation from the point of view of the food supplies, and success has not been so much greater from observation of the birds. If waders ever do come up against a food threshold during winter this must surely be obvious in one way or another.

It has already been seen in earlier chapters that waders tend to move out of a particular environment *before* things get too difficult for them. Perhaps, then, the most obvious indication that waders might be faced with feeding difficulties, particularly in the case of continental, inland feeding birds, is that a general exodus takes place to a better feeding area. With estuarine feeding birds in the British Isles, this is a relatively infrequent occurrence, though many estuaries have peak numbers of particular species at different times of the year. The Ribble peak in Knot numbers occurs in August and September, whereas in Morecambe Bay and the Wash, peaks occur in January. Probably all that this indicates is that in winter, birds in the north-west of England find better feeding on Morecambe Bay than on the Ribble, as those remaining seem to experience no difficulty feeding. The very fact that birds do not move away from our estuaries during the winter almost certainly indicates that they are obtaining sufficient food, and are not near a food ceiling.

Some waders change their diet during the course of the winter. Bar-tailed Godwits, for example, feed extensively on *Nereis* in autumn and early winter on the Ribble and this forms 59% of the diet until the end of January (66); in February *Macoma* predominates and *Nereis* falls to only 27% of the diet. One possible explanation of this is that *Nereis* is no longer present in the quantities in which it can be easily obtained during late winter, but it is much more likely that *Macoma* becomes more easily available to the Godwits at this time than is *Nereis*. Such a transfer in food preference could be a possible indication of food shortage but it is much more likely to reflect a choice for a better food source.

There are other behavioural traits which might indicate that the numbers of waders in a particular habitat are approaching the maximum carrying capacity for the area. The fact that birds spend most of the available time feeding may well indicate that they are having to put in a maximum effort in order to achieve their required energy intake. It has already been seen that some species, e.g. Dunlin, require to feed for much longer periods than other species, e.g. Oystercatcher, and in mid-winter an even greater proportion of the available time is spent feeding. This may be due to greater difficulty in finding food items, to the fact that the energy content of each item is smaller at this time of the year than at others, or to the fact that a greater gross energy intake is necessary to maintain body heat in cold weather. No matter what the reason, there can be little doubt that this indicates that the population is nearer the maximum carrying capacity than at other times, but the important question is – how near? Again the observation that waders are undergoing periods of feeding difficulty, due perhaps to low temperatures, is another indication of this, but again no quantitative estimate has yet been possible of a food threshold. Low weights and emaciation are clear indicators of insufficient intake of energy, but generally speaking these are rare, and are found only in times of extreme cold, and hardly at all during normal temperate winters.

Where food is short, fighting between individuals might be expected and this tends to occur where feeding territories are set up on the shore. Redshanks, Grey Plovers and Curlews may set up such territories and defend them against other individuals of the same species. Not all individuals in an area behave in this way and it is common to see birds of the same species feeding together near the low water mark whilst others may hold feeding territories in mid-shore. These latter birds will frequently display aggression and it is difficult to see what benefit they gain from occupying feeding areas in this way, particularly since they appear to waste good feeding time in aggressive encounters with others of the same species but ignore waders of a different species which are quite clearly taking the same prey species from their feeding territories. Possibly such territorial defence ensures a better feeding rate but this type of aggression appears to show that they have time to waste indulging in it, rather than it being an indication of food limitation.

Perhaps the clearest indication of food limitation comes from obvious signs of starvation with emaciated corpses being found. This only occurs when food is virtually unobtainable due to gales or very cold conditions and where a combination of the freezing over of the feeding grounds combines with sub-zero temperatures in which poorly fed birds are unable to maintain their body temperatures. This has little to do with the carrying capacity of habitats and such situations occur only infrequently. Clearly, from an evolutionary point of view, such mortality, must on average, be lower than that incurred were the population to perform a more extensive southerly migration.

The carrying capacity of a particular habitat is the maximum population of waders which that habitat can support. This may well vary from year to year, as the food supplies undoubtedly vary, but is there really any evidence to suggest that wading birds are anywhere near the limits which can be supported by the available food supply? Despite all the work that has been done on winter feeding ecology, the answer to this question is that we still do not know. The weight of evidence points to numbers on all our estuaries which are well below theoretical carrying capacities, but we are very little nearer determining for any wintering area the spare carrying capacity, that is the additional numbers which could be added to any single habitat without adversely affecting the already resident birds.

On the Wash, Goss-Custard (62) obtained results consistent with the suggestion made by Zwarts (255) that high densities of waders on preferred feeding areas cause additional birds moving into the area to feed elsewhere. In the case of both the Knot and the Oystercatcher, Goss-Custard found that numbers in preferred areas continued to increase as additional birds moved into the area, but at a slower rate of increase than in the initially less preferred areas. These findings led him to predict that where enclosures were made on estuaries the consequences might be threefold; firstly, there would be an increase in density in the remaining preferred feeding areas; secondly, there would be an increase in the use of less preferred areas; and thirdly, there was likely to be an increase in the range of size of prey species taken. All these factors might well lead to an overall reduction in ingestion rate, the consequences of which are difficult to predict. Clearly numbers would be brought nearer to the carrying capacity of the area, but in practice the result could vary from merely increasing the time spent feeding, to the other extreme of seeking an alternative wintering area. The situation also varies from species to species and habitat loss would obviously affect species nearer to a maximum carrying capacity than those well below it. Goss-Custard (62) predicts that on the Wash, Knots would be more affected by proposed enclosures than would Oystercatchers, so that the possible effects of such modifications to the intertidal areas must be monitored for each species separately. Some species may be particularly susceptible to loss of feeding habitat and such a possibility should be borne in mind in further work in this area.

Most of this discussion on carrying capacity has, of necessity, centred around food and its availability. The importance of the presence of suitable roosts throughout the tidal cycle should not be lost sight of, but bearing this in mind for the design of future research it is worth reflecting that work carried out so far has centred upon two main possible situations. In the first of these, birds might be considered to reach maximum numbers only when they come up against a food limit after depleting the available food supplies to the extent that they are then unable to feed efficiently. In the second situation, birds might be considered to have evolved the capacity to regulate their own numbers well below any food limit, either through density dependent agencies or through behaviour. In the first case we might expect numbers to reach levels at or near the maximum carrying capacity for a given habitat; in the second considerable spare carrying capacity would be likely. The evidence available tends to support the second case, but there is a third alternative so far not considered. This is the situation where population regulation occurs on the breeding grounds and the numbers present on the wintering areas are dependent on limits determined elsewhere. In these circumstances, wintering populations could well be far below the maximum possible and the winter distribution would result from a dispersion of birds, determined by settlement in an area where food was most easily obtained, and where suitable roosting sites occurred. The available information on the ecology of wading birds throughout the year fits this third alternative best. It is likely that the concept of carrying capacity is at present only of theoretical interest, but this does not mean to say that it has no practical value in the future. The main problem of the present time is to find some reliable method of estimating the spare carrying capacity which undoubtedly exists on most, if not all, our estuaries. Pressures on wader habitats are such that the carrying capacities of estuaries may change overnight from a purely academic problem to one of stark practicality. It is important to know how many waders a particular habitat can support, in order to plan any conservation strategy in which this group of birds is involved. It may be that some estuarine areas will have to be sacrificed for water storage purposes, or reclaimed for agriculture, and it is the ecologists' job to provide the information on which conservationists can base a policy. Unfortunately, we are dealing with a situation in which the facts may well not be available until the situation which it is sought to prevent has occurred. In practice it is likely that the only way in which information can be obtained on carrying capacity is by reducing very significantly the areas available to waders on our estuaries; if this could be done experimentally, so that such areas could revert to their original state afterwards, then we may well obtain the information which would enable us to predict the extent to which birds displaced from one area could be accommodated in others. The grave danger is that our experimental situations will arise only in the form of permanent reclamation schemes but if, and when, they do arise every advantage must be taken to make use of them. The likelihood is that our estuaries are not close to their maximum carrying capacity in winter; however, this does not mean that significant reclamation will leave the wintering wader populations unaffected. Different reclamation schemes will have different effects upon the birds and conservation strategies must be based, as far as possible, on a knowledge of these; this will be considered further in the final chapter.

CHAPTER 13

COCKLES AND CONSERVATION

WADERS probably cause fewer economic problems than any other group of birds, and in the British Isles only one species, the Oystercatcher, has at any time been considered a serious pest against which some sort of action should be taken to reduce its numbers. As has been seen in previous chapters probably the main single food species of the Oystercatcher in the British Isles is the cockle which is cropped in significant numbers in certain areas. Davidson (29) estimated that the feeding rate of Oystercatchers on the Burry Inlet, one of the main commercial fisheries, varied from 0.73 cockles per minute to 2.1 cockles per minute, depending on the flesh volume of the cockles. Assuming that on average some 55% of the intertidal period during which cockles are available is used for feeding, he estimated that in three two-monthly winter periods 280, 205 and 280 were the mean numbers of cockles consumed by a single Oystercatcher during one daylight tide. During the three winters (1961–62, 1962–63, 1964–65) Davidson calculated that Oystercatchers removed between 557×10^6 and 1237×10^6 second winter and older cockles from total stocks of $1001 \times 10^6 - 3232 \times 10^6$ of the same ages. This compared with the fished catches of $46 \times 10^6 - 128 \times 10^6$ and whilst survey times were different and areas other than the fished ones were available to the Oystercatchers, these figures certainly give a comparison of the relative orders of magnitude of the cropping by Man and birds.

The Burry Inlet became more important as a commercial fishery than it had previously been after the crash of the Morecambe Bay and Dee cockle populations in the winter of 1962–63. Prior to this, both had been of great importance in terms of the weight of the annual crop, the other two important areas for cockle fisheries being the Wash and the Thames Estuary. The Thames supports only a small Oystercatcher population, and whilst the Wash population is much bigger, of the order of 15,000 birds, they are very dispersed at low water and in a low density which, according to Davidson (30) has little effect on the cockle population. The same author claims that Oystercatchers contributed significantly to the demise of the cockle on the Dee and Morecambe Bay, as cockles become moribund with increasing cold and are unable to close tightly or quickly, and so they are easy prey to Oystercatchers. Even when few cockles remained numbers of Oystercatchers were supported by *Macoma* (and possibly even at this early stage by earthworms) so that virtually all cockles were taken by the birds which did not have to move elsewhere as cockle numbers fell. Hancock and Urquhart (79) showed that in samples from the Burry Inlet there was an unusually high mortality (91%) for second year winter cockles compared with 48% for first year and only 20% for older shellfish. It was demonstrated that this was not a result of fishing, as cockles inside a fenced area where fishing was prohibited, had the same pattern of mortality; nor was it thought to be associated with disease or parasites. The most likely cause was considered to be selective feeding by a predator. Fish take large numbers of small cockles during the summer months but could not account for the pattern of mortality shown in second year cockles. This left only Oystercatchers, and observations showed that they took considerable numbers of second winter cockles. Where they were excluded from some cockle beds by nets the mortality of second winter cockles was significantly reduced, so that it appeared that the cockles were taken by Oystercatchers in large numbers. As second winter cockles form the bulk of the commercial fishery stocks there appeared to be sufficient evidence to justify studies which might provide the background for future control measures. However, Drinnan's (36) studies showed that there was also a large natural wastage of cockles which was entirely unrelated to Oystercatcher predation.

For many years prior to Drinnan and Cole's (37) study the South Wales Sea Fisheries Committee had maintained that the Oystercatcher was a serious pest of the fishery. This study, however, concluded that Oystercatchers were not a serious threat to the fishery, but complaints from fishermen continued, as they held that competition with Oystercatchers reduced their own fishing rate. At first sight, considering the annual value of the cockle industry at the time of the initiation of the main studies (c. £200,000), it is surprising that the Ministry of Agriculture, Fisheries and Food thought this worthwhile. It is probable that because the fisheries are often concentrated in very small communities, where the effects of a failing fishery might be very large (30) the decision was taken to carry out studies on the predation of cockles by Oystercatchers.

However, this was not the first interest that the Ministry had shown in cockle fisheries. In 1954, after the cockle fishermen in Morecambe Bay had claimed that Oystercatchers were affecting their livelihood, a study was initiated which culminated in a comparison between the situation in More-cambe Bay and in Brancaster Harbour, Norfolk (36). At first sight the data collected in Morecambe Bay might be interpreted as indicating that if Oystercatcher predation had ceased in 1954 there would have been an increase of over 80% of cockles surviving the winter of 1954–55. But, often, so very much depends on how data are interpreted and Drinnan points out that disregarding the interaction of all the relevant factors may well be 'a grave omission' in forecasting the effects of Oystercatcher control; it is perhaps surprising that effects took the course they did following upon this. It was shown that, of an annual mortality of 74%, only some 22% could be accoun-ted for by the Oystercatchers. In Brancaster Harbour, cockles were more readily accessible to the birds, and a shorter period of time was taken in obtaining the same amount of food, so that Brancaster birds did not feed for such a long period of time. Drinnan pointed out the well known fact that spat fall in cockles is very variable, and this results in high populations of cockles in years immediately following a high spat fall, and low numbers following poor spat fall. At this stage the relationship between the size of the Oystercatcher flocks and the cockle populations was not well known, but at Brancaster in 1947–48 there was a dense settlement of cockles. This was followed by an increase in numbers of the Oystercatcher population to between 3000 and 4000, a much higher figure than during Drinnan's work. As cockle popu-lations declined so did the Oystercatcher population. In Morecambe Bay, at this time, the Oystercatcher population numbered between 30,000 and 37,000; the crash of the cockle population during the winter of 1962–63 reduced these numbers drastically.

Two very important factors are pointed to in this initial research; firstly, probably in the region of half the cockles taken by Oystercatchers would be subject to other natural mortality during the winter had they not been taken; secondly, where there are large cockle populations Oystercatchers move in, and when the cockles go so do the birds. It is surprising that so little attention was paid to these matters in the subsequent actions of the Ministry, particu-larly since similar results were obtained in subsequent work. This work was carried out from two different points of view, that of the cockle (79, 75, 76, 77, 78) and that of the Oystercatcher (25, 26, 29, 30, 100).

Hancock and Urquhart (79) again found a high rate of natural mortality which was attributable to effects other than predation by Oystercatchers; they also showed that the flesh content decreases between mid-October and mid-May, so that birds need to take more cockles during this period to obtain the necessary energy intake. Hancock (76) showed that at high densities the percentage survival of cockles is little affected by predation or fishing, but that at low densities both fishing and predation are reduced. This is clearly to be expected, but fishing is more severely affected in that the birds can move elsewhere, whereas the fishermen cannot. Hancock concluded that it is at moderate cockle densities that Oystercatchers have their greatest effect, reducing the spawning stock. Between 1958 and 1962 the reduction in the numbers of spawners due to the combined effects of fishing and predation resulted in a higher level of recruitment to the Burry Inlet population. This, however, allowed only a low-level of fishing. Following the heavy spat fall after the 1962–63 winter cockle populations built up with a better survival of cockles through their second winter but this in turn gave rise to both greater predation and heavier fishing. The industry increased from a landing of 18,240 cwt, valued at £12,000 in 1963, to 80,000 cwt, valued at £80,000 in 1970, though it must be appreciated that the 1963 figure was abnormally low following the bad winter.

Hancock (77) discusses spat fall in relation to cold winters and other possible causative factors of heavy falls. Where few young (first year) cockles occur spat fall is often high so that there is an inverse relationship between succeeding year classes. On this basis it is possible to argue that Oyster-catchers may, in certain circumstances, increase the population of cockles by reducing numbers to an extent which causes a heavy spat fall. Kristensen (119) believes that the presence of adult cockles affects the survival of the young to the extent that, until older cockles die or are removed, a new year class does not establish itself.

On the basis of the winter weight loss, Hancock and Franklin (78) argue that, if instead of harvesting cockles during the winter months it was done before November, the increase in meat yield over a year would be of the order of 10%. Clearly this would involve deep freezing the harvest, as most of it is sold as fresh meat, but there would be clear advantages, particularly in harvesting before the natural winter mortality occurred, and before Oyster-catchers took a large percentage of the population. The meat content of second winter cockles in the period May–July is twice that of winter collected shellfish, so that if they were harvested at this time there would be a much improved yield. There are arguments against the adoption of these tech-niques, not least of which would be the seasonal unemployment of some fishermen, and the possible associated necessary increase in the harvest, but matched against the Oystercatchers they are surely worthy of consideration. It has been suggested that the money spent on research on Oystercatchers might well have been better spent on work on the cockles (23) but in fairness there is a vast amount of information available on the biology of cockles though, of course, there is still much to be learnt, particularly in relation to spat fall. However, it was clearly of importance to know more about Oyster-catchers in relation to cockles, since, if any control measures were to be instigated, a full knowledge of the biology of the species would be an ad-vantage in making recommendations on how to go about it.

Dare (25) estimated that in the winters of 1963–64 and 1964–65 the

population of Oystercatchers in the British Isles numbered some 95,000–
175,000; these estimates compare with counts of 207,000 in September 1974
and 184,000 in January 1975. These birds are distributed in 35 main haunts
with the Solway Firth, Morecambe Bay, the Burry Inlet and the Wash being
the most important of these. From the discussions in previous chapters, it
can be concluded that these birds were spread over the best feeding areas,
and it does not take more than a little common sense to realise that the
removal of the birds from a good feeding area will almost certainly result in
others moving in. In this context we are discussing not only the British
wintering population of 200,000+ but others which might remain here rather
than move to the shores of the continental mainland, should populations in
Britain be smaller. These number some 558,000 in western Europe
(Table 18).

Dare (26), in his study of the movements of Oystercatcher, showed from
both ringing and colour marking that birds tended to 'home' annually to
particular wintering areas where they tended to remain until the spring
northward movement. Only limited exchanges occurred between flocks on
the west coast wintering grounds in Wales and north-west England, and there
was virtually no interchange with other haunts in Scotland, Ireland and the
south-east of England. It was concluded that under relatively stable conditions of prey distribution and abundance Oystercatchers were normally
faithful to a particular wintering area. The evidence is such that there is no
reason to doubt these conclusions, but they apply only to Oystercatcher
populations which have found their own levels. To assume that possible
control measures, resulting in the removal of several thousand birds from the
Burry Inlet, would result in a reduced Burry wintering population, on a
permanent basis, is assuming too much. This is not a reasonable conclusion to
draw, though clearly the work on Oystercatcher movements was initiated
with just such possibilities in mind. Davidson (30) pointed out that the
question whether removed birds would be replaced by others is a question
which can only be solved by studying the results of a control programme; it
was, however, well known that where cockles became abundant Oystercatchers moved in. These birds did not stay in their traditional wintering
areas, and there were no good reasons to assume that birds from elsewhere
would not move into the vacant Burry Inlet after the removal of the normally
resident winter birds.

On the Burry Inlet itself, Davidson (29) estimated that maximum winter
numbers of Oystercatchers varied from 5500 (1963–64) to 15,800 (1965–66)
and he later (30) calculated (1968) that on average one bird consumes over
500 cockles per day, which is equivalent to about 325 g live weight of flesh. He
concluded that substantial reduction in the birds' predation would be expected to lead to a marked increase in the number of cockles available to the
fishery and, if the fishery was to maintain a steady high level of production,
control of the Oystercatcher was necessary.

So long as cockling remained a local tradition, control measures involving the killing of large numbers of birds could not be justified. However, following the heavy spat fall of 1963, the industry expanded six fold, as has already been discussed, and fluctuations in the cockle harvest were blamed on the Oyster-catcher. After such a dramatic increase in the cockle harvest, it came as a surprise that the Secretary of State for Wales and the Ministry of Agriculture, Fisheries and Food gave the South Wales Sea Fisheries Board permission to kill 11,000 Oystercatchers. It was even more surprising that such a decision was made in the light of the scientific data collected on both the birds and the cockles. This was a political decision with little scientific basis.

The criticism that money spent on Oystercatcher research would have been better spent on work on the cockle (23) is to some extent justified by the lack of information on cockle mortality resulting from pollution by sewage and industrial effluents, which has occurred. In addition, the river channel altered its position as a result of the collapse of an old training wall, and this resulted in the scouring of some cockle beds and the silting up of others. The spread of *Spartina* also affected cockle beds, yet how these factors affected the variation in the cockle harvest remained unknown. The central factor in taking the decision to cull Oystercatchers was clearly that they were sup-posedly taking more than twice the weight of cockles fished. That many of these were taken away from the main fished cockle beds was ignored. Taking into account this fact, together with the likely overestimate of the cockle intake of Oystercatchers, and the fact that the cockle harvest is invariably underestimated because of the small quantities of cockles taken by private individuals and licenced gatherers possibly concealing landings in excess of the legal limits, the probability is that Oystercatchers and fishermen take about the same quantities of cockles. Another important factor was the estimated number of Oystercatchers present in the Inlet, said to be 21,000. This is now known to be a gross overestimate, only some 15,000 birds being counted during the Birds of Estuaries Enquiry in the same year.

If there was one thing more remarkable than the decision to cull 11,000 birds, it was the method by which the Ministry chose to carry it out. To elect to shoot the birds, and to offer a bounty of 25p per head to authorised marksmen who were themselves licenced cockle fishers was, to say the least, surprising, particularly as the Ministry had previously decided that it would not subsidise cartridges for the destruction of wood pigeons during the winter months because, as a means of controlling the population, it was thought to be a waste of time and money.

Culling first took place in the autumn of 1973 and 7000 Oystercatchers were slaughtered – more than half the Burry Inlet's normal wintering population, and in the early winter of 1974 3000 more were killed. Not un-reasonably, this totally unnecessary action resulted in an international outcry, and it is unlikely to be repeated, but the unfortunate principle of political expediency over-riding scientific advisability and plain common sense will almost certainly be repeated in other, and probably more important, fields of conservation. The original data collected during the work on the Burry Inlet have recently been re-analysed by Horwood and Goss-Custard (100) who constructed a mathematical model of the cockle fishery and bird predation. To a certain extent this raises doubts about the general conclusions of the original work. These were that predation by Oystercatchers greatly reduced the numbers of second winter cockles available to the fishery and that a reduction in the numbers of birds would therefore lead to higher yields in the fishery. The re-analysis shows a relationship between the pattern of predation and the density of the cockle stocks. At high cockle densities the numbers of cockles taken are great, but the effect small. At low densities Oystercatchers could theoretically remove all second winter cockles, but this does not happen because there is a threshold value, of the order of 50–100 per m², below which Oystercatchers turn to other age groups. The earlier conclusion, that up to 90% of the second winter cockle mortality was caused by Oyster-catchers appears to be invalid, and the correct figure is significantly smaller (30–47%). In addition, it is likely that the commercial cockle beds are regarded as preferred feeding sites by Oystercatchers; removal of the feeding birds is therefore likely to attract birds from elsewhere to feed on them. Had this analysis been available at the time when it was decided to cull 11,000 birds, this decision might well not have been taken, but since the decision was political this is by no means certain. What is certain is that in the long-term the measures taken will be totally ineffective.

As far as possible, conservation measures should result in a balance between Man's need and the environment, and clearly action must often be taken against proven pest species when the available scientific evidence indicates this. Such action should only be approved where there is a real problem and where the action is likely to provide an acceptable solution to the problem. Such was clearly not the case for the Burry Inlet Oystercatchers.

Unfortunately, political rather than fully reasoned practical decisions play an important part in the conservation of our natural environment and whilst waders, as such, present few problems as a result of their activities, the preservation of the habitats in which they occur becomes increasingly more difficult. For our native breeding birds, improvement and drainage of rough land for agricultural purposes and the increasing use of the coastal littoral zone for leisure pursuits have had a significant effect this century. Of most significance is the shoreline which, with the possible exception of some montane habitats and the areas immediately adjacent to water courses, is probably the only truly natural habitat remaining. The shore is one of very few habitats now occupied by birds for which they originally evolved the adaptations they possess. There can be little doubt that both Oystercatchers and Ringed Plovers (and formerly Kentish Plovers) occupied the strand line to the exclusion of all other nesting habitats in Britain until relatively recently. The Oystercatcher has shown itself to be more versatile in the breeding season than the Ringed Plover, as their nesting beaches have become more disturbed, and has moved onto grassland habitats and rivers whereas, in general, Ringed Plover numbers have fallen considerably. Occasionally they will nest on salt marshes but they are almost exclusively birds of pebbly beaches, though they will nest a few miles inland on river beds. On the Lancashire coastline, where they are now relatively uncommon, Ringed Plovers have nested regularly for some time on the edges of the runways on the BAC airfield at Warton, where the chipping concrete provides a habitat very similar to a pebbly beach. The species, however, is declining in numbers, and disturbance is probably the major causative factor. Few beaches outside nature reserves are sufficiently quiet for the birds to remain undisturbed, and more and more beaches each year are deserted by Ringed Plovers as a result of recreational pressure. Salt marsh is not so attractive a recreational habitat so that each year a higher proportion of our nesting Oystercatchers find sanctuary there, but as more people have more leisure time even salt marshes are more disturbed than they used to be. There is a very clear need for us to have more beaches and salt marsh areas as reserves than we have now, particularly since they are entirely natural habitats, relatively unaffected by Man.

When we complain of loss of habitat it is worth reflecting that in most cases what we are losing had been created largely by human influences in the first place. The Lapwing population of Britain must be many times what it was when the major plant cover was oak woodland and it is likely that at that time the Redshank and Snipe were limited to coastal wetlands and river valleys, whereas both species now occur on agricultural land. It is true that recent draining of wetlands may well have reduced populations of both species but in many cases these wetlands had initially been created by human influences. Both the Snipe and Redshank now nest commonly on wet, rough pasture, up to nearly 2000 ft in the northern Pennines, and these habitats are largely man-made, as are the adjacent grouse moors where Dunlins, Curlews and Golden Plovers nest. The populations of all these species have certainly increased as a result of Man's activities, and it is likely that this, at one time, was the case with the Stone Curlew, though the reclamation of heathland for agriculture is now causing the population of this species to fall. With the possible exception of the two shore-breeding species, and the Dotterel and Red-necked Phalarope, human influences probably resulted in the increase of the breeding populations of all waders in the British Isles. Because the breeding populations of these latter two species were small they may well have been affected by egg collecting, though the Greenshank, subjected to the same treatment, seems to have fared better.

The Woodcock may well be holding its own despite loss of habitat. Since it is encouraged as a game species this may have combatted the reduction in the availability of suitable woodland in which to nest. The species may well have increased as a result of conservation by gamekeepers, as has the Dunlin as a result of increased upland grazing. Breeding Common Sandpipers, which nest beside streams were probably one of the most recent species to be affected by human influences, in this case beneficially, as gravel pits similarly favoured Little Ringed Plovers. Only during the last hundred years has suitable new habitat been created for this species round reservoirs. Many Man-made lakes have attracted this species where previously it nested less commonly and there can be little doubt that there has been a recent increase in the breeding population.

We have seen that the winter habitat of most waders is along the coastline, and that the British Isles accommodates many more waders in winter than during the breeding season. The argument has been put that there is spare capacity for additional birds on our present estuarine complex, but many estuaries have been under threat of reclamation for one reason or another for some time now, e.g. Morecambe Bay, the Dee, the Wash and others have had reclamation schemes implemented, e.g. the Tees. There are two main problems for the waders associated with such reclamation. Firstly, there may be the physical removal of feeding and roosting areas, which are made unavailable by development of one sort or another or, secondly, there may be the removal of salt marsh areas for industrial development or agriculture. On the face of it this latter may not seem so important, but it could have effects much more far-reaching than the limits of the reclaimed areas. The detritus from the salt marsh forms a large part of the food supply of the mud-flat invertebrates, as was seen in Chapter 9, and if this is removed there can be little doubt that it will have an adverse effect on the food supply of the waders over the entire estuary. It might be argued that salt marsh has been reclaimed for centuries, and so it has, but as the reclaimed areas get nearer to the main river channels, and to the sea, development of new salt marsh is slower and physically limited by the extent of the mud flats available for colonisation. And there is a further problem. The spread of *Spartina* has resulted in a different form of initial colonisation, and instead of the *Puccinellia* dominated vegetation, much new salt marsh is formed initially by cord-grass. This tends to form a cover completely unsuitable for most waders to roost on and in places it is likely to cover greater areas of mud flat than *Puccinellia*, so making them useless for feeding waders.

If reclamation of estuarine habitat continues at its present rate in western Europe it seems likely that we will eventually reach a point when estuaries will be unable to support the present numbers of wading birds. This will have far-reaching consequences. If we assume, as has been argued, that populations are limited on the breeding grounds, and the wintering grounds could no longer accommodate these numbers, then the whole mechanism of both population limitation, and population regulation will be altered. It may no longer be profitable in some species for birds of one sex to leave the breeding area after the hatch; by remaining on the breeding ground they may well affect the survival of the brood and thus reduce the numbers surviving, which in turn may well reduce the breeding populations and possibly allow other species to breed in the area. In such circumstances migration patterns as well as breeding strategies may be affected and the whole pattern of wader ecology significantly altered. It is not possible to predict what might happen if the wintering grounds were so reduced as to affect breeding populations, but it is likely that the effects would be far-reaching for those waders wintering on the coasts.

From the point of view of conservation, it is clearly of greater importance to concentrate effort on the preservation of habitat than on the birds themselves. There have been success stories, such as the return of the Avocet to the British Isles, which have depended on protecting birds as much as on the creation of the right habitat, but in the long run it is habitat conservation which is the more important. This is not to say that we should not protect the birds. The wholesale slaughter of wading birds which takes place in Denmark, and is surprisingly tolerated there, would result in an outcry in Britain. In Copenhagen, wader corpses by the crate are available in the market after a weekend's shooting and it is fortunate that shooting of waders on this scale is not prevalent in other countries in western Europe. However, waders have provided hunters with sport in this country for some centuries and Snipe and Woodcock are still shot commonly, as are Curlews in some parts, but on nothing like the scale in Denmark. Fortunately, few waders are shot in the British Isles now, and the majority of people derive much more enjoyment from merely seeing the birds than from shooting them. The days when records were set for the numbers of Dunlin shot by the single loading of a punt gun are past; 300 at one discharge is a record unlikely to be increased and perhaps this is one area in which significant advances have been made in protection. Nor do we now see large numbers of Plovers' eggs on sale at the beginning of April, and for many such acts of conservation the RSPB has been responsible in influencing the Bird Protection Laws. Waders' eggs were always popular with egg collectors, and whilst there was a time when such people added to our scientific knowledge, and their activities could be justified on this basis, this time is now past. Possibly, they affected the populations of Dotterel, Greenshank and Red-necked Phalarope, but fortunately all these have survived in the British Isles, again largely thanks to the RSPB who have also carefully nursed our small populations of Avocet, Black-tailed Godwit and Ruff. Whilst we cannot claim to have significant populations of any of these species, the fact that they are there at all points to a general acceptance of the principles of conservation. It is to be hoped that we are able to preserve our wader habitats as well as we have done our small rare wader populations; it will be difficult, but there are grounds for optimism.

This chapter began within a situation in which one wader, the Oyster-catcher, is regarded as a pest species, and it is perhaps appropriate that we should end with another, but one in which there is an alternative to putting waders into the class of pests. Where animals and plants adversely affect human activities they are always regarded as pests. The alternative to the removal of the pest is to avoid the situation in which the organism concerned acts as such and very often this is a real possibility. This is the case with many waders where they cause problems to aircraft. If the siting of airfields was more carefully selected in the first instance, problems with birds may not arise to the extent which they do. Problems with Lapwings are probably unavoidable and about 12% of all bird strikes are caused by this species. The cost of bird strikes tend to be measured in engine damage rather than in actual crashes, which fortunately are few and far between. Even so, much of this could be avoided if the siting of airports was away from sea-bird colonies and estuarine environments. The proposal to build an international airport on Saltholm in the strait between Denmark and Sweden would certainly result in a high incidence of bird strikes, many of which would be with wading birds. Had the third London airport been developed on the Maplin sands a similar situation would have resulted there, and whilst bird strikes may have caused only enginge damage over a long period of time the chances of a major crash are clearly higher where the incidence of strikes is higher. The problems are increased several fold where dense flocks are concerned, and waders present a very serious strike hazard in some areas.

Certain waders also cause particular problems to aircraft that other species do not. Dunlin at Vancouver airport adopt a behaviour pattern typical of a situation where they are attacked by an avian predator, and zig zag down the runway in front of planes (133); even if Dunlins are crossing the runway they turn into the paths of planes taking off and landing. The use of falcons is at present being considered against large Dunlin flocks at Vancouver airport, and their use has been successful against other waders, e.g. Stone Curlew at Barajas Madrid Airport.

Lapwings, Oystercatchers and other Plovers cause minor problems no matter where airports are sited, but it is the dense flocks of estuarine waders which are likely to cause the biggest problems. Ironically, it may well be as a consequence of serious bird strikes that planners will seek the advice of ecologists, in this and other fields, in the future. Several Local Authorities in the United Kingdom now employ ecologists in their planning teams, and some, such as Merseyside, have gone as far as appointing Natural Resources Officers whose remit is wider than conservation and land use. With vision of this sort we can perhaps have real hopes of preserving large areas of our natural habitat, not only for our native birds but for those which spend only the winter season with us.

Vast numbers of waders use our estuaries and wetlands as staging posts and wintering areas outside the breeding season and we are privileged to act as hosts to them at these times. Fortunately, it is becoming more extensively recognised that they are a natural resource which is well worth conserving, and one which we have a duty to conserve. This wider appreciation of our wading birds is timely and with forethought and planning we might yet preserve sufficient of their natural habitats to ensure their continued arrival each autumn. Further work on the biology of these birds, particularly on their breeding grounds, will go a long way towards providing information on which sensible conservation strategies might be based. There are few sights more exciting than flocks of wading birds performing aerial evolutions in the autumn sunlight, and few biological problems as fascinating as those presented by the waders.

The classification and world distribution of wading birds
Main region(s) of breeding only indicated.

Cosmopo

SUB-ORDER CHARADRII

Super-family **Jacanoidea**

Family Jacanidae
Jacanas – 7 species

Microparra capensis (A. Smith, 1839) Smaller Jacana	
Actophilornis africana (Gmelin, 1789) African Jacana	
Actophilornis albinucha (I. Geoffrey St. Hilaire, 1882) Madagascar Jacana	
Irediparra gallinacea (Temminck, 1828) Comb-crested Jacana	
Hydrophasianus chirurgus (Scopoli, 1786) Pheasant-tailed Jacana	
Metopidius indicus (Latham, 1790) Bronze-winged Jacana	
Jacana spinosa (Linné, 1758) American Jacana	

Family Rostratulidae
Painted Snipe – 2 species

Rostratula benghalensis (Linné, 1758) Painted Snipe	
Nycticryphes semi-collaris (Vieillot, 1816) South American Painted Snipe	

Super-family **Charadrioidea**

Family Haematopodidae
Oystercatchers – 6 species

Haematopus ostralegus Linné, 1758 Oystercatcher	
Haematopus bachmani Audubon, 1838 Black Oystercatcher	

Neotropical	Nearctic		Palaearctic		Ethiopian	Oriental	Australasian
	South	North	South	North			
					●		
					●		
					●		
							●
						●	
						●	
					●	●	●
●							
	●	●					

Haematopus palliatus Temminck, 1820 American Oystercatcher	
Haematopus leucopodus Garnot, 1926 Magellanic Oystercatcher	
Haematopus fuliginosus Gould, 1845 Sooty Oystercatcher	
Haematopus ater Vieillot & Oudart, 1825 Blackish Oystercatcher	

Family Recurvirostridae
Avocets and Stilts – 6 species

Himantopus himantopus (Linné, 1758) Black-winged Stilt	●
Cladorhynchus leucocephala (Vieillot, 1816) Banded Stilt	
Recurvirostra avosetta Linné, 1758 Avocet	
Recurvirostra americana Gmelin, 1789 American Avocet	
Recurvirostra novae-hollandiae Vieillot, 1816 Red-necked Avocet	
Recurvirostra andina Philippi & Landbeck, 1861 Andian Avocet	

Family Burhinidae
Stone Curlews – 9 species

Burhinus oedicnemus Linné, 1758 Stone Curlew	
Burhinus senegalensis (Swainson, 1837) Senegal Tick-knee	
urhinus vermiculatus (Cabanis, 1868) Water Thick-knee	
Burhinus capensis (Lichtenstein, 1823) Spotted Thick-knee	
Burhinus bistriatus (Wagler, 1829) Double striped Thick-knee	
Burhinus superciliaris (Tschudi, 1843) Peruvian Thick-knee	
Burhinus magnirostris (Latham, 1801) Southern Stone Curlew	
Esacus recurvirostris (Cuvier, 1829) Great Stone Curlew	
Orthorhamphus magnirostris (Vieillot, 1818) Beach Stone Curlew	

| Neotropical | Nearctic | | Palaearctic | | Ethiopian | Oriental | Australasian |
	South	North	South	North			
•	•						
•							
							•
•							
							•
			•				
	•						
							•
•							
			•		•	•	
					•		
					•		
					•		
•							
•							
							•
						•	
						•	•

Family Charadriidae
Plovers – 62 species
  Sub-family Vanellinae

Chettusia leucura (Lichtenstein, 1823)
White-tailed Plover

Chettusia gregaria (Pallas, 1771)
Sociable Plover

Vanellus vanellus (Linné, 1758)
Lapwing

Belanopterus chilensis (Molina, 1782)
Southern Lapwing

Hemiparra crassirostris (Hartlaub, 1855)
Long-toed Lapwing

Tylibyx melanocephalus (Ruppell, 1845)
Spot-breasted Plover

Microsarcops cinereus (Blyth, 1842)
Grey-headed Lapwing

Lobivanellus indicus (Boddaert, 1783)
Red-wattled Lapwing

Xiphidiopterus albiceps (Gould, 1834)
White-crowned Plover

Rogibyx tricolor (Horsfield, 1821)
Banded Plover

Lobibyx novae-hollandiae (Stephens, 1819)
Australian Spur-winged Plover

Lobibyx miles (Boddaert, 1783)
Masked Plover

Afribyx senegallus Linné, 1766
Wattled Plover

Stephanibyx lugubris (Lesson, 1826)
Senegal Plover

Stephanibyx melanopterus (Cretzschmar, 1829)
Black-winged Plover

Stephanibyx coronatus (Boddaert, 1783)
Crowned Lapwing

Hoplopterus spinosus (Linné, 1758)
Spur-winged Lapwing

Hoplopterus armatus (Burchell, 1822)
Blacksmith Plover

Hoplopterus duvaucelii (Lesson, 1826)
Indian Spur-winged Lapwing

Hoploxypterus cayanus (Latham, 1790)
Pied Plover

Neotropical	Nearctic South	Nearctic North	Palaearctic South	Palaearctic North	Ethiopian	Oriental	Australasian
			•				
			•				
			•				
•							
					•		
					•		
			•				
						•	
					•		
						•	
							•
							•
					•		
					•		
					•		
					•		
			•		•		
					•		
						•	
•							

	Cosmopolit●
Ptiloscelys resplendens (Tschudi, 1843) Andean Lapwing	
Zonifer tricolor (Vieillot, 1818) Black-breasted Wattled Lapwing	
Anomalophrys superciliosus (Reichenow, 1886) Brown-chested Plover	
Lobipluvia malarbarica (Boddaert, 1783) Yellow-wattled Lapwing	
Sarciophorus tectus (Boddaert, 1783) Black-headed Plover	
Sub-family Charadriinae	
Squatarola squatarola (Linné, 1758) Grey Plover	
Pluvialis apricaria (Linné, 1758) Golden Plover	
Pluvialis dominica (P. L. S. Müller, 1776) Lesser Golden Plover	
Pluviorhynchus obscurus (Gmelin, 1789) Red-breasted Dotterel	
Charadrius rubricollis Gmelin, 1789 Hooded Dotterel	
Charadrius hiaticula Linné, 1758 Ringed Plover	
Charadrius semipalmatus Bonaparte, 1825 Semipalmated Plover	
Charadrius melodus Ord, 1824 Piping Plover	
Charadrius dubius Scopoli, 1786 Little Ringed Plover	
Charadrius alexandrinus Linné, 1758 Kentish Plover	●
Charadrius venustus Fischer & Reichenow, 1884 White-fronted Sand Plover	
Charadrius falklandicus Latham, 1799 Two-banded Plover	●
Charadrius alticola (Berlepsch & Stolzmann, 1902) Puna Plover	●
Charadrius bicinctus Jardine & Selby, 1827 Banded Dotterel	
Charadrius peronii Schlegel, 1856 Malay Plover	
Charadrius collaris Vieillot, 1818 Collared Plover	●

Neotropical	Nearctic South	Nearctic North	Palaearctic South	Palaearctic North	Ethiopian	Oriental	Australasian
●							
							●
					●		
						●	
					●		
		●		●			
			●	●			
		●		●			
							●
							●
		●	●	●			
		●					
	●						
			●			●	
					●		
							●
							●

	Cosmopol.
Charadrius pecuarius Temminck, 1823 Kittlitz's Plover	
Charadrius sanctae-helenae (Harting, 1873) Wire Bird	
Charadrius thoracicus (Richmond, 1896) Black-banded Sand Plover	
Charadrius placidus Gray and Gray, 1863 Long-billed Ringed Plover	
Charadrius vociferus Linné, 1758 Kildeer Plover	
Charadrius tricollaris (Vieillot, 1818) Three-banded Plover	
Charadrius mongolus Pallas, 1776 Mongolian Plover	
Charadrius wilsonia Ord, 1814 Wilson's Plover	
Charadrius leschenaultii Lesson, 1826 Greater Sand Plover	
Elseyornis melanops (Vieillot, 1818) Black-fronted Plover	
Eupoda asiatica (Pallas, 1773) Caspian Plover	
Eupoda veredus (Gould, 1848) Oriental Plover	
Eupoda montana (J. K. Townsend, 1837) Mountain Plover	
Oreophilus ruficollis (Wagler, 1829) Tawny-throated Dotterel	
Erythrogonys cinctus Gould, 1838 Red-kneed Dotterel	
Eudromias morinellus (Linné, 1758) Dotterel	
Zonibyx modestus (Lichtenstein, 1823) Rufous-chested Dotterel	
Thinornis novae-seelandiae (Gmelin, 1789) New Zealand Shore Plover	
Anarhynchus frontalis Quoy & Gaimard, 1830 Wrybill	
Pluvianellus socialis G. R. Gray, 1846 Magellanic Plover	

Sub-family Phegornithinae

Phegornis mitchellii (Fraser, 1844) Diademed Sandpiper–Plover	

Neotropical	Nearctic		Palaearctic		Ethiopian	Oriental	Australasian
	South	North	South	North			
					●		
					●		
					●		
			●				
	●						
					●		
			●				
●	●						
			●				
							●
			●				
			●				
	●						
●							
							●
			●	●			
●							
							●
							●
●							
●							

Family Glareolidae
Coursers and Pratincoles – 17 species
  Sub-family Cursoriinae

    Pluvianus aegyptius (Linné, 1758)
    Egyptian Plover

    Cursorius cursor (Latham, 1787)
    Cream coloured Courser

    Cursorius temminckii Swainson, 1822
    Temminck's Courser

    Cursorius coromandelicus (Gmelin, 1789)
    Indian Courser

    Rhinoptilus africanus (Temminck, 1807)
    Two-banded Courser

    Rhinoptilus cinctus (Heuglin, 1863)
    Heuglin's Courser

    Rhinoptilus chalcopterus (Temminck, 1824)
    Violet-tipped Courser

    Rhinoptilus bitorquatus (Blyth, 1848)
    Jerdon's Courser

    Peltohyas australis (Gould, 1840)
    Australian Dotterel

  Sub-family Glareolinae

    Stiltia isabella (Vieillot, 1816)
    Long-legged Pratincole

    Glareola pratincola (Linné, 1766)
    Collared Pratincole

    Glareola maldivarum J. R. Forster, 1795
    Eastern collared Pratincole

    Glareola nordmanni Fischer, 1842
    Black-winged Pratincole

    Glareola ocularis Verreaux, 1833
    Madagascar Pratincole

    Glareola nuchalis G. R. Gray, 1840
    White collared Pratincole

    Glareola cinerea Fraser, 1843
    Grey Pratincole

    Glareola lactea Temminck, 1820
    Little Pratincole

277

Neotropical	Nearctic South	Nearctic North	Palaearctic South	Palaearctic North	Ethiopian	Oriental	Australasian
					●		
			●		●	●	
					●		
						●	
					●		
					●		
					●		
						●	
							●
							●
			●		●	●	
			●			●	
			●				
					●		
					●		
					●		
						●	

	Cosmopol

Family Scolopacidae
Sandpipers and Snipe – 85 species
  Sub-family Tringinae
    Tribe Numenini	

Bartramia longicauda (Bechstein, 1812) Upland (Bartram's) Sandpiper	
Numenius minutus Gould, 1840 Little Curlew	
Numenius borealis (J. R. Forster, 1772) Eskimo Curlew	
Numenius phaeopus Linné, 1758 Whimbrel	
Numenius tahitiensis (Gmelin, 1789) Bristle-thighed Curlew	
Numenius tenuirostris Vieillot, 1817 Slender-billed Curlew	
Numenius arquata (Linné, 1758) Eurasian Curlew	
Numenius madagascariensis (Linné, 1766) Far-eastern Curlew	
Numenius americanus Bechstein, 1812 Long-billed Curlew	
Limosa limosa (Linné, 1758) Black-tailed Godwit	
Limosa haemastica (Linné, 1758) Hudsonian Godwit	
Limosa lapponica (Linné, 1758) Bar-tailed Godwit	
Limosa fedoa (Linné, 1758) Marbled Godwit	
Tribe Tringini	
Tringa erythropus (Pallas, 1764) Spotted Redshank	
Tringa totanus (Linné, 1758) Redshank	
Tringa flavipes (Gmelin, 1789) Lesser Yellowlegs	
Tringa stagnatalis (Bechstein, 1803) Marsh Sandpiper	
Tringa nebularia (Gunnerus, 1767) Greenshank	
Tringa melanoleuca (Gmelin, 1789) Greater Yellowlegs	

Neotropical	Nearctic South	Nearctic North	Palaearctic South	Palaearctic North	Ethiopian	Oriental	Australasian
	●	●					
			●				
		●					
	●	●	●	●			
		●					
			●				
			●				
			●				
●							
			●				
		●					
				●			
●							
				●			
			●				
		●					
			●				
				●			
●							

Cosmopol‹

Tringa ocrophus Linné, 1758 Green Sandpiper	
Tringa solitaria Wilson, 1813 Solitary Sandpiper	
Tringa glareola Linné, 1758 Wood Sandpiper	
Pseudototanus guttifer (Nordmann, 1835) Spotted Greenshank	
Xenus cinereus (Güldenstaedt, 1774) Terek Sandpiper	
Actitis hypoleucos (Linné, 1758) Common Sandpiper	
Actitis macularia (Linné, 1766) Spotted Sandpiper	
Catoptrophorus semipalmatus (Gmelin, 1789) Willet	
Heteroscelus brevipes (Vieillot, 1816) Grey-rumped Sandpiper	
Heteroscelus incanus (Gmelin, 1789) Wandering Tattler	

Tribe Prosobonini

Aechmorhynchus parvirostris (Peale, 1848) Tuamatu Sandpiper	

Sub-family Arenariinae

Arenaria interpres (Linné, 1758) Turnstone	
Arenaria melanocephala (Vigors, 1828) Black Turnstone	

Sub-family Phalaropodinae

Phalaropus fulicarius (Linné, 1758) Grey Phalarope	
Steganops tricolor Vieillot, 1819 Wilson's Phalarope	
Lobipes lobatus (Linné, 1758) Red-necked Phalarope	

Sub-family Scolopacinae

Scolopax rusticola Linné, 1758 Eurasian Woodcock	

Neotropical	Nearctic		Palaearctic		Ethiopian	Oriental	Australasian
	South	North	South	North			
			●				
	●	●					
			●	●			
			●				
			●	●			
			●	●			
●							
●							
			●				
		●					
							●
		●		●			
		●					
		●		●			
●							
		●		●			
			●				

	Cosmopol
Scolopax saturata Horsfield, 1821 East Indian Woodcock	
Scolopax celebensis Riley, 1921 Celebes Woodcock	
Scolopax rochussenii Schlegel, 1866 Obi Woodcock	
Philohela minor (Gmelin, 1789) American Woodcock	

Sub-family Capellinae

Limnodromus griseus Gmelin, 1789 Short-billed Dowitcher	
Limnodromus scolopaceus (Say, 1823) Long-billed Dowitcher	
Limnodromus semipalmatus (Blyth, 1848) Asian Dowitcher	
Coenocorytha aucklandica G. R. Gray, 1845 Sub-antarctic Snipe	
Capella solitaria (Hodgson, 1831) Solitary Snipe	
Capella hardwickii (J. E. Gray, 1831) Japanese Snipe	
Capella nemoricola (Hodgson, 1836) Wood Snipe	
Capella stenura (Bonaparte, 1839) Pintail Snipe	
Capella megala (Swinhoe, 1861) Swinhoe's Snipe	
Capella nigripennis (Bonaparte, 1839) African Snipe	
Capella macrodactyla (Bonaparte, 1839) Madagascar Snipe	
Capella media (Latham, 1787) Great Snipe	
Capella gallinago (Linné, 1758) Common Snipe	●
Capella delicata (Ord, 1825) American Snipe	
Capella paraguaiae (Vieillot, 1816) Pina Snipe	
Capella nobilis (Sclater, 1856) Noble Snipe	
Capella undulata (Boddaert, 1783) Giant Snipe	

Neotropical	Nearctic South	Nearctic North	Palaearctic South	Palaearctic North	Ethiopian	Oriental	Australasian
						•	
						•	
						•	
	•						
	•	•					
	•	•					
			•				
							•
			•				
			•				
						•	
			•				
			•				
					•		
					•		
			•				
	•	•					
•							
•							
•							

	Cosmopol
Chubbia imperialis (Sclater & Salvin, 1869) Banded Snipe	
Chubbia jamesoni (Bonaparte, 1855) Jameson's Snipe	
Chubbia stricklandii (G. R. Gray, 1845) Cordilleran Snipe	
Lymnocryptes minima (Brünnich, 1764) Jack Snipe	

Sub-family Calidriinae (= Eroliinae)

Calidris canutus (Linné, 1758) Knot	
Calidris tenuirostris (Horsfield, 1821) Great Knot	
Calidris alba (Pallas, 1764) Sanderling	
Calidris pusillus (Linné, 1766) Semi-palmated Sandpiper	
Calidris mauri (Cabanis, 1856) Western Sandpiper	
Calidris pygmeus (Linné, 1758) Spoon-billed Sandpiper	
Calidris ruficollis (Pallas, 1776) Red-necked Stint	
Calidris minuta (Leisler, 1812) Little Stint	
Calidris temminckii (Leisler, 1812) Temminck's Stint	
Calidris subminuta (Middendorff, 1853) Long-toed Stint	
Calidris minutilla (Vieillot, 1819) Least Sandpiper	
Calidris fuscicollis (Vieillot, 1819) White-rumped Sandpiper	
Calidris bairdii (Coues, 1861) Baird's Sandpiper	
Calidris melanotus (Vieillot, 1819) Pectoral Sandpiper	
Calidris acuminata (Horsfield, 1821) Sharp-tailed Sandpiper	
Calidris maritima (Brunnich, 1764) Purple Sandpiper	
Calidris ptilocnemis (Coues, 1878) Rock Sandpiper	

| Neotropical | Nearctic | | Palaearctic | | Ethiopian | Oriental | Australasian |
	South	North	South	North			
●							
●							
●							
			●	●			
		●		●			
				●			
		●		●			
		●		●			
		●					
			●	●			
		●		●			
				●			
				●			
			●	●			
		●					
		●					
		●		●			
		●					
				●			
		●		●			
		●		●			

Calidris alpina (Linné, 1758) Dunlin	
Calidris testacea (Pallas, 1764) Curlew Sandpiper	
Limicola falcinellus (Pontoppidan, 1768) Broad-billed Sandpiper	
Micropalama himantopus (Bonaparte, 1826) Stilt Sandpiper	
Tryngites subruficollis (Vieillot, 1819) Buff-breasted Sandpiper	
Philomachus pugnax (Linné, 1758) Ruff	
Sub-family Aphrizinae	
Aphriza virgata (Gmelin, 1789) Surf Bird	

Super-family **Ibidorhynchoidea**

Family Ibidorhynchidae
Ibis-bills – 1 species

Ibidorhyncha struthersii Vigors, 1832 Ibis-bill	

Super-family **Dromadoidea**

Family Dromadidae
Crab Plovers – 1 species

Dromas ardeola Paykull, 1805 Crab Plover	

Super-family **Chionidoidea**

Family Thinocoridae
Seedsnipes – 4 species

Attagis gayi I. Geoffrey St.-Hilaire & Lesson, 1830 Rufous-bellied Seed Snipe	
Attagis malouinus (Boddaert, 1783) White-bellied Seed Snipe	
Thinocorus orbignyianus I. Geoffrey St.-Hilaire & Lesson, 1830 Grey-breasted Seed Snipe	
Thinocorus rumicivorus Eschscholtz, 1829 Least Seed Snipe	

Neotropical	Nearctic		Palaearctic		Ethiopian	Oriental	Australasian
	South	North	South	North			
		●		●			
				●			
				●			
		●					
		●					
			●	●			
		●					
			●			●	
					●	●	
●							
●							
●							
●							

	Cosmopo
Family Chionididae Sheathbills – 2 species	
Chionis alba (Gmelin, 1788) Snowy Sheathbill	
Chionis minor Hartlaub, 1841 Black-faced Sheathbill	

| Neotropical | Nearctic | | Palaearctic | | Ethiopian | Oriental | Australasian |
	South	North	South	North			
●							
							●

APPENDIX 2

The occurrence of rare waders in the British Isles

TABLE I. Monthly records of rarities prior to 1958, 1958–72 and 1972–76. (Total numbers recorded in brackets.) B = breeding.

	J	F	M	A	M	J	J	A	S	O	N	D
Black-winged Stilt (157)												
>1958					←		100		→			
1958–72				9	14	5	5	4	13	3		1
1972–76					1					1		1
Hastings rarities					2				2	1		
White-tailed Plover (1)												
>1958												
1958–72												
1972–76							1					
Hastings rarities												
Sociable Plover (16)												
>1958									←	5	→	
1958–72	1				1		1		2	2		
1972–76										4		
Hastings rarities					8							
Lesser Golden Plover (42)												
>1958								←	6	→		
1958–72					1	1		2	10	8		
1972–76						1	1	2	9	1		
Hastings rarities									8			
Kildeer Plover (24)												
>1958	9 ——→										←——→	
1958–72		5	1								3	
1972–76	1		3				.			1	1	
Hastings rarities				3				1			2	
Caspian Plover (2)												
>1958					2							
1958–72												
1972–76												
Hastings rarities				1			2					

	J	F	M	A	M	J	J	A	S	O	N	D
Cream Coloured Courser (30)												
>1958										←26→		
1958–72										4		
1972–76												
Hastings rarities		2			2			1				
Pratincole (Collared) (51)												
>1958		1			7	3	1	8	5	2	4	
1958–72					3		2			2		
1972–76				1	6	2	2	1	1			
Hastings rarities				1	2	1	2	1				
Black-winged Pratincole (15)												
>1958					1		1	3				
1958–72							1	3	3			
1972–76								3				
Hastings rarities				1	4	1	1					
Upland Sandpiper (31)												
>1958										←15→		
1958–72								3	7	1		
1972–76							1	1	3			
Hastings rarities							2					
Eskimo Curlew (7)												
>1958									4	1	2	
1958–72												
1972–76												
Hastings rarities												
Slender-billed Curlew (1)												
>1958												
1958–72												
1972–76							.				1	
Hastings rarities					2				4			
Lesser Yellowlegs (127)												
>1958					←35→							
1958–72			1	2	4	1	2	10	24	15	2	1
1972–76				1	3			6	10		4	
Hastings rarities								2				
Marsh Sandpiper (23)												
>1958					←6→				←6→			
1958–72		2					1	2	2			
1972–76					2				2			
Hastings rarities					2	2	1					

Greater Yellowlegs (21)

	J	F	M	A	M	J	J	A	S	O	N	D
>1958				3			←	6		→		3
1958–72				1			1	2	1	1	1	
1972–76							1	1				
Hastings rarities										1		

Solitary Sandpiper (17)

	J	F	M	A	M	J	J	A	S	O	N	D
>1958							1	1	2	2		
1958–72								2	4			
1972–76							1		4			
Hastings rarities			1	1				2				

Terek Sandpiper (13)

	J	F	M	A	M	J	J	A	S	O	N	D
>1958					1	1		1				
1958–72					3	1		1				
1972–76					1	2		1				1
Hastings rarities					7							

Spotted Sandpiper (33)

	J	F	M	A	M	J	J	A	S	O	N	D
>1958			←	3	→		←	3	→			1
1958–72					2	1		2	5	4	1	
1972–76					2(1B)			4		3		2
Hastings rarities					8							

Wilson's Phalarope (76)

	J	F	M	A	M	J	J	A	S	O	N	D
>1958										1		
1958–72					2	8	1	10	24	7		
1972–76					1	1	3	4	11	2	1	
Hastings rarities					1							

Long-billed Dowitcher (32)

	J	F	M	A	M	J	J	A	S	O	N	D
>1958								←	9	→		
1958–72					2				7	3	3	
1972–76								1	4	3		
Hastings rarities												

Short-billed Dowitcher (6)

	J	F	M	A	M	J	J	A	S	O	N	D
>1958									1	3		
1958–72				1					1			
1972–76												
Hastings rarities												

	J	F	M	A	M	J	J	A	S	O	N	D
All Dowitchers (131)												
>1958								←—	31	—→		
1958–72		I		2	6	I		5	20	34	9	3
1972–76	I			I	I		I	2	8	3	I	I
Hastings rarities					I			I				
Great Snipe (222+)												
>1958							←——		(180)	—→		
1958–72	3	2	I	I	I		I	2	5	4	2	5
1972–76			I	I	I			2	7	3		
Hastings rarities								I		I	I	
Semi-palmated Sandpiper (c. 18)												
>1958									2			
1958–72							I	2	9	2	I	
1972–76					I			I		I		
Hastings rarities									I			
Western Sandpiper (5)												
>1958					I							
1958–72									I	I		
1972–76							I		I			
Hastings rarities												
Red-necked Stint (3?)												
>1958												
1958–72												
1972–76										3?		
Hastings rarities												
Least Sandpiper (21)												
>1958								←—	6	—→		
1958–72						I		4	6	2		
1972–76										2		
Hastings rarities												
White-rumped Sandpiper (134)												
>1958	←———								24	—→		
1958–72	I	2	I					2	15	28	31	7
1972–76								5	7	6	4	I
Hastings rarities				I		I		I				

	J	F	M	A	M	J	J	A	S	O	N	D
Baird's Sandpiper (61)												
>1958					1			4				
1958–72							1	7	19	10	1	
1972–76						1	1	4	9	3		
Hastings rarities									2	1		
Pectoral Sandpiper (646+)												
>1958					2 or 3		←——	158	——→			
1958–72					2	7	5	24	98	246	105	1
1972–76				not regarded as rare								
Hastings rarities					2				3	1	1	
Sharp-tailed Sandpiper (14)												
>1958		1							1	2	1	
1958–72									1	2		
1972–76									3	1	1	1
Hastings rarities												
Broad-billed Sandpiper (51)												
>1958						←——		23	——→			
1958–72					5	1	2	7	4			
1972–76					7	1		1				
Hastings rarities									2	4	1	
Stilt Sandpiper (12)												
>1958								1				
1958–72			1				3	3	1	1		
1972–76								2				
Hastings rarities												
Buff-breasted Sandpiper (250)												
>1958								←——	33	—→		
1958–72					1	2	1	9	73	14	1	
1972–76				1	1	2		9	88	14	1	
Hastings rarities												

TABLE 2. American waders in the British Isles.

	Total	Before 1958	Hastings rarities	1958–76
Lesser Golden Plover	36	3	1	33
Kildeer	24	9	6	15
Upland Sandpiper	31	15	2	16
Eskimo Curlew	1	1	0	0
Lesser Yellowshank	127	35	2	92
Greater Yellowshank	21	12	1	9
Solitary Sandpiper	17	6	4	11
Spotted Sandpiper	33	7	8	26
Dowitcher	131	31	2	100
Semi-palmated Sandpiper	18	2	1	16
Western Sandpiper	5	1	0	4
Red-necked Stint	3	0	0	3
Least Sandpiper	21	6	0	15
White-rumped Sandpiper	137	24	3	113
Baird's Sandpiper	61	5	3	56
Pectoral Sandpiper	646	158	7	488
Stilt–Sandpiper	12	1	0	11
Buff-breasted Sandpiper	250	33	0	217
Wilson's Phalarope	76	1	1	75
	1651	350	41	1301

TABLE 3. Rare Eurasian waders in the British Isles.

	Total	Before 1958	Hastings rarities	1958–76
Black-winged Stilt	157	100	4	57
Sociable Plover	16	5	8	11
White-tailed Plover	1	0	0	1
Lesser Golden Plover	5	3	7	2
Caspian Plover	2	2	0	0
Cream-coloured Courser	30	26	5	4
Black-winged Pratincole	15	5	7	10
Collared Pratincole	51	31	7	20
Slender-billed Curlew	1	0	6	1
Great Snipe	222+	180+	3	42
Marsh Sandpiper	23	12	5	11
Terek Sandpiper	13	3	7	10
Sharp-tailed Sandpiper	14	5	0	9
Broad-billed Sandpiper	51	23	7	28
	601	395	66	206

TABLE 4. Other Hastings rarities – species struck off the British List.

	No.	Date
Semi-palmated Ringed Plover	1	8.4.1916
Grey-rumped Sandpiper	1	23.9.1914
	1	27.9.1914

TABLE 5. Species not considered now as rarities.

	J	F	M	A	M	J	J	A	S	O	N	D
Little Ringed Plover												
>1920				1	3		1	3		2		
Hastings rarities				1								

BIBLIOGRAPHY

1. ALLEN, J.A. 1877. The influence of physical conditions in the genesis of species. *Radical Rev. 1*: 108–140.
2. ANDERSON, S.S. 1972. The ecology of Morecambe Bay II. Intertidal Invertebrates and factors affecting their distribution. *J.Appl.Ecol. 9*: 161–178.
3. ARNOLD, E.C. 1924. British Waders. Cambridge.
4. ASHMOLE, N.P. 1962. The Black Noddy *Anous tenuirostris* on Ascension Island. *Ibis. 103b*: 235–319.
5. ATKINSON, J.M.S. 1976. Inland Wintering and Urban Roosting by Redshanks. *Bird Study. 23*: 51–55.
6. BAINBRIDGE, I. P. & MINTON, C.D.T. 1978. The Migration and Mortality of the Curlew in Britain and Ireland. *Bird Study. 25*: 39–50.
7. BAKER, M.C. & BAKER, A.E.M. 1973. Niche Relationships among six species of shore birds on their wintering and breeding ranges. *Ecol. Monog. 43*: 193–212.
8. BANNERMAN, D.A. 1961. The Birds of the British Isles vol. X. Edinburgh.
9. BELLROSE, F.C. & GRABER, R.R. 1963. A radar study of the flight directions of nocturnal migrants. *13th Int.Orn.Congr.* : 362–389.
10. BENGTSON, S.A. 1975. Timing of the moult of the Purple Sandpiper *Calidris maritima* in Spitzbergen. *Ibis. 117*: 100–102.
11. BENGTSON, S.A., NILSSON, A., NORDSTROM, S. & RUNDGREN, S. 1976. Effect of Bird Predation on Lumbricid Populations. *Oikos. 27*: 9–12.
12. BERGER, M. & HART, J.S. 1974. Physiology & Energetics of Flight; in Avian Biology, Farner, D.S. & King, J.R. New York p.415–477.
13. BERGMAN, G. 1946. Der Steinwalzer, *Arenaria i. interpres(L.)* im seiner Beziehung mur Umwelt. *Acta Zool.Fenn. 47*: 1–144.
14. BOERE, G.C. 1977. The significance of the Dutch Waddenzee in the annual life cycle of Arctic, Subarctic and Boreal Waders. Part 1. The function as a moulting area. *Ardea 64*: 210–291.
15. BOYD, H. 1962. Mortality and Fertility in European Charadrii. *Ibis. 104*: 368–387.
16. BOYD, H. & OGILVIE, M.A. 1966. The primary moult of Waders. *Ibis. 108*: 454.
17. BRANSON, N.J.B.A. & MINTON, C.D.T. 1976. Moult measurements and migrations of the Grey Plover. *Bird Study. 23*: 257–266.
18 BRUDERER, B. 1971. Radarbeobachtungen uber den Frühlingszug in Schweizerischen Mittelland. *Orn.Beob. 68*: 89–158.
19. BUB, H. 1962. Planberingungen am Sandregenpfeifer (*Charadrius hiaticula*). *J.Orn. 103*: 243–249.
20. CADIEUX, F. 1970. Capacité de vol et routes de migration autumnale de certains oiseaux de rivage. *MSc Thesis*, University of Montreal.
21. CASEMENT, M.B. 1966. Migration across the Mediterranean observed by radar. *Ibis. 108*: 461–491.

22   CATESBY, M. 1731. The Natural History of Carolina, Florida and Bahama Islands. London.

23. CONDER. 1974. Ministerial Ignorance. *Birds* (RSPB Magazine). *5*: 6.

24. CUMMINS, K.W. & WUYCHECK, J.C. 1971. Calorie equivalents for investigation in ecological energetics. *Mitt.Int.Ver.Limnol. 18*: 1–158.

25. DARE, P.J. 1966. The breeding and wintering population of the Oystercatcher (*Haematopus ostralegus* L.) in the British Isles. *Fishery Invest.Lond.Ser.II. 25(5)*, 1–69.

26. DARE, P.J. 1970. The movement of Oystercatchers *Haematopus ostralegus* L., visiting or breeding in the British Isles. *Fishery Invest.Lond.Ser.II. 25(9)*: 1–137.

27. DARE, P.J. 1977. Seasonal changes in body weight of Oystercatchers *Haematopus ostralegus*. *Ibis. 119*: 494–506.

28. DARE, P.J. & MERCER, A.J. 1973. Foods of the Oystercatcher in Morecambe Bay, Lancashire. *Bird Study, 20*: 173–184.

29. DAVIDSON, P.E. 1967. A Study of the Oystercatcher (*Haemotopus ostralegus L.*) in relation to the Fishery for Cockles (*Cardium edule L.*) in the Burry Inlet, South Wales. *Fishery Invest. Lond.* Ser.II. *25(7)*: 1–28.

30. DAVIDSON, P.E. 1968. The Oystercatcher – a pest of shellfisheries; in *The Problems of Birds as Pests* ed. Murton, R.K. & Wright, E.N., London.

31. DEMENTIEV, C.T. & GLADKOV, N.A. 1951. Birds of the Soviet Union. Israel Program of Scientific Translation, Jerusalem, 1969.

32   DICK, W.J.A. 1975. Oxford and Cambridge Mauritanian Expedition Report. Cambridge.

33. DICK, W.J.A., PIENKOWSKI, M.W., WALTNER, M. & MINTON, C.D.T. 1976. Distribution and Geographical Origins of Knot *Calidris canutus* wintering in Europe and Africa. *Ardea. 64*: 22–46.

34. DIRCKSEN, R. 1932. Die Biologie des Austernfischers, der Brandseeschwalbe und der Kustenseeschwalbe nach Beobachtungen. *J. Orn. 80*: 427–521.

35. DORST, J. 1961. The Migrations of Birds. London.

36. DRINNAN, R.E. 1957. The winter feeding of the Oystercatcher (*Haematopus ostralegus*) on the edible cockle (*Cardium edule*) *J.Anim.Ecol. 26*: 441–469.

37. DRINNAN, P.E. & COLE, H.A. 1957. Oystercatchers (*Haematopus ostralegus*) as pests of cockle and mussel beds. *Nat.in Wales. 3*: 499–503.

38. DWIGHT, J. 1900. The moult of the North American shore birds, *Limicolae*. *Auk. 17*: 368–385.

39. EADES, R.A. & OKILL, D.J. 1977. Weight changes of Dunlins on the Dee estuary in May. *Bird Study. 24*: 62–63.

40. EASTWOOD, L. 1967. Radar Ornithology. London.

41. ELLIOTT, C.C.H., WALTNER, M., UNDERHILL, C.G., PRINGLE, J.S.S. & DICK, W.J.A. 1976. The Migration system of the Curlew-Sandpiper *Calidris ferruginea* in Africa. *Ostrich. 47*: 191–213.

42. ENNION, E.A. 1949. The Lapwing. London.

43. EVANS, P.R. 1966a. Wader migration in North-East England. – *Trans.Nat.Hist.Soc. Northumb., 16*: 126–151. Newcastle upon Tyne.

44. EVANS, P.R. 1966b. Autumn movements, moult & measurements of the Redpoll *Carduelis flammea cabaret*. *Ibis. 108*: 183–216.

45. EVANS, P.R. 1968. Autumn movements and orientation of Waders in North-East England and Southern Scotland studied by radar. *Bird Study. 15*: 53–64.

46. EVANS, P.R. 1976. Energy balance and optimal foraging strategies in shore

birds: some implications for their distribution and movements in the non-breeding season. *Ardea. 64*: 117–139.

47. EVANS, P.R. & SMITH, P.C. 1975. Studies of Shore Birds at Lindisfarne, Northumberland. Fat and pectoral muscle as indicators of body condition in the Bar-tailed Godwit. *Wildfowl. 26*: 64–76.

48. FEDYUSHIN, A.V. & DOLBIK, M.S. 1967. The Birds of Byelorussia. *Nauka i Tekhnika Publishing House* Minsk.

49. FJELDSÅ, J. 1977. Guide to the young of European Precocial Birds. Denmark.

50. FRENZEL, B 1968. Grundzüge der Pleistozänen vegetation-geschichte nord Eurasiens. *Steiner Verlag GMBH*. Weisbaden.

51. FUCHS, E. 1973. Durchzug und Uberwinterung des Alpenstrandlaufer *Calidris alpina* in der Camargue. *Orn. Beob. 70*: 113–134.

52. FURNESS, R.W. 1973a. Roost selection by Waders. *Scott.Nat. 7*: 281–287.

53. FURNESS, R.W. 1973b. Wader populations at Musselburgh. *Scott.Birds. 7*: 275–281.

54. GEIST, V. In Press. Life strategies, human evolution, environmental design; towards a theory of health.

55. GLUTZ VON BLOTZHEIM, U.N., BAUER, K.M. & BEZZEL, E. 1975–1977. Handbuch der Vögel Mitteleuropas. Vols. 6 & 7. Weisboden.

56. GOODYER, L.R. 1976. Lapwing weights and moult. *W.S.G.Bull. 18*: 9–12.

57. GORDON, S.P. 1915. Hill birds of Scotland. London.

58. GOSS-CUSTARD, J.D. 1969. The winter feeding ecology of the Redshank *Tringa totanus*. *Ibis. 111*: 338–356.

59. GOSS-CUSTARD, J.D. 1970. The responses of Redshank (*Tringa totanus (L)*) to spacial variations in the density of their prey. *J.Anim.Ecol. 39*: 91–113.

60. GOSS-CUSTARD, J.D. 1973. Current problems in studying the feeding ecology of estuarine birds. *CERS Research Paper. 4*: 1–33.

61. GOSS-CUSTARD, J.D. 1977a. Predator responses and prey mortality in Redshank *Tringa totanus* (L) and a preferred prey *Corophium volutator* (Pallas). *J.Anim.Ecol. 46*: 21–35.

62. GOSS-CUSTARD, J.D. 1977b. The Ecology of The Wash: III. Density related behaviour and the possible effects of a loss of feeding grounds on wading birds (Charadrii). *J.Appl.Ecol. 14*: 721–739.

63. GOSS-CUSTARD, J.D. & CHARMAN, K. 1976. Predicting how many wintering waterfowl an area can support. *Wildfowl Ecol.Sym. 27*: 157–158.

64. GOSS-CUSTARD, J.D., JENYON, R.A., JONES, R.E. NEWBERRY, P.E. & WILLIAMS, R.B. 1977. The ecology of The Wash. II. Seasonal variation in the feeding conditions of wading birds. *J.Appl.Ecol. 14*: 701–719.

65. GOSS-CUSTARD, J.D. & JONES, R.E. 1976. The diets of Redshank and Curlew. *Bird Study. 23*: 233–243.

66. GREENHALGH, M.E. 1975. Studies on the foods and feeding ecology of wading birds. Ph.D. Thesis, Liverpool Polytechnic.

67. GRIMES, L.G. 1974. Radar tracks of Palaearctic waders departing from the coast of Ghana in spring. *Ibis. 116*: 165–171.

68. GROSSKOPF, G. 1958. Zur Biologie des Rotschenkels (*Tringa t. totanus L*) I. *J. Orn. 99*: 1–17.

69. GROSSKOPF, G. 1959. Zur Biologie des Rotschenkels (*Tringa t. totanus L*) II. *J. Orn. 100*: 210–236.

70. GROSSKOPF, G. 1964. Sterblichkeit und Durcheschnittsalter einiger Kusten-vogel. *J. Orn. 105*: 427–449.
71. HALDANE, J.B.S. 1955. The calculation of mortality rates from ringing data. *11th Int.Orn.Congr.* Basel. *45*: 454–458.
72. HALE, W.G. 1956. The lack of territory in the Redshank. *Ibis. 98*: 398–400.
73. HALE, W.G. 1971. A revision of the taxonomy of the Redshank. *Zool.J.Linn.Soc. 50*: 199–268.
74. HALE, W.G. 1973. The distribution of the Redshank, *Tringa totanus*, in the winter range. *Zool.J.Linn.Soc. 53*: 177–236.
75. HANCOCK, D.A. 1967. Growth and mesh selection in the edible cockle. *J.Appl.Ecol.4.* 137–157.
76. HANCOCK, D.A. 1971. The role of predators and parasites in a fishery for the mollusc *Cardium edule* L. Dynamics of Populations. (ed. der Boer, P.J. and Gradwell, G.R.) *Proc.Adv.Study Inst. Oosterbeek.* pp 419–439. Wageningen.
77. HANCOCK, D.A. 1973. The relationship between stock and recruitment in exploited invertebrates. *Rapp.P.-V. Reun.Cons.int.Explor.Mer. 164*: 113–31.
78. HANCOCK, D.A. & FRANKLIN, A. 1972. Seasonal changes in the condition of the edible cockle (*Cardium edule* L). *J.Appl.Ecol. 9*: 567–579.
79. HANCOCK, D.A. & URQUHART, A.E. 1965. Determination of natural mortality and its causes in an exploited population of cockles. *Fisheries Investigation.* Series II Vol. *24(2)*: 1–40.
80. HARRISON, J.M. 1968. Bristow and the Hastings Rarities Affair. St. Leonards on Sea.
81. HELDT, R. 1966. Zur Brutbiologie des Alpenstrandlaüfers. *Corax. 1*: 173–188.
82. HEMMINGSEN, A.M. 1950. The relation of bird migration in North Eastern China to body weight and its bearing on Bergmann's Rule. *10th Int.Orn.Congr.* 289:294.
83. HEMMINGSEN, A.M. 1951. Observations on birds in North-Eastern China, especially the migration at Pei-tai-beach. *Spolia Zool. Mus. Hauniensis*, Copenhagen.
84. HEPPLESTON, P.B. 1971. The feeding ecology of Oystercatchers (*Haematopus ostralegus* L) in winter in northern Scotland. *J.Anim.Ecol. 40*: 651–672.
85. HEPPLESTON, P.B. 1972. The comparative breeding ecology of Oystercatchers (*Haematopus ostralegus* L) in inland and coastal habitats. *J.Anim.Ecol. 41*: p.23–51.
86. HILDEN, O. 1961. Uber den Beginn des Wegzuges bei den Limikolen im Finland. *Orn.Fenn. 38*: 2–31.
87. HILDEN, O. 1965. Zur Brutbiologie des Temminckstrandlaufers *Calidris temminckii* (Leisl.). *Orn.Fenn.* Vol. *42*: 1–5.
88. HILDEN, O. & VUOLANTO, S. 1972. Breeding biology of the Red-necked Phalarope *Phalaropus lobatus* in Finland. *Orn.Fenn. 49*: 57–85.
89. HOGAN-WARBURG, A.J. 1966. Social behaviour of the Ruff. *Ardea. 54*: 109–229.
90. HÖHN, E.O. 1967. Observations on the breeding biology of Wilson's Phalarope (*Steganopus tricolor*) in Central Alaska. *Auk. 84*: 220–244.
91. HÖHN, E.O. 1968. Some observations on the breeding of Northern Phalaropes at Seammon Bay, Alaska. *Auk. 85*: 316–317.
92. HÖHN, E.O. 1971. Observations on the breeding behaviour of Grey and Red-necked Phalaropes. *Ibis. 113*: 335–348.

93. HOLMES, R.T. 1966a. Breeding ecology and annual cycle adaptions of the Red-backed Sandpiper (*Calidris alpina*) in Northern Alaska. *Condor. 68*: 3–46.

94. HOLMES, R.T. 1966b. Feeding ecology of the Red-backed Sandpiper (*Calidris alpina*) in Arctic Alaska. *Ecology. 47*: 32–45.

95. HOLMES, R.T. 1970. Differences in population density, territoriality and food supply of Dunlin on Arctic and Subarctic Tundra; in: Watson, A. (Ed.) Animal Populations in relation to their food resources. *Oxford and Edinburgh*.

96. HOLMES, R.T. 1971a. Density, Habitat, & the Mating System of the Western Sandpiper (*Calidris mauri*). *Oecologia. 7*: 191–208.

97. HOLMES, R.T. 1971b. Latitudinal differences in the breeding and moult schedules of Alaskan Red-backed Sandpipers. *Condor. 73*: 93–99.

98. HOLMES, R.T. 1972. Ecological factors influencing the breeding season schedule of Western Sandpipers (*Calidris mauri*) in Subarctic Alaska. *Am.Midl.Nat. 87*: 472–491.

99. HOLMES, R.T. & PITELKA, F.A. 1968. Food overlap among co-existing Sandpipers on Northern Alaskan Tundra. *Systematic Zoology. 17*: 305–318.

100. HORWOOD, J.W. & GOSS-CUSTARD, J.D. 1977. Predation by the Oystercatcher (*Haematopus ostralegus L.*) in relation to the cockle (*Cerastoderma edule L*) fishery in the Burry Inlet, South Wales. *J.Appl.Ecol. 14*: 139–158.

101. HUGHES, R.N. 1970. An energy budget for a tidal flat population of the bivalve *Scrobicularia plana*. (Da Costa). *J.Anim.Ecol. 39*: 357–378.

102. HULSCHER, J.B. 1974. An experimental study of the food intake of the Oystercatcher *Haematopus ostralegus L.* in captivity during the summer. *Ardea. 62*: 155–170.

103. HULSCHER, J.B. 1976. Localisation of cockles (*Cardium edule L.*) by the Oystercatcher (*Haematopus ostralegus L.*) in darkness and daylight. *Ardea. 64*: 292–311.

104. HUMPHREY, P.S. & PARKES, K.C. 1959. An approach to the study of moults and plumages. *Auk. 76*: 1–31.

105. HUXLEY, J.S. 1912. A first account of the courtship of the Redshank. *Proc.Zoo.Soc.Lond. 33*: 647–655.

106. ISAKOV, J.A. 1949. K voproso ob elementarnych populjatsiach ptits. *Akad.Nauk SSSR Moskva – Leningrad. Biol.Ser. 1*: 54–70.

107. JACKSON, A.C. 1918. The moults and sequence of plumages of the British Waders *Brit. Birds*. I–V; *11*: 55–64, 83–85, 105–116, 177–182, 228–230. VI–X; *12*: 4–13, 39–41, 104–113, 146–151, 172–179.

108. JAMES, F.C. 1970. Geographic size variation in birds and its relationship to climate. *Ecology. 51*: 365–390.

109. JEHL, J.R. 1968. Relationships in the Charadrii *Sandiego Soc.Nat.Hist. 3*.

110. JOHNS, J.E. 1969. Field Studies of Wilson's Phalarope. *Auk. 86*: 660–670.

111. JOHNSTON, D.W. & McFARLANE, R.W. 1967. Migration and bioenergetics of flight in the Pacific Golden Plover. *Condor. 69*: 156–168.

112. JUNGFER, W. 1954. Uber Paartreue, Nistplatztreue und Alter der Austernfischer (*Haematopus o. ostralegus*) auf Mellum. *Vogelwarte. 17*: 6–15.

113. KEIGHLEY, J. 1949. Oystercatchers. *Skok.Bird. Obs.Rep.* 6–9.

114. KENDEIGH, S.C. 1967. Data (unpublished) in Cummins & Wuycheck (1971).

115. KING, J.R. & FARNER, D.S. 1966. The adaptive role of winter fattening in the White-crowned Sparrow with comments on its regulation. *Amer.Nat. 100*: 403–418.

116. KITTLE, T. 1975. Weights and moult of Green Sandpipers in Britain. *Ringing & Migration. 1*: 52–55.

117. KLOMP, H. 1953. Die Terreinkeus van de Kievit *Vanellus vanellus. Ardea. 41*: 1–139.

118. KOZLOVA, E.V. 1962. Water Birds, Limicolae (concluded). Fauna of the USSR. *Vol.2 Sect.1, Pt.3.* Moscow.

119. KRISTENSEN, I. 1957. Difference in density and growth in a cockle population in the Dutch Waddenzee. *Archs.neerl.Zool. 12*: 351–453.

120. KUMARI, A. 1958. The food of waders in the peat bogs of Estonia. *Ornitoloogiline Kogumik. 1*: 195–215.

121. LACK, D. 1943. The age of some more British birds. *Brit.Birds. 36*: 193–197, 214–221.

122. LACK, D. 1944. The problem of partial migration. *Brit.Birds. 37*: 122–130, 143–150.

123. LACK, D. 1954. The natural regulation of animal numbers. Oxford.

124. LACK, D. 1962. Migration across the southern North Sea studied by radar. Part 3. Movements in June and July. *Ibis. 104*: 74–85.

125. LACK, D. 1963a. Migration across the southern North Sea studied by radar. Part 4. Autumn. *Ibis. 105*: 1–54.

126. LACK, D. 1963b. Migration across the southern North Sea studied by radar. Part 5. Movements in August, winter and spring and Conclusion. *Ibis. 105*: 461–492.

127. LACK, D. 1966. Population studies of birds. Oxford.

128. LACK, D. 1968a. Ecological adaptions for breeding in birds. London.

129. LACK, D. 1968b. Bird Migration and Natural Selection. *Oikos. 19*: 1–9.

130. LARSON, S. 1957. The Suborder Charadrii in Arctic and Boreal areas during the Tertiary and Pleistocene. *Acta Vertebratica. 1*: 1–84.

131. LATHAM, J. 1785. A General Synopsis of Birds. London.

132. LAVEN, H. 1940. Beitrage zur Biologie des Sandregenpfeifers. *J.Orn. 88*: 183–281.

133. LGL LTD. 1974. The bird hazard problem at Vancouver International Airport. Autumn 1973. *Rept. of the National Research Council of Canada.* p. 101.

134. LILJA, S. 1969. On the post-nuptial wing moult of migratory Dunlin *Calidris alpina. Ann.Reptr.Orn.Soc.Pori.* 40–43.

135. LINCOLN, F.C. 1935. The migration of North American birds. *Circular 363 U.S. Dept. of Agriculture, Washington, DC.* p.72.

136. LISCINSKY, S.A. 1972. The Pennsylvanian Woodcock management study. *Res.Bull.171 Pennsylvania Game Commission.*

137. LISTER, M.D. 1964. The Lapwing habitat enquiry. *Bird Study. 11*: 128–147.

138. LONGSTREET, R.J. 1930. Notes on speed of flight of certain birds. *Auk. 47*: 428–429.

139. LOW, G.C. 1924. The Literature of the Charadriiformes 1894–1924, London. 139a. 1894–1928 (2nd Edn. 1931). London.

140. MACLEAN, G.L. 1972. Clutch size and evolution in the Charadrii. *Auk. 89*: 299–324.

141. MACLEAN, S.F. 1969. Ecological Determinants of Species Diversity of Arctic Sandpipers near Barrow, Alaska. *PhD Thesis.* University of California, Berkeley.

142. MACLEAN, S.F. 1973. Life cycle and growth energetics of the arctic crane fly *Pedicia hannai antenatta. Oikos. 24(4)*: 426–443.

143. MACLEAN, S.F. 1974. Primary Production, Decomposition and the Activity of Soil Invertebrates in Tundra ecosystems: A Hypothesis; in *Soil Organisms & Decomposition in Tundra. ed. A.J.Holding et al.* Stockholm.

144. MACLEAN, S.F. & PITELKA, F.A. 1971. Seasonal Patterns of Abundance of Tundra Arthropods near Barrow. *Arctic. 24:* 19–40.

145. MASCHER, J.W. 1966. Weight variations in resting Dunlins (*Calidris a. alpina*) on autumn migration in Sweden. *Bird Banding. 37:* 1–34.

146. MAYR, E. 1963. Animal species and evolution. Cambridge, Mass.

147. McCABE, T.T. 1942. Types of Shorebird Flight. *Auk. 59:* 110–111.

148. McCLURE, H.E. 1974. Migration and Survival of the Birds of Asia. Bangkok.

149. McNEIL, R. 1968. Hivernage et estivage d'oiseaux aquatiques nord-americains dans le Nord-Est du Venezuela. *PhD Thesis.* University of Montreal.

150. McNEIL, R. 1969. La determination du contenu lipidique et de la capacité de vol chez quelques especies d'oiseaux de rivage (Charadriidae et Scolopacidae). *Can.J.Zool. 47:* 525–536.

151. McNEIL, R. 1970. Hivernage et estivage d'oiseaux aquatiques Nord-americains dans la Nord-Est du Venezuela avec accumulation de graisse, capacité de vol et routes de migration. *L'Oiseau et R.F.O. 40:* 185–302.

152. McNEIL, R. & CADIEUX, F. 1972a. Numerical formulae to estimate flight range of some North American shore birds from fresh weight and wing length. *Bird Banding. 43:* 107–113.

153. McNEIL, R. & CADIEUX, F. 1972b. Fat content and flight range capacities of some adult spring and fall migrant North American shore birds in relation to migration routes on the Atlantic coast. *Naturalite can. 99:* 589–605.

154. MEINERTZHAGEN, R. 1955. The speed and altitude of bird flight. *Ibis. 97:* 81–117.

155. MERCER, A.J. 1968. Individual weight changes in breeding Oystercatchers. *Bird Study. 15:* 93–98.

156. MIDDLEMISS, E. 1961. Biological aspects of *Calidris minuta* while wintering in south west Cape. *Ostrich. 32:* 107–121.

157. MILNE, H. & DUNNET, G.M. 1971. Standing crop, productivity and trophic relations of the fauna of the Ythan estuary. In "The Estuarine Environment". Barnes, R.S.K. & Green, J. Applied Science Publishers Ltd., London.

158. MINTON, C.D.T. 1975. Waders of The Wash – ringing and biometric studies. *WWRG/Wash Feasibility Study.*

159. MINTON, C.D.T. 1977. The moult of Waders. *3rd Bird Watchers Book* ed. J. Gooders.

160. MOREAU, R.E. 1960. Climatic correlations of size in *Zosterops. Ibis. 102:* 137–138.

161. MOREAU, R.E. 1972. The Palaearctic African Bird Migration Systems. London.

162. MORRISON, R.E.G. 1976. Moult of the Purple Sandpiper *Caladris maritima* in Iceland. *Ibis. 118:* 237–246.

163. NETHERSOLE-THOMPSON, D. 1951. The Greenshank. London.

164. NETHERSOLE-THOMPSON, D. 1973. The Dotterel. London.

165. NETTLESHIP, D.N. 1973. Breeding ecology of Turnstones *Arenaria interpres* at Hazen Camp, Ellesmere Island, N.W.T. *Ibis. 115:* 202–217.

166. NETTLESHIP, D.N. 1974. The Breeding of the Knot *Calidris canutus* at Hazen Camp, Ellesmere Island, N.W.T. *Polarforschung. 44*: 8–26.

167. NEWTON, I. 1966. The moult of the Bullfinch *Pyrrhula pyrrhula*. *Ibis. 108*: 41–67.

168. NEWTON, I. 1967. Feather growth and moult in some captive finches. *Bird Study. 14*: 10–24.

169. NEWTON, I. 1969. Winter fattening in the Bullfinch. *Physiol.Zool. 42*: 96–104.

170. NICHOLSON, E.M. 1938–39. Report on the Lapwing Habitat Enquiry 1937. *British Birds. 32*: 170–191; 207–279; 255–259.

171. NICHOLSON, E.M. & FERGUSON-LEES, I.J. 1962. The Hastings Rarities. *British Birds. 55*: 299–384.

172. NISBET, I.C.T., DRURY, W.R. & BAIRD, J. 1963. Weight loss during migration. Pt. 1 Deposition and consumption of fat by the Blackpoll Warbler *Dendroica striata*. *Bird Banding. 34*: 107–121.

173. NORDBERG, S. 1950. Researches on the bird fauna of the marine zone in the Aland Archipelago. *Acta Zool.Fenn. 63*: 1–62.

174. NORTON, D.W. 1972. Incubation schedules of four species of Calidridine Sandpipers in Barrow, Alaska. *Condor. 74(2)*: 164–176.

175. NORTON, D.W. 1973. Ecological Energetics of Calidridine Sandpipers in Northern Alaska. *PhD Thesis*. University of Alaska.

176. ODUM, E.P. 1971. Fundamentals of Ecology. Third Edition. London.

177. ODUM, E.P. & SMALLEY, A.E. 1959. Comparison of population energy flow of a herbivorous and a deposit feeding invertebrate in a salt-marsh ecosystem. *Proc.Nat.Acad.Sci. 45*: 617–622.

178. ODUM, E.P., CONNELL, C.E. & STODDARD, H.J. 1961. Flight energy and estimated flight range of some migratory birds. *Auk. 78*: 515–527.

179. OWEN, M. 1972. Some factors affecting food intake and selection in White-fronted Geese. *J.Anim.Ecol. 41*: 79–92.

180. OWEN, R.B. & KROHN, W.B. 1973. Moult pattern and weight changes of the American Woodcock. *Wilson Bull. 85*: 31–41.

181. PAGE, G. & WHITACRE, D.F. 1975. Raptor predation on wintering shore birds. *Condor. 77*: 73–83.

182. PARMELEE, D.F. 1970. Breeding behaviour of the Sanderling in the Canadian high arctic. *Living Bird. 9*: 97–146.

183. PARMELEE, D.F. & PAYNE, R.B. 1973. On Multiple broods and the breeding strategy of Arctic Sanderlings. *Ibis. 115*: 219–226.

184. PEARSON, D.J. 1974. The timing of wing moult on some Palaearctic Waders wintering to East Africa. *W.S.G.Bull. 12*: 6–12.

185. PEARSON, D.J., PHILLIPS, J.H. & BACKHURST, G.C. 1970. Weights of some Palaearctic Waders wintering in Kenya. *Ibis. 112*: 199–209.

186. PEARSON, O.P. 1950. The metabolism of humming birds. *Condor. 52*: 145–152.

187. PENNYCUICK, C.J. 1969. The mechanics of bird migration. *Ibis. 111*: 525–556.

188. PIENKOWSKI, M.W. (Ed.) 1972. University of East Anglia Expedition to Morocco 1971 Report. *University of East Anglia*.

189. PIENKOWSKI, M.W. (Ed.) 1975. Studies on coastal birds and wet-lands in Morocco. *University of East Anglia Expedition to Morocco 1971–72*.

190. PIENKOWSKI, M.W. 1976. Recurrence of Waders on autumn migration at sites in Morocco. *Wag.Die.Vogelwarte. 28*: 293–297.

191. PIENKOWSKI, M.W. & DICK, W.J.A. 1975. The migration and wintering of Dunlin *Calidris alpina* in North West Africa. *Ornis Scand.* 6: 151–167.

192. PIENKOWSKI, M.W. & GREEN, G.H. 1976. Breeding biology of Sanderlings in North East Greenland. *Brit. Birds.* 69: 165–177.

193. PIENKOWSKI, M.W., KNIGHT, P.J., ARGYLE, F.B., STANYARD, D.J. 1976. The primary moult of waders on the Atlantic coast of Morocco. *Ibis.* 118: 347–365.

194. PIMM, S. 1976. Estimation of the duration of bird moult. *Condor.* 78: 550.

195. PRATER, A.J. 1972. The ecology of Morecambe Bay. III. The food and feeding habits of Knot (*Calidris canutus* L.) in Morecambe Bay. *J.Appl.Ecol.* 9: 179–194.

196. PRATER, A.J. 1974. Breeding biology of the Ringed Plover *Charadrius hiaticula*. *Proc.Wader Symp.Warsaw 1973.* 15–22.

197. PRATER, A.J. 1974. The population and migration of the Knot in Europe. *Proc.Wader Symp.Warsaw 1973.* 99–115.

198. PRATER, A.J. 1975. Fat and weight changes of waders in winter. *Ringing & Migration.* 1: 43–47.

199. PRATER, A.J. 1976. The distribution of coastal waders in Europe & North Africa. *5th Int.Orn.Congr.* 255–271.

200. PRATER, A.J. 1977. Birds of Estuaries Enquiry 1974–75. *BTO/RSPB/WT.*

201. PRATER, A.J., MARCHANT, J.H., VUORINEN, J. 1977. Guide to the Identification and ageing of Holarctic Waders. *BTO Guide 17.*

202. PULLIAINEN, E. 1970. On the breeding biology of the Dotterel. *Orn.Fenn.* 47: 69–73.

203. RAND, A.L. 1936. Altitudinal variation in New Guinea birds. *Am.Mus.Novit.* 890: 1–14.

204. RATCLIFFE, D.A. 1976. Observations on the breeding of the Golden Plover in Great Britain. *Bird Study.* 23: 63–116.

205. READING, C.J. & McGRORTY, S. 1978. Seasonal variations on the burying depth of *Macoma balthica (L)* and its accessibility to wading birds. *Est. Coast. Mar. Sci.,* 6: 135–144.

206. VAN RHIJN, J.G. 1973. Behavioural dimorphism in male Ruffs *Philomachus pugnax* (L). *Behaviour* 47: 153–229.

207. RICHARDS, G.A. 1965. A checklist of the birds of Ayrshire. *Duplicated MS.*

208. RITTINGHAUS, H. 1956. Untersuchungen am Seeregenpfeifer auf der Insel Oldeoog. *J.Orn.* 97: 117–155.

209. RITTINGHAUS, H.1961. Der Seeregenpfeifer. Wittenberg.

210. SALOMONSEN, F. 1950. The Birds of Greenland. Copenhagen.

211. SALOMONSEN, F. 1954. The migration of the European Redshank (*Tringa totanus* L.). *Dansk.Ornith.For.Tiddskrift.* 48: 94–122.

212. SALOMONSEN, F. 1955. The Evolutionary significance of bird migration. *Dan.Biol.Medd.* 22: 1–62.

213. SALOMONSEN, F. 1972. Zoogeographical and ecological problems in arctic birds. *15th Int.Orn.Congr.* 25–77 Leiden.

214. SALT, G.W. 1963. Avian body weight adaptation and evolution in western North America. *13th Int.Orn.Congr.* 905–917.

215. SAUER, E.G.F. 1962. Ethology and ecology of Golden Plovers on St. Lawrence Island, Bering Sea. *Psychologische Forschung.* 26: 399–470.

306   BIBLIOGRAPHY

216. SCHOENER, T.W. 1965. The evolution of bill size differences among sympatric congeneric species of birds. *Evolution. 19*: 189–213.
217. SEEBOHM, H. 1887. The geographical distribution of the Family Charadriidae. London.
218. SELOUS, F. 1906. Observations tending to throw light on the question of sexual selection in birds, including a day-to-day diary on the breeding habits of the Ruff (*Machetes pugnax*). *Zoologist. 4*: 60–65; 161–182; 285–294; 367–381; 419–428.
219. SHELDON, W.G. 1967. The Book of the American Woodcock.
220. SIBLEY, C. 1960. The electrophoretic pattern of avian egg white proteins. *Ibis. 102*: 215–84.
221. SMITH, P.C. 1975. A study of the winter feeding ecology and behaviour of the Bar-tailed Godwit *Limosa lapponnica*. PhD Thesis, University of Durham.
222. SMITH, P.H. & GREENHALGH, M.E. 1977. A four-year census of wading birds on the Ribble Estuary, Lancs/Merseyside. *Bird Study. 24*: 243–258.
223. SMITH, S. BAYLISS 1950. British Waders in their haunts. London.
224. SNOW, D.W. 1954. Trends in geographical variation in Palaearctic members of the Genus Parus. *Evolution. 8*: 19–28.
225. SNOW, D.W. 1965. The moult enquiry fourth report June 1965. *Bird Study. 12*: 135–142.
226. SNOW, D.W. & SNOW, B. 1976. The post breeding moult of the Lapwing. *Bird Study. 23*: 117–120.
227. SOIKKELI, M. 1967. Breeding cycle and population dynamics in Dunlin. *Ann.Zool.Fenn. 4*: 158–198.
228. SOIKKELI, M. 1974. Size variation of breeding Dunlins in Finland. *Bird Study. 21*: 151–154.
229. SPENCER, K.G. 1953. The Lapwing in Britain. London.
230. STANLEY, P.I. 1972. The W.W.R.G. visit to Denmark and Sweden, August 1972. *W.S.G.Bull. 7*: 9–10.
231. STANLEY, P.I. & MINTON, C.D.T. 1972. The unprecedented westward migration of Curlew-Sandpipers in Autumn 1969. *Brit. Birds. 65*: 365–380.
232. STAPLES, C.P. & HARRISON, J.G. 1949. Further as to colour change without moult with particular reference to the Snow Bunting. *Bull. B.O.C. 69*: 33–37.
233. STOUT, G.D. 1967. The Shorebirds of North America. New York.
234. SUMMERS, R.W., PRINGLE, J.S. & COOPER, J. 1976. The status of coastal waders in the South Western Cape, South Africa. *Western Cape Wader Study Group.*
235. SVARDSEN, G. 1952. Verksamheten vid Ottenby fagelstation 1951. *Var Fagelvarld. 11*: 158–176.
236. SWENNEN, C. 1971. Het voedsel van de Groenpootruiter *Tringa nebularia* tijdeus het verblijf in het Nederlandse Waddengebied. *Limosa. 44*: 71–83.
237. TAYLOR, R.C. 1978. Geographical variation in the Ringed Plover *Charadrius hiaticula*. PhD Thesis, Liverpool Polytechnic.
238. TEAL, J.M. 1957. Community metabolism in a temperate cold spring. *Ecol.Monogr. 27*: 283–302.
239. TEDD, J.G. & LACK, D. 1958. The detection of bird migration by high power radar. *Proc.Roy.Soc.,B. 149*: 503–510.
240. THOMAS, J.F. 1942. Report on the Redshank Enquiry 1939–40. *Brit.Birds. 36*: 5–14, 22–34.

241. THOMAS, D.G. & DARTNALL, A.J. 1971. Moult of the Curlew-Sandpiper in relation to its annual cycle. *Emu. 71*: 153–158.
242. TINBERGEN, N. 1951. The study of instinct. Oxford.
243. TUCK, L.M. 1972. The Snipes. Ottawa.
244. TUCKER, V.A. 1971. Flight energetics in birds. *Amer.Zool. 11*: 115–124.
245. VÄISÄNEN, R.A. 1969. Evolution of the Ringed Plover (*Charadrius hiaticula* L) during the last hundred years in Europe. *Ann.Acad.Sci.Fenn. 149*: 1–90.
246. VÄISÄNEN, R.A. 1977. Geographic variation in timing of breeding and egg size in eight European species of Waders. *Ann.Zool.Fennici. 14*: 1–25.
247. VERWEY, J. 1927. Maturity and breeding dress in birds. III & IV. The plumages of *Tringa canutus* L. & *Tringa crassirostris* Temm. & Schlegel. *Zool.Mededeel (Leiden). 10*: 158–183.
248. VESSEY-FITZGERALD, B. 1939. A Book of British Waders. London.
249. WARD, P. & ZAHAVI, A. 1973. The importance of certain assemblages of birds as information centres for food-finding. *Ibis. 115*: 517–534.
250. WHITE, E. & GITTINS, J.C. 1954. The value of Wader measurements in the study of Wader migration, with particular reference to the Oystercatcher. *Bird Study. 11*: 257–261.
251. WILLIAMSON, K. 1958. Bergmann's Rule & obligatory overseas migration. *Brit. Birds. 51*: 209–232.
252. WILLIAMSON, K. 1974. The changing flora and fauna of Britain.
253. WITHERBY, H.F., JOURDAIN, F.C.R., TICEHURST, N.F. & TUCKER, B.W. 1940. Handbook of British Birds. London.
254. WYNNE EDWARDS, V.C. 1962. Animal dispersion in relation to social behaviour. Edin. and London.
255. ZWARTS, L. 1974. Vogels van het brakke getijgebied. Amsterdam.

INDEX